LIBERATION FROM SAMSARA

Kyabjé Dodrupchen Rinpoché

LIBERATION
FROM SAMSARA

ORAL INSTRUCTIONS ON THE PRELIMINARY
PRACTICES OF LONGCHEN NYINGTHIK

by
Kyabjé Dodrupchen Rinpoché

Translated by Tulku Thondup Rinpoché
and Sonam Paljor Dejongpa

DODRUP CHEN

Wisdom

Wisdom Publications
199 Elm Street
Somerville, MA 02144 USA
wisdomexperience.org

Library of Congress Cataloging-in-Publication Data
Names: Thub-bstan-phrin-las-bzang-po, Rdo Grub-chen IV, 1927– author. |
    Thondup, Tulku, translator. | Paljor, Sonam, translator.
Title: Liberation from Samsara: oral instructions on the preliminary practices of
    Longchen Nyingthik / by Kyabjé Dodrupchen Rinpoché; translated by Tulku
    Thondup Rinpoché and Sonam Paljor Dejongpa.
Other titles: Longchen Nyingtik.
Description: First wisdom edition. | Somerville: Wisdom Publications, 2022. |
    Includes index.
Identifiers: LCCN 2021042902 (print) | LCCN 2021042903 (ebook) |
    ISBN 9781614296638 (hardcover) | ISBN 9781614296645 (ebook)
Subjects: LCSH: Guru worship (Rite)—Buddhism.
Classification: LCC BQ7662.6 .T578 2022 (print) | LCC BQ7662.6 (ebook) |
    DDC 294.3/61—dc23
LC record available at https://lccn.loc.gov/2021042902
LC ebook record available at https://lccn.loc.gov/2021042903

ISBN 978-1-61429-663-8   ebook ISBN 978-1-61429-664-5

26 25 24 23 22
5 4 3 2 1

Cover and interior design by Gopa & Ted2, Inc. Cover photo by Lama Chödak
Gyatso Nubpa.

CONTENTS

EDITOR'S PREFACE

KYABJÉ DODRUPCHEN RINPOCHÉ is one of the most important living masters in the Nyingma and Dzokchen traditions of Tibetan Buddhism. He was born in 1927 in the Golok province of Far Eastern Tibet (see "About the Author" for the short biography by Tulku Thondup). Rinpoché made frequent visits to the West, first in 1973 when he established the Mahasiddha Temple in Massachusetts. Early on, Rinpoché gave a series of teachings on how to practice Ngöndro, a Dharma practice of guru yoga. Dodrupchen Rinpoché called Ngöndro the most fundamental and complete path to liberation from samsara.

The first two chapters of this book were translated by Tulku Thondup and the rest by Sonam Paljor Dejongpa. The appendix, notes, and Tibetan transliterations were graciously provided by Tulku Thondup. The transcription of Rinpoché's oral teaching was started by Jean Cowles and finished with the help of Mahasiddha members, especially Deborah Schneider, who did extensive editing of the transcript. David Devore provided computer graphic and editing help. The transmission of oral teachings into the medium of a book for a wider audience required the creation of a certain structure and additional editing by the publisher, yet the content remains faithful to the original teaching.

Most of the deity photos in this book were taken from original thangka paintings commissioned and supervised by Kyabjé Dodrupchen Rinpoché himself.

—K. Lee, PhD

Shakyamuni Buddha

TRANSLATOR'S INTRODUCTION

Embodiment of all the enlightened masters of the Vajrayana,
source of esoteric teachings of the Heart Essence,
principle doctrine-holder of the Longchen Nyingthik lineage—
to you we pray to awaken the enlightened nature of our mind.

THE TEACHINGS of the Longchen Nyingthik Ngöndro were first revealed by Rikzin Jikmé Lingpa (1729–98). The texts were then compiled by the First Dodrupchen (1745–1821) as the *Namkhyen Lamzang, the Excellent Path of Omniscience.* Since then, a great many commentaries on them, including *The Words of My Perfect Teacher*, were composed by Patrul Rinpoché and others. After studying the Ngöndro teachings thoroughly, we must meditate on them thoroughly from the depth of our hearts.

When the Fourth Kyabjé Dodrupchen Rinpoché (1927–) gave teachings on the Longchen Nyingthik Ngöndro at the Mahasiddha Nyingmapa Center in Massachusetts, he repeatedly explained that the main title of this teaching is the Ngöndro—that is, the preliminary trainings. However, although the teachings start with ways to turn our mind toward Dharma, they end with meditations on and realizations of unifying one's mind with Guru Rinpoché's wisdom mind. So the Ngöndro provides a complete path of training for becoming a Buddhist and attaining buddhahood.

Teachings on the Ngöndro begin with meditations on the common preliminary practices, including (1) the difficulties of obtaining a life of a fortunate human being; (2) the changing and impermanent nature of life; (3) the implacability of karma, with the impacts of virtuous, unvirtuous, and neutral karmic causations dictating our life; and (4) the suffering nature of the cycle of life. Also, they offer (5) three different paths to liberation and (6) stress the importance of having a Dharma teacher. If we follow these instructions, our precious human life will not be wasted but will be fully devoted to pursuing pure Dharma from the heart.

Next are the uncommon practices: (1) taking refuge in the Triple Jewels with total trust, (2) developing enlightened aspiration for all beings, (3) purifying all evil deeds (karmas) through Vajrasattva training, and (4) accumulating meritorious deeds through mandala offerings. If we do these, then instead of sinking into the ocean of evil deeds and suffering, whatever we think or do, everything will turn us to taking the right steps toward the realization of enlightenment.

Third is guru yoga, the actual practice. In this stage we (1) visualize Guru Rinpoché and the details of his pure land, (2) invite him with the Vajra Seven-Line Prayer, (3) accumulate the sevenfold merits,[1] (4) pray with heartfelt devotion, (5) invoke him with the vajra secret mantra, (6) pray to the lineage masters, (7) and make aspirational prayers to realize the various stages of the path. Then from Guru Rinpoché we receive (8) the vase, the body empowerment; (9) the secret, the speech empowerment; (10) the wisdom, the mind empowerment; and (11) the precious word (*tshig dbang rin po ch'e*) empowerment. Then (12) finally, with strong devotion, we merge into Guru Rinpoché and remain in union with him—in the awakened awareness nature, the Dzokpa Chenpo.

Fourth is the concluding practice. We dedicate all the dual accumulations—merits and wisdom—that we have ever accumulated to all mother beings as the cause of their happiness and attainment of enlightenment, and we make heartfelt aspirations for all to enjoy happiness and attain enlightenment.

If we think, feel, and remain as one in such true Dharma experiences and accomplishments, then our attainments will not only progress but will also be fully perfected—the perfection of buddhahood.

PLEASE NOTE

For ease of reading, transliterated Tibetan and Sanskrit terms are rendered phonetically. Unless otherwise noted, italicized terms are Tibetan. "Sutra" often refers to Sutrayana and "Tantra" to Tantrayana—the Sutra Vehicle and Tantra Vehicle, respectively. When these two words are not capitalized, they refer to two types of scriptures: sutras and tantras. The meaning of all philosophical terms accords with the presentation of the Nyingma tenet system.

—Tulku Thondup

INTRODUCTION BY
KYABJÉ DODRUPCHEN RINPOCHÉ

OM AH HUNG VAJRA GURU PADMA SIDDHI HUNG

SINCE YOU ARE COMING from a far distance, we will not do long prayers. Time is a consideration, and for our current context it is better to transmit and hear the teachings than to engage in long prayer sessions.[2]

First, I would like to express my thanks to many of my old disciples who almost accomplished half of the *bum nga*[3] and have done much practice of Ngöndro.[4] I am very happy.

I will explain in some detail how to practice our daily prayers because they are so important to our practice. You should know the meaning of these prayers and how to practice them. Then after knowing how to practice, you should practice.

Before you practice, it is necessary to receive instruction from a teacher and obtain knowledge through study. In Tibet we studied at least ten or fifteen years before practicing, because without knowledge practicing has less results. Receiving such guidance from a teacher is called *thöpa* ("hearing") and is very important. Otherwise it is like a person without hands trying to climb a rocky mountain. Next is pondering, examining, and analyzing the teachings. It is difficult and ineffective to practice and recite without understanding the meaning of the words. After receiving the teachings, it is important to practice and to meditate on their meaning. Just receiving teachings without practice has no value. The result is attained by the practice, not just by receiving teachings. So practicing Dharma has three important aspects: the first is receiving teachings, the second is pondering and analyzing them, the third is practicing and meditating on those teachings. Also, just to know how to meditate or practice is not sufficient for either student or teacher. It is very important that you have an interest in receiving the teachings. This is called "faith." Buddha himself said, "Faith is very important in order to have a mind that is clean from defilements."

Everybody likes a practice through which one can attain buddhahood without difficulty or hard work. But Buddha himself said, "I am showing you the path to liberation, or buddhahood. Now it depends on you to attain buddhahood. It's up to you to practice." Very hard and diligent practice is necessary because we, from beginningless time, have been involved in worldly affairs and our minds are defiled or covered over by very strong defilements. So long practice is a must. People used to tell me, "I am trying to practice but there is not much progress." That's because just short practice is not enough. Progress is obtained only by long practice. Practice for a long time.

Everybody also likes a short path to buddhahood. Tantra is the shortest path to attain the result. That's why we practice tantra. In tantra there are two stages of practice. The first is practicing with effort. The practitioner uses his own body, veins, wind, semen, visualization, and so on. This visualization practice is called "the development stage" (*thab lam*). Each person has a different capacity, so different paths are necessary. And there are many people who like to generate visualization. The second stage in tantra practice is the accomplishment stage. Practicing with effort, the development stage, is not enough. One should practice the accomplishment stage (*jor-lam*) as well, which is the meditative practice without generating visualization. It is important to practice both the development stage and accomplishment stage together.

Every person has a different capacity for practice, so different paths are necessary. And there are many people who like to generate visualization—that's why it is necessary for them to practice with effort. It is important for the teacher to explain the proper stages, making it clear that visualization alone is not correct. But there are two kinds of teachers: one who takes disciples to the right path, and the other who takes disciples to a wrong path. If one is going to cross the ocean and doesn't have a good pilot, one might take the boat in the wrong direction. Therefore it is necessary to have a good teacher first, so one can go in the right direction.

There are many ways to practice, but for us it is necessary to take one path. So I will teach you one path, not all paths. A path has many parts, just as a chair has four legs and other parts. I chose to give you this practice with fewer words that are more meaningful than many words. Traditionally, and in general, the Guru Prayer is much longer. However, I thought it better to shorten it to make it easier for you. But it has all the necessary parts and is complete. One may attain buddhahood just by practicing the prayer. It is a full and complete practice.

You can call this prayer "Guru Yoga" or "Lama Yoga" or "Practice of the Lama." Generally, guru yoga starts from *Emaho* (Part 4), and the prayers at the beginning are the preliminary practices (Parts 1–3). All the prayers of these practices (Parts 1–5) are guru yoga.

I am teaching you each characteristic of this Ngöndro practice by pointing out "this is like this" and "that is like that." I am teaching them to you in that manner, since you haven't had an opportunity to study over the course of many years.

THE GURU PRAYER

I. SHAKYAMUNI BUDDHA

To you who knows the method (for the liberation of sentient beings)
    and (who is) compassionate, born of the Shakyan race,
who cannot be conquered by others, who overcomes demonic forces,
whose body is radiant like golden Mount Sumeru—
to you, King of the Shakyas, I pay homage.

By (the power of) the intentions of the Bliss Gone (Buddha)
    and all his children,
by the might of enlightened deeds, aspirations, wisdom, compassion,
    and power
that are the illusory manifestation of the unexcelled wisdom
    (of the Buddha),
may I and others become the very same.

(Repeat many times)

II. SEVEN-LINE PRAYER TO GURU RINPOCHÉ PADMASAMBHAVA

Hung! In the northwest in the country of Oddiyana,
(born) on the pistil stem of a lotus,
endowed with the marvelous supreme attainment,

renowned as the lotus-born,
surrounded by a retinue of many dakinis—
following you, I shall practice.
Please come and bless (me), Guru Padma Siddhi Hung.

III. PRAYER TO LINEAGE LAMAS

To Samantabhadra, Vajrasattva, Prahevajra, Shri Singha,
and to Padmakara (and his) twenty-five (disciples): king
    and subjects,
To So, Zur, Nub, Nyak, and the hundred Dharma treasure
    discoverers, etc.,
I pray to you, the lamas of (the lineages of) canonical and
    Dharma treasure teachings.

IV. PRAYER TO KUNKHYEN LONGCHEN RABJAM (LONGCHENPA)

The Six Ornaments, the adornments of the Jambu continent,
    and the Two Supreme Ones:
to you who are endowed with compassion, learning, and
    realization equal to them,
yet by practicing in secret in the midst of sacred forests
accomplished the perfection of samsara and nirvana
    as the dharmakaya Longchenpa—
Trinle Özer, at your feet I pray.

V. PRAYER TO KUNKHYEN JIKMÉ LINGPA

To (you) who know all the knowable, treasure of compassion
    for sentient beings,
remanifestation of Trinle Özer and source of mind treasures,

sky yogi of the luminescent vast expanse—
Jikmé Lingpa, at your feet I pray.

VI. PRAYER TO THE FIRST DODRUPCHEN RINPOCHÉ

By Padmasambhava, all-knower of the three times,
empowered as master of the profound dharma treasure,
    universal king of Dharma.
Sangyé Lingpa, his manifestation who follows a hidden way—
Kunsang Shenphen, at (your) feet (I) pray.

VII. PRAYER TO THE ROOT LAMAS

In the Palace of Unexcelled Dharmadhatu,
I essence of all the buddhas of the three times,
who bring about the direct introduction to one's own mind,
    the dharmakaya—
root lamas, to you I pray.

PART 1

Prayers to Buddhas and Lineage and Root Lamas

THE NGÖNDRO TEXT starts with a number of prayers to the lineage masters. People who have studied Ngöndro will understand their relevance. Since you haven't studied and don't understand it, you might think that the prayers are not about meditation, but in fact they are important for Ngöndro meditation. They will help to pacify the obstructions and invoke the blessings for Ngöndro training. The first is the prayer to Shakyamuni Buddha, the source of Buddhadharma.

Buddha was born in Lumbini garden (now in Nepal) beneath a sal tree, as the son of King Shuddhodana of the Shakya clan and Queen Mayadevi. As soon as he was born, he took seven steps toward each direction as flowers bloomed in his wake. He proclaimed, "I am supreme in the three realms." Eventually he married Princess Yashodhara and sired a son, Rahula. Buddha lived in Kapilavastu, the capital city of the Shakyas, until the age of twenty-nine. His father tried to protect him from seeing any suffering and provided all the comforts of the world. The king did not want his son to renounce the imperial household life for an ascetic path. However, Buddha witnessed the sufferings of life, old age, sickness, and death. He realized that whatever is born ends in death, whatever is brought together ends in separation, and whatever is joy ends in pain. Seeing these sights, Buddha determined to find the way to freedom from the cycle of suffering and lead all beings to freedom. Then he saw an ascetic, a seeker of liberation from samsara, the cycle of suffering. Buddha knew that to attain liberation he had to renounce the samsaric traps of the royal palace.

When Buddha requested the king's permission to renounce mundane life, the king said, "Please don't leave, I will provide anything that you like." The Buddha answered, "I will stay, if you can assure me that I don't have to die." At that the king had no answer and was forced to give the Buddha permission to renounce the kingdom.

Buddha left for Magadha in Central India. He cut his own hair, took the robes of a renunciate, and adopted a life of renunciation. He went to a number of well-known Indian sages and meditated according to their instructions, achieving the highest goals, but none of this satisfied him.

Then Buddha, with his five companions, practiced severe austerities on the banks of the Nairanjana River. He meditated for six years. For the first two years, he ate a very small amount of wheat. During the second term he consumed only water, and in the last term, nothing at all. Then according to Hinayana, the Common *Yana*, or Vehicle, he went to Bodhgaya and attained buddhahood. According to Tantra, when he practiced near the Nairanjana River, he left his body at the bank of the river and his consciousness went to the unexcelled pure land, where he attained buddhahood. It is also said that he gave different kinds of teachings, attaining Mahaparinirvana and so on.[5]

Let us understand that these enlightened beings are just manifestations. They are not at all real, merely manifestations of sentient beings. These stories of Buddha's life are different interpretations of the indescribable. The actual Buddha nature or the performance of the Buddha is beyond description. Further, all these manifestations or exhibitions of Buddha appear according to the different capacities of disciples. What I told you about Buddha is just one interpretation. There are many different interpretations, many ways of describing the Buddha's actions.

ཆོས་སྐུ་ཀུན་ཏུ་བཟང་པོ།

Chuku Kuntu Sangpo

ལོངས་སྐུ་རྡོ་རྗེ་སེམས་དཔའ།

Longku Dorjé Sempa

སྤྲུལ་སྐུ་དགའ་རབ་རྡོ་རྗེ།

Tulku Garab Dorjé

རིག་འཛིན་ཤྲཱི་སིང་ཧ།

Rikzin Shri Singha

པཎ་ཆེན་བི་མ་ལ་མི་ཏྲ།

Panchen Vimalamitra

རྒྱལ་བ་ཀློང་ཆེན་རབ་འབྱམས།

Gyalwa Longchen Rabjam

རིག་འཛིན་འཇིགས་མེད་གླིང་པ།

Rikzin Jikmé Lingpa

རྡོ་གྲུབ་ཆེན་དང་པོ་འཇིགས་མེད་ཕྲིན་ལས་འོད་ཟེར།

First Dodrupchen Jikmé Trinlé Öser

According to commonly accepted history, after the completion of six years of meditation by the Nairanjana River, Buddha went to Bodhgaya. On the way there, a grass seller named Tashi Mongol gave him kusha grass. Buddha blessed the grass as an auspicious substance. That's why kusha grass is now considered one of eight auspicious signs in our ritual. Then he sat below the bodhi tree on the kusha grass and concentrated on his final meditation. At that time, Mara appeared and tried to obstruct him from attaining buddhahood. But the demon could not obstruct him. Buddha subdued Mara and attained buddhahood. The demon had said to him, "You are the son of a king. How can you be a Buddha? It's beyond your capacity. Don't think about attaining buddhahood." And Buddha had answered, "You have power and got your powerful birth because of your single merit. I accumulated numerous merits for three countless kalpas. That's why I am going to attain buddhahood." The demon then raised his two fingers and said, "If you accumulated such merits, bring the witnesses here." Buddha answered, "The earth is the best of beings and known beings. This is my witness." And he touched the earth with his hand. At his touch, the golden-colored goddess of the earth came up from the earth and said, "I can count the atoms of the earth, but I cannot count the Buddha's sacrifices: giving his heads, legs, and arms for the benefit of sentient beings. I am the witness to the Buddha's accumulation of merits. Buddha is the one who can attain buddhahood."

So Mara was beaten back. Then the demon came back with the forces of other demons. But because of the power of Buddha's contemplation, all the instruments thrown by the forces of the demons became the offering of flowers. They could not harm Buddha, and he attained buddhahood.

Then Buddha said, "I received the final attainment, but people will not understand its meaning. So I am not going to teach this. I will stay in the forest." And he stayed there for seven weeks without giving any teachings.

And then the gods Brahma and Indra came to Buddha and offered a white conch shell. Brahma offered him the golden wheel and asked for teachings. Buddha accepted their requests and went to the city of Varanasi. There he set in motion three Dharma chakras, the Dharma wheels. And then the teaching of Buddha became like light, or a path, for his followers. So that's why the source of sutras and tantras (Buddhist esoteric teachings) is Buddha. And that's why we have to pray to him in the beginning of our prayers. *Om Muni Muni Maha Muni Ye So Ha* is the name of the Buddha.

It is stated in sutra that even one piece of a special teacher's body, a bit of bone or material, will help to purify one's defilements.

Generally buddhas are always present before us. In appearance, the original body of Buddha is gone. He is dead, but in actuality, Buddha is present before us all the time. Because of our defilements we cannot see the Buddha, but he is there. Buddha said, "In a dark age, I will appear for sentient beings as a teacher."

There are three manifestations of Buddha bodies: dharmakaya, the ultimate body, the pure nature of buddhahood and the basis for all the qualities of the Buddha; samboghakaya, the pure form-body buddhahood that can be seen only by buddhas; and nirmanakaya, the manifested body in various forms and actions that appear according to the needs and capacities of ordinary human beings. The forms and sounds of the Buddha that we ordinary beings can perceive belong to the nirmanakaya. Shakyamuni Buddha is like a body of nirmanakaya. Because of defilements we cannot see the supreme dharmakaya and samboghakaya. That's what is said in sutra.

In tantric teachings, it is said the lama is the united body of all divinities. And if one pays homage to him, one will be paying homage to all the divinities. In general one tries to practice both the development stage and the accomplishment stage. These have many different kinds of practices and it would be very difficult to understand them all. That's why I gave you guru yoga: it does not have all those different practices, it is very easy to practice, and it is very important.

Next is the "Seven-Line Prayer to Guru Rinpoché Padmasambhava"—a prayer and invitation to Guru Rinpoché, asking him to come and bless us. He is very important. He came to Tibet at the time of King Tri Songdetsen and founded Buddhism, building Samyé Monastery, the main temple, and eight small temples. He translated many tantra and sutra texts. In Dragya Ling, one of the temples, he preached the tantra in Tibet. Because of him, Buddhist tantra teachings still exist and are available for practice.

As we said, in the displays and actions of buddhas, there are three kinds of bodies, or *kayas*: dharmakaya, sambhogakaya, and nirmanakaya. Each kaya has three divisions—for example, dharmakaya of dharmakaya, samboghakaya of dharmakaya, and nirmanakaya of dharmakaya. The same three divisions exist for samboghakaya and nirmanakaya. In the Nyingma tradition, the image of Kuntu Sangpo (Skt. Samantabhadra) symbolizes the dharmakaya. He is a blue-colored buddha in naked form. Dorjé Sempa represents sambhogakaya of nirmanakaya. Garab Dorjé represents nirmanakaya of nirmanakaya.

Just as there are many ways of dividing the three kayas, there are many different systems and interpretations. In this prayer, we are mainly praying to the lineage teachers belonging to the Dzokchen tradition. The Dzokchen teaching was transmitted by Garab Dorjé to Shri Singha, Shri Singha to Padma Jungé or Padmakara (Guru Rinpoché) and his disciples. Guru Rinpoché had numerous disciples, but only twenty-five main disciples. After Padmakara, or Guru Rinpoché, and his twenty-five disciples, the teaching came through the lineage of lamas without a break, transmitted one to the next, until it came to my teacher. That is called the "long transmission."

THE LINEAGE OF LONGCHEN NYINGTHIK
—— indicates the main transmission line of the Dodrupchen lineage

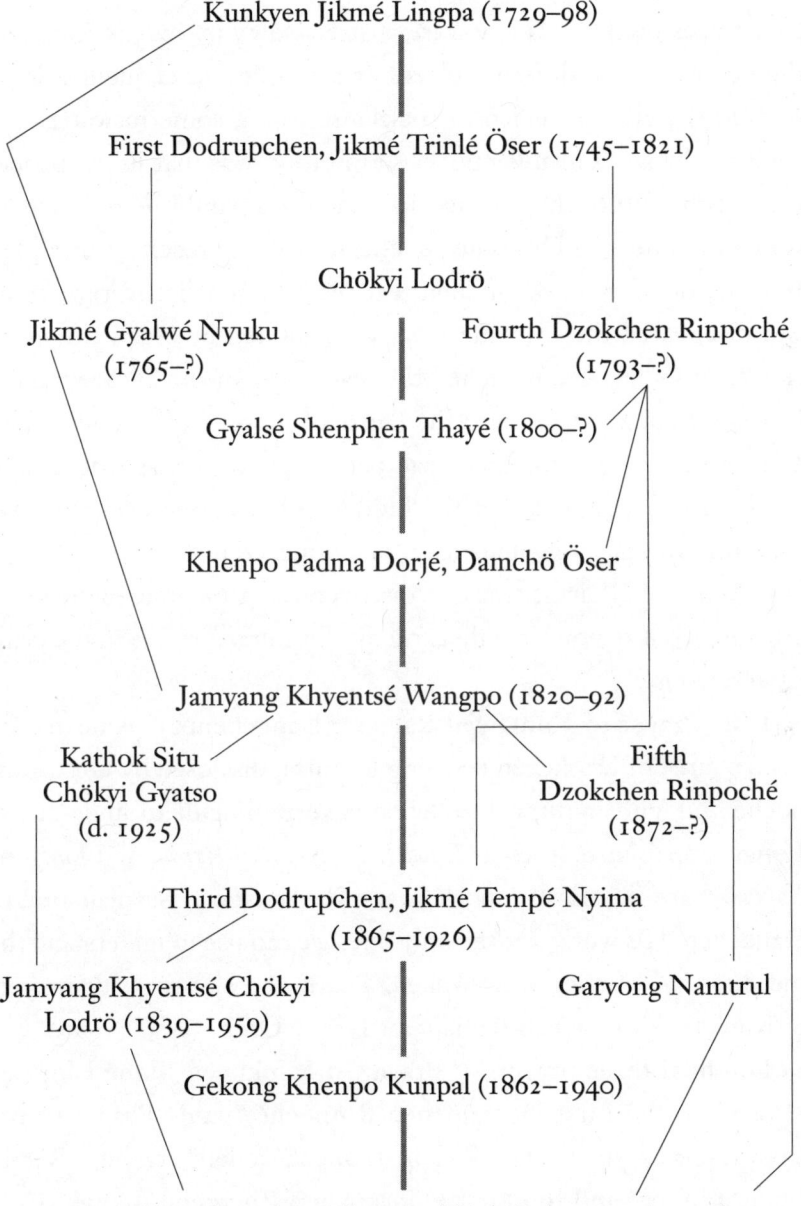

Kunkyen Jikmé Lingpa (1729–98)

First Dodrupchen, Jikmé Trinlé Öser (1745–1821)

Chökyi Lodrö

Jikmé Gyalwé Nyuku (1765–?)

Fourth Dzokchen Rinpoché (1793–?)

Gyalsé Shenphen Thayé (1800–?)

Khenpo Padma Dorjé, Damchö Öser

Jamyang Khyentsé Wangpo (1820–92)

Kathok Situ Chökyi Gyatso (d. 1925)

Fifth Dzokchen Rinpoché (1872–?)

Third Dodrupchen, Jikmé Tempé Nyima (1865–1926)

Jamyang Khyentsé Chökyi Lodrö (1839–1959)

Garyong Namtrul

Gekong Khenpo Kunpal (1862–1940)

Fourth Dodrupchen, Thupten Trinlé Palsangpo (1927–)

The "Prayer to the Lineage Lamas" is next. All Nyingma[6] teach-ings can be classified as *kama*, meaning "canon," and *terma*, the hidden texts or tradition. These are oral teachings Guru Rinpoché gave to his disciples. They were written down by his disciples and then concealed in different places and in different elements. Some teachings were concealed in rocks and earth, some in water, and some in the sky. Guru Rinpoché's aspiration was that in the proper time in the future these concealed teachings would be revealed by various teachers and become beneficial to all the teacher's disciples. In time, the *tertons*, the hidden text revealers or discoverers, came and discovered the teachings that were hidden by Guru Rinpoché and his disciples and preached the teachings. In the "Prayer to the Lineage Lamas" we pray to the lamas of these two lineages (kama and terma). Sur, Nub, and Nyak belong to the lamas who taught the long transmission, not the hidden texts. In the prayer it says "Tertön Gya Tsa Sog," meaning "one hundred text discoverers," or "the hundred Dharma treasure discoverers," though actually there are numerous tertons in Tibet and the "hundred" refers to the prin-cipal tertons.

The "Prayer to Kunkhyen Rabjam (Longchenpa)" is next. The main source of Dzokchen teaching is tantra, disclosed by Guru Rin-poché and Vimalamitra. Dzokchen is very difficult to understand. Longchenpa's texts (such as *Dzod Dun*, *Ngalso Korsum*, and *Rangdrol Korsum*)[7] are the most important and the most clear explanation of Dzokchen. His works are the only ones we can use to understand the meaning and practice of Dzokchen. That's why we have to do prayers to Kunkhyen Longchen Rabjam, or Drime Öser.

The final three prayers—"Prayer to Kunkhyen Jikmé Lingpa," "Prayer to the First Dodrupchen Rinpoché," and "Prayer to the Root Lamas"—are to the root lamas, one's teachers' teachers: Rikzin Jikmé Lingpa[8] and the First Dodrupchen Rinpoché, Jikmé Trinlé

Öser. The root lamas appeared in different forms, but in actuality they are all the same. So we do prayers to them as one united body. By praying to one's *tsawai* lama, or root lama, you are praying to all the lamas.

PART 2

The Four Common Preliminary Practices

THE FOUR COMMON preliminary practices are the four turnings away from samsara.

SESSION 1. Fortunate Human Birth
It is exceedingly difficult to obtain human life with (the eight)
   freedoms and (ten) endowments.
When I have the chance to fulfill the aim of humanity,
if I do not take advantage of it,
how can I get this opportunity afterward?

SESSION 2. The Impermanence of Human Life
The three worlds are as impermanent as the clouds of autumn.
The births and deaths of beings are like watching a dance.
The speed of human lives is like lightning in the sky;
it passes as swiftly as a stream down a steep mountain.

SESSION 3. Karma: Cause and Result
If, when his time comes, even a king should die,
his wealth and his friends and relatives shall not follow him;
wherever men go, wherever they remain,
karma like a shadow will follow them.

Session 4. The Suffering of Samsara: The Six Realms

*Due to ignorance, craving, and becoming
in the realms of men, gods, and the three inferior spheres,
in all five realms beings revolve foolishly,
like the turning of a potter's wheel.*

FORTUNATE HUMAN BIRTH

It is exceedingly difficult to obtain human life with (the eight)
freedoms and (ten) endowments.
When I have the chance to fulfill the aim of humanity,
if I do not take advantage of it,
how can I get this opportunity afterward?

THE EIGHT FREEDOMS AND THE
TEN ENDOWMENTS OF A PRECIOUS HUMAN LIFE

AFTER THE PRAYERS to buddhas and the lineage and root lamas, one does the four common preliminary practices. This involves mind training, a mind-reversing practice. It is necessary to turn the mind away from attachment to this world, which can be summed up in four practices. The reason we cannot practice Dharma is because we are so attached to this world that we don't have the appetite to practice Dharma. If one is attached to something, then one is not free to practice Dharma. If one does not have a busy life, then one is free. There are many ways of practicing; all serve this purpose of turning away from attachment. So we devote ourselves to these four common preliminary practices to turn away from this attachment.

The first common preliminary practice is to realize the difficulty of obtaining a human life. The first four lines of the above verse mention the difficulty of obtaining a human life. Recite these lines and meditate on the difficulty of obtaining a human life. To meditate means to think in one-pointed concentration. You should know what the eight freedoms (*tal*) and the ten endowments (*jor*) are. The first freedom is that we have a human life and are not born in hell. If we were born in hell, we would have no time to practice Dharma because we would always be suffering. The second freedom is that we are not born as a hungry ghost. If we were in the hungry-ghost realm, we would be suffering from hunger and thirst. We wouldn't have time to practice Dharma. At present, we are not born as a hungry ghost, so we are free from that state. The third freedom is that we have not taken birth as an animal. If we were in the animal realm, we would have no time to practice. Animals do not know what to practice and they are always busy trying to harm one another. They are chased by people. Fortunately we are free from that state. The fourth freedom is that we are not born as long-life gods. These are gods who have no thoughts and have no suffering, so they have no will to practice Dharma and no desire to do anything. We are free from that state. The fifth freedom is not being in a barbarous country where there is no Buddha or Dharma, and so no way to practice Dharma. But we are in a place where there is Dharma, so we are free from that state. The sixth freedom is being free from a wrong religion. Some religions practice human and animal sacrifice. Buddhism's basic teaching is nonviolence, to not harm any sentient beings. If one becomes the follower of a religion that preaches the sacrifice of living beings, one would not be free to practice Dharma. But we are followers of Dharma and free from that kind of wrong religion.

The Buddhadharma was preached in many eras, but in many others eras it did not exist at all. If you are born where Dharma does not exist, there is no way of practicing Dharma. The seventh freedom is not being born in a place or time where Buddha and Dharma don't exist. At this time we are free from such conditions. The eighth and last freedom is that we are free from being physically helpless or mentally dumb or foolish. If one is dumb, one cannot understand the meaning of the teaching. We are neither physically nor mentally helpless. So we are free from that kind of state.

It is so easy for us to have a wrong view, like not having faith in Dharma, not having faith in a teacher, and not having a pure perception of phenomena. As humans, we have obtained all eight freedoms, yet it is still not easy for us to be free from wrong views. We must make an effort to keep away from wrong views. Having wrong views is one of the reasons or causes to take rebirth in hell. At the time of Buddha there was a monk named Legpe Karma. He became an attendant of Buddha for twenty-six years but he never had faith in Buddha. He told Buddha, "You can teach twelve aspects of Dharma by memory without looking at a text. So can I. The only difference between us is you have a light around your body." If Buddha can have someone close by who lacks faith, it can easily happen to others.

Along with eight kinds of freedoms we have ten kinds of endowments: five personal and five external endowments. I will talk about personal endowments first.

We have a human life, and that is the first personal endowment. If we don't have a human life, there is no way we can practice. The second personal endowment is to take birth in a country where Buddhadharma exists. In the beginning, India was the center of Buddhism. Originally Tibet was not a Buddhist country, but later it became one of the centers of Buddhism. Then the Buddhadharma became almost nonexistent in India. So the existence of Buddha and Dharma is not permanent in space and time, and you should not take this second personal endowment for granted. The third is having the proper faculties. If one does not have the faculty of sight or hearing or speech, it would be difficult to practice Dharma. We have all our faculties, so we have the third endowment. The fourth personal endowment is not having a reverse life, not leaving the Dharma. If one practices accordingly and learns the Dharma, and does not get attached to worldly life, one has reversed one's life of being attached to worldly affairs. Fortunately, we have the personal endowment to practice Dharma and continuously practice Dharma. And the fifth personal endowment is having faith. If one has no faith in Dharma, there is no reason to practice. You all have faith in Dharma. These five personal endowments should be completely integrated within ourselves. Practicing Dharma is one of the most important and necessary requirements for liberation.

Now for the five external endowments. The sixth endowment is having Buddha, meaning Buddha came to this age. If Buddha had not come, there would be no possibility for his teaching to exist and we could not practice. But Buddha came in this age. The seventh endowment is the giving of teaching by the Buddha. If Buddha had come but not given teachings, we could not practice. Fortunately, not only did Buddha come but he also gave three levels of teachings. The eighth endowment is the existence of the Buddhadharma, meaning Buddha came, gave teachings, and those teachings remained. The Dharma of Buddha still exists. The ninth endowment is entering into the Dharma. If one does not practice Dharma, then even if it exists, there is no way of getting the benefits of Dharma. For example, even if the sun is shining, if one is blind, one cannot see. Even if there is a stream, if you do not drink the water, you cannot quench your thirst. Likewise, even if the Dharma exists but you do not try to enter into the Dharma by practicing it, there is no way of getting the benefit. But we entered into the Dharma and have this endowment. The tenth and last external endowment is having a teacher. Even if one enters into the Dharma, if one has no teacher, it would be difficult to know how to practice.

In ancient times, Atisha, the eleventh-century Buddhist teacher from India, went to Tibet. His disciples asked him, "Which is more important, studying the text or having instruction from a lama?"

Atisha answered, "Instruction from a lama." He also said, "If one understands and even preaches the meaning of the three teachings of Buddha (the *pratyeka*), if one has no instruction on how to practice them, it would be difficult for one's mind to benefit from the teachings." Another person asked, "To perceive the precepts of the three levels of teachings without instruction from a lama, or observing these precepts with instruction from a lama, are they the same?" Atisha replied, "It is not the same. If someone observes the precepts of three levels of worlds, but does not repent samsara, there will be no benefit for him by just observing the precepts." He also said, "After doing practices, you should dedicate the merit to all sentient beings. Otherwise if you experience defilements, such as anger, it will destroy your past merit. And you should feel repentance for getting lost in worldly affairs, or pretending to do Dharma practice, or just doing Dharma practice for a show." So one must have a teacher and get instructions from them on how to practice, not just read and pretend you know how to practice.

KNOWING HOW TO PRACTICE: MIND TRAINING

To begin with, you should know how to practice. You should know the eighteen different qualities—the eight freedoms and the ten endowments—of a precious human life well. Stop for a while and think about the qualities. This is the first of the mind trainings of the four common preliminary practices. Examine whether you have all those qualities. If you don't, you should try to have them because you must have them to practice Dharma. If one has these eighteen qualities, then one has a precious human life. If one doesn't recognize and realize the importance of all eighteen qualities, then one has an ordinary human life that is wasted. Most of us have the eighteen qualities inherently, so we are all capable of practicing Dharma.

You should also know how rare human life is; how difficult it is to have this life. Go to a place where there are other human beings. You can see each individual person has the quality of a precious human life but does not realize it. So realize how fortunate we are that we have this kind of precious human life. Do the prayers and recite the first lines of the common preliminary practices: "It is exceedingly difficult to obtain human life with (the eight) freedoms and (ten) endowments. When I have the chance to fulfill the aim of humanity, if I do not take advantage of it, how can I get this opportunity afterward?"

This is the first of the mind trainings of the fourfold common preliminary practices. When you feel the need for entertainment, or when you feel you cannot practice, think about your precious human life. When one realizes the difficulty of obtaining a human life, one will realize the value of human life and will not waste time and get lost in entertainment. So it is very important to think about the difficulty of obtaining a precious human life. It is said that when you have a precious human life, that is the threshold that determines if you will be happy or unhappy in the future. That is the border crossing for us. Decide whether to be happy in the future by practicing Dharma or to be unhappy by wasting your precious human life. We are at the border and have to decide which way to go. It is like riding a horse and coming to a point where one has to turn left or right. It is time to decide whether to go on the right path or the wrong path. It is time for you to decide.

This is the mind-training practice. This is the basic foundation practice. It is very important. You should not think about only the higher practice. Try to do this main practice and build a solid base. I will explain the practice step by step so you can proceed according to my instructions. At the end of each practice, dedicate the merit to all sentient beings for their happiness and for attaining buddhahood. If one dedicates the merit to sentient beings, the merit accumulated shall not be destroyed by defilement. Consider this analogy: if a drop of water falls into a large body of water, until that large body of water dries, the drop of water will not dry. It's like that. So it is necessary to dedicate the merit to all sentient beings.

THE DEDICATION

We will now say some prayers, dedicating the merit of what we have taught and what we have learned to all sentient beings. Even if you do not know the verses or the meaning of the verses, you should think: "The merit accumulated by receiving the teachings, and the merit accumulated in the past, present, and future, I am distributing to all sentient beings for their happiness and for the attainment of buddhahood."

Questions and Answers

Q: In the "Seven-Line Prayer to Guru Rinpoché," should we visualize Padmasambhava (Guru Rinpoché)?
A: It is good to visualize Padmasambhava and do the seven-line prayer with confidence in him. If you can do that, that is good.

Q: The "Prayer to Longchen Rabjam"—is he the same as *Longchenpa*?
A: Yes.

Q: Do we do the "Prayer to Tsawai Lamas" (root lamas), to lamas in general, or to to just one specific teacher like Dodrupchen?
A: To all the tsawai lamas, all the root teachers of spiritual teachings.

Q: What is the esoteric meaning of Dharmadhatu?
A: The Palace of Unexcelled Dharmadhatu is given as an example of a palace. It is not an actual palace. It is the state of nature of all existence—the final goal that we should attain.

Q: What is the essence of Buddha in the three times?
A: The three times are the past, present, and future.

Q: In the "Prayer to Kunkhyen Jikmé Lingpa," are So, Zur, Nub, and Nyak among the twenty-five disciples of Guru Rinpoché?
A: Only Nub and Nyak are among the twenty-five disciples. Sur is not.

Q: And are tertons among the twenty-five disciples?
A: Most of the tertons are incarnations of the twenty-five disciples.

Q: What are the six ornaments of Dzambuling?
A: They are the most distinguished scholars of ancient India, like Nagarjuna, Asanga, and so on.

Q: Who are the two supreme ones?
A: There are many ways to count superiority, but according to one way, Guna Parba and Shakya Parba are the two most excellent ones.

Q: What are the special effects of the *Om muni muni* mantra?
A: That is the name of Shakyamuni Buddha. By praying to him through his name, you will invoke him to give you blessing, just as if one calls your name and asks for help.

Q: Is there an esoteric or special symbolic meaning about the Uddiyana, the northern realms of the northwest?
A: Yes. Here it is just a common way of explanation. It has an esoteric meaning, but here we practice the common way.

Q: Did the teacher say anything about the esoteric meaning?
A: Just to practice according to the common way.

Q: Are there many other teachers, like Longchenpa, who left lots of books?

A: Yes, there are many lamas in the lineage who have left many books: Patrul Rinpoché, Jikmé Garyung Luku, Mipham Rinpoché, and many others.

Q: Are most of the books kept by Rinpoché?

A: No, I do not have all those books, just a few.

Q: In the very first verse, Shakyamuni Buddha's body is golden. Is that just an ornamental way of speaking, or does it mean his body was really golden?

A: Not real gold. The Buddha's color is yellow, yellow like Manjushri.

THE IMPERMANENCE OF HUMAN LIFE

THE INTENTION

VIRTUOUS KARMA, unvirtuous karma, and neutral karma originate from your intention. During a teaching, the teacher and the students must formulate good intention. How should you formulate the intention? The intention should be to understand that there is not a single sentient being who has not been your parent. Like your present parents, they have been very kind to you. All sentient beings desire happiness. However, they do not know how to perform dharmic actions, which are the source of happiness.

THE TEACHING

The three worlds are as impermanent as the clouds of autumn.
The births and deaths of beings are like watching a dance.
The speed of human lives is like lightning in the sky;
it passes as swiftly as a stream down a steep mountain.

This is a quote on impermanence from the Buddha himself, as Shantideva tells us in the *Bodhisattva's Way of* Life.[9] The first line summarizes today's teaching and includes all meanings possible. This is done in order to suit your requirements, given the society you live in and your desire to practice Dharma. Relatively shorter teachings are not my cultural tradition but is an adaption to your ability to practice. That is because one must not practice with any feeling of resentment. If one practices Dharma with discomfort in one's mind, that practice will turn adharmic. When a practice becomes longer, you may have a tendency to get tired and feel resentment toward it or feel you have to change your schedule to accommodate the practice. In order to eliminate that eventuality, the teaching has been shortened.

There is perpetual suffering in samsara, and that is caused by adharmic or anti-dharmic actions. Sentient beings desire happiness. However, they act just the opposite, as if they desire suffering. Because of that contradiction between desire and action, the suffering perpetuates. So you must formulate compassion, realizing all sentient beings are under the influence of ignorance and suffering. These suffering sentient beings must be helped. There is no other way but to help them. So you must formulate your intention of compassion, bodhichitta. Now, bodhichitta has two aspects. The first one is the formulation of a goal—that is, a desire to go someplace. Second, a person actually goes to that place. The formulation of the goal is, "I will liberate all sentient beings." The intention of mind is that by listening to this Dharma and inculcating its tenets, I will try to liberate all sentient beings across the wide horizon of the sky from this existence of suffering.

Practicing Dharma is hearing the Dharma, understanding the Dharma, and the process of reaching the goal. Once you have formulated the intention of liberating all sentient beings from suffering, then you participate in the process of reaching that goal. As well, you must listen to teachings with pure intentions. It is not like collecting some deep philosophical ideas just to extend your knowledge.

As I explained, we are not proceeding according to the traditional teaching method of hearing and pondering, and it is difficult to just jump right into the kernel of the meditation. However, there are many ways to grasp one's path—for example, through visualization and an empty state of mind. Slowly this will be explained. I am teaching you the path that is guru yoga, complete in all its elements. Regarding chanting, there is a longer version in the regular text, but because of language barriers and your limited time to practice, I condensed the whole text into a compact and short chant. In Tibet, half of the chanting and so on is clearly Dharma, but the other half could be just a monastic tradition.[10]

The essence of this Dharma is not to help you immediately but to acquire eternal happiness. So that's how you should formulate your intention at this time. If you wonder what the Dharma teaching is going to be—there are many paths. Within one path, you must have all the elements to make it a complete path. Just as if you want to drive a car, the engine and all its parts must be complete. Otherwise you cannot drive. Our teaching, although shortened, provides all the elements to make it a complete path.

In Dharma, there is philosophy and action. You cannot say, "Just get the philosophy and abandon the action." That is not correct. If you say, "Don't worry about the philosophy, just do the action," that is also faulty. Philosophy and action must be grafted together. Dharma is not practiced by one person forcing another person to practice. Ultimately it depends on the desire and the yearning of the students. Take the example of deities. There are many, many deities. One cannot say some deities are good and others are bad. Some of you are attracted to a particular deity and some are not. That's because of your karmic relation to that deity.

During the empowerment ceremony, all the dharmic gods are brought together. They are classed into five different buddha families. During the ceremony, a lama will invoke all the buddhas. A student, with supplication in her mind, picks up a flower and puts it on the mandala placed at the altar, praying, "Let my karmic deity be identified." When the flower is placed on the mandala, the place where the flower ends up is his buddha family. It is identified at that time.

The path of experiencing the personal deity (*yidam*)[11] is found that way also. And the Dharma is the same way. Whichever Dharma path you have strong faith in and a karmic relationship with, that is the way to practice.

Some of my students really wish to practice Dzokchen. Teaching Dzokchen is very hard. The difficulty comes from the differences in the nine paths. These can be summarized into three paths: low, middle, and high. Among those, the highest and the superior path is Dzokchen, the Great Accomplished.

In Tibet, first you have to listen to the teaching. You have to study the teaching. Then you must proceed from the bottom path to the higher path. That's because if you are not taught in that sequence, you might not be able to understand the teaching. The sequence is very important. It is analogous to entering a house: you must come through the door of the first floor, then proceed to the second and the third floors. It is of great importance that the teacher expound the path as clearly as possible. A mistaken path will lead the student to the wrong end and can result in drastic consequences to the teacher himself.

Deep esoteric teaching is not available to everyone. If that teaching is provided, it follows a sequence: first you get permission to practice, then you receive an explanation of the practice, after which you get the empowerment of practice, the *wang*. That sequence must be followed. If esoteric teachings are opened to people who do not meet these requirements, that is breaking the seventh vow of tantric samaya.

Yes, we know everything regarding the paths, but even in Tibet, if one is asked to teach Dzokchen from the very beginning, it would be considered very strange. However, because people gathered here demonstrate great endeavor and devotion to take the teaching, it is not right to say that you cannot take the teaching or you are not proceeding accordingly. Because of your endeavor and your desire, I feel that by giving this teaching, it might be possible that, with your karmic relationship, you might attain enlightenment. So the teaching of Dzokchen shall be approached broadly at this time. Enlightenment of one sentient being means countless sentient beings can be enlightened. If you do not become enlightened, still you have sown the seed of buddhahood.

That is my intention toward my students and toward other people. Superficially, when looking from outside, when the Dzokchen teaching is taught to people who don't even know the gestures, who don't even know how to read, and who don't know all the background basic requirements for Dzokchen, the attempt will sound very strange. The actual teaching of Dzokchen to such people is offensive to other lamas. Other Nyingmapa lamas don't consider that this follows the tradition. However, whatever other people say, my intention is clearly to sow the seeds of buddhahood among my students. Among yourselves, as students, you must realize the preciousness of this teaching and practice as hard as possible.

Do not think that you can practice later on when you have free time. Life is impermanent. It is uncertain when death will arrive. So you must think and meditate on impermanence, which will inspire you to practice and to practice now.

This meditation also provides you with a clear perception of the impermanence of your relationships in your immediate environment. We are so involved in being attached to our friends and staying away from our enemies. This is one aspect of life: making friends and having enemies. We distinctively divide humanity into two kinds of people: some are friends and some are enemies. We help our friends but bring down our enemies, or whoever we consider to be our enemies.

If you meditate on impermanence, the true nature of relationship will be discovered—that is, the indefiniteness of relationship. Look at the parents who have children. They try to protect their children, do the best things they possibly can for them. But at the end, that could be the cause of their death. On the other hand, the enemy whom you do not like, whom you hate, could come to your aid when you need help. That enemy could also marry into your family and become a close relative. Since human relationships are indefinite and changing, meditation on impermanence should provide you with clear perception, making you less attached to samsaric relationships.

Meditation on impermanence can also provide you with the preciousness of the Dharma doctrine. All the buddhas, realizing impermanence itself, practiced Dharma for the enlightenment of all sentient beings. If you realize impermanence by itself, you will feel sad or get depressed, or you might feel despair and think you have no alternative. But once you have Dharma, once you know the existence of Dharma and the path, when you get depressed or your mind is in turmoil, you can turn to it into Dharma. If you don't know that path, just the realization of impermanence can lead you to a mental institution. That's why meditation on impermanence becomes the reason to practice Dharma.

Meditation on impermanence is the motivation for complete practice. When you are practicing meditation, if the practice is too long and you become tired, you might say, "I am going to leave it right here and continue after taking a break and stretching my body." Or when you have to practice, you might think, "I am going to go away for my vacation and complete it later." When you put off your practice, or keep on procrastinating and never practice, the meditation on impermanence will make you realize that you have no time to procrastinate. Since your life is indefinite and the termination of your life is imminent at any moment and at any second, you cannot put off the practice of Dharma.

Realizing that you have only a little time, you must complete the practice of Dharma. The great Buddha said, "If you acquire a complete and true realization of impermanence, that in itself is one of the full paths." Now, if you would like to know what is the sign of true realization, or the complete realization of impermanence, here is an example. The hermit Karkar Gomchen was meditating in a cave in central Tibet. Right in front of the doorway of the cave was a thorny bush, which continually obstructed his movement in and out of the cave. One time he thought, "Maybe I should cut this bush so I can move freely." Then the second thought originated in his mind: "Why should I waste time cutting down the bush! I never know when I will die. I might die while cutting this bush, and I will be away from practicing Dharma. So I am not going to waste time cutting the bush. Instead, I will practice Dharma."

Here is another example: Jikmé Lingpa used to meditate by a pond with a special karma. At night when stars shone in the sky, the water from the pond turned into medicinal water. If you took a bath during that time, your body would be healed. In order to get down to the pond, you needed a ladder. Some lama suggested to Jikmé Lingpa, "You should build a ladder." Jikmé Lingpa said, "I never know when I will return to this pond. There is no sense in wasting time to build the ladder." That is the measurement of the realization of impermanence.

About the actual meditation or contemplation of impermanence: One way is to meditate on this universe—our planet, the sun, moon, and stars, and the many other planets. You people are more knowledgeable than we are. You have photographs and telescopes to see everything, like how big the planets are, how round they are, how big the sun or moon is. Now think that this whole universe will be destroyed. It will be like empty space. Nothing will be left. Seven suns and one water—seven days of continuous sun—will burn everything, and then the destruction will be completed by the rain and the wind.

Take a piece of rock and see how hard it is. Compare it to the universe that is filled with mountains and planets and everything. It will all be destroyed to dust. Then compare your life to a bubble on water.

Like that bubble, it can burst at any time. Even so you carry on with your life and are so attached to it. When you pursue that bubble, or when you are not successful in that bubble, you cause your own death. If you now realize the impermanence of the universe, there is no time to care for your mere bubble of life.

In Tibetan, our Earth is called "Dzambuling." There are countless planets like this one. When it is time for the destruction of this planet, of this universe, all the sentient beings will vacate here and be reborn in the gods' realm. The gods' realm has six floors, six regions of gods. The lowest one, the sun and moon and stars, is the closest to the Earth. On top of that there are five floors called "the gods of existence of desire"—these are the gods of desire, the region of desire. On top of that is the gods of form region.

When it is time for this Earth to be destroyed, all the beings on it will die and be reborn on the first floor of the form realm of the gods. Then the extremely hot rays of the sun will shine for seven days and burn the six realms of desire and the first floor of the form realm. When the flame turns upward and reaches the first floor of the form realm of the gods, they will see the flame rising. The young gods will ask the older gods for the cause of this flame. The elder gods will explain, "This flame was there a long time ago and has returned."

After the destruction, after seven days of fire, there will be rain, the destruction by rain. Each raindrop will be as big as a plow or a yoke of oxen and as long as an arrow. It will rain for seven days. The first floor of the form realm will flood. That's when all the sentient beings of the first floor will be born in the second floor. According to the Dharma, this world is ruled by a wind called "cross Dorjé" that holds the world from underneath. This wind now rises and breaks through the floor. It destroys the second floor of the form realm. At that time, the entire second floor will be born in the third floor. The empty space will remain like that for a long, long time.

Compared with this impermanence of the universe, your life is as short as an insect's, a mite that hatches in the morning and dies in the evening, a one-day existence. That is the length of our life. Compared with the destruction of the universe, realize how insignificant your life is, how unimportant and time consuming, and how important you make your life to be just to pursue samsaric goals. Realize the impermanence from this comparative sense, the impermanence of the whole universe that you believed to be permanent. This endeavor should arouse a deep realization of impermanence. You must then turn toward the Dharma. This is one way of getting to know impermanence.

Another way to meditate on impermanence is to think about the existence of phenomena. Think of phenomena in terms of planets, rocks, and all the formations. Now meditate on the impermanence of those planets and the beings on those planets. It is true fact that not a single being can escape death. Everyone must die at some point and must accept death as the termination of life. Everyone must come to that point, especially when we have so many kinds of diseases that we cannot understand. Even scientists and doctors have a hard time understanding all the diseases human beings are vulnerable to. This means the causes of death are increasing.

When we are born and as we grow up, we think, "I am growing up. My life is long." We do not think, "I am nearing death." But in reality, it is not life that is extending but death that is closing in. Yet even when we realize that death is coming nearer and nearer, we still grasp onto our samsaric existence.

You must realize that death, the phenomenon of death, is not new but happened to your father, your grandfather, your great-great grandfather, and so on. If you look deep into the past, you can see the extermination of your lineage by death. All beings suffer due to the impermanence wreaked by death. So before death takes your life, you must attain the goals of this precious human life. The immediate goal is doing away with suffering. You must realize that Dharma is happiness forever. You must practice Dharma as hard as possible. One of the most important points of Dharma is to subjugate all the five poisons. You must listen to the teaching and reflect on it; this will affect your mind and purify the defilements of your mind.

The words that are spoken in Dharma do not sound good. It is not the sound of joy and happiness. It is contradictory to what you usually use in samsara. Samsaric words provide physical and mental pleasure, like when you are tired, you rest or take a vacation to recuperate. In Dharma, it is the opposite—your physical body or mental body should work toward enlightenment. That's why the teachings of Dharma do not sound that great. They do not talk about pleasure or happiness or immediate happiness.

Lamas who act according to the Dharma do not get along with people who are involved in samsara. That's why many people do not like lamas who pursue their lives according to the Dharma. The root of the Dharma experience is guru yoga. Guru yoga is the root practice, but it should be preceded by attaining realization of how hard it is to get a human life, the impermanence of life, karma and its effect, and the bad consequences of samsara. For real practice, Dzokchen, the highest and most definitive path to enlightenment in the Nyingma tradition, should come after guru yoga. When I am teaching guru yoga, people desire Dzokchen, and some might see the preliminary practices as useless. However, think of it like going up stairs: you must first enter the first floor and find the stairs to climb to the second floor. That is the path. You must not undermine the preliminary work.

A lama and a doctor have almost the same responsibilities. Lamas are devoted to showing the path to enlightenment for all sentient beings. They are always in pursuit of a shorter path to get enlightened. However, the Dharma cannot be given in the form of a medicinal dose: "Take this now and get enlightenment right away." As Buddha said, "I will show you the path to liberation. However, whether you get enlightened or not depends on you." Thus lamas will find the nearest and clearest path for students, but the practice and experience of that path depends on the students themselves.

It seems you people think that you will get a sort of soothing message for your mind from Dharma. That is false. Do not expect that. First of all, these teachings are to bring your mind down to reality. They could cause troubles in your mind, bring sorrows to your mind. They do not have a soothing message. That's why you must listen to the message carefully. In order to have a very clear Dharma practice, you must have a mind that will turn away from samsara. At this moment, in every minute of your life you are completely involved in how to live in samsara better than before. Every time you get involved like that, you will not see its empty nature. Since you are not detached from samsara, and instead perpetuate the creation of samasaric action, you will go around and around in samsaric existence.

Take a sharp knife and put honey on the knife edge. If you are attached to the sweetness of honey and lick it, you are bound to cut and split your tongue in two. Likewise, since we are too attached to the pleasures of samsara, we risk cutting ourselves and being caught in the perpetual pursuit of pleasure. We get overly attached to our bodies. A moth that is attracted to the light of a lamp will go round and round. I don't know what it sees in the lamp, but it gets so attached it will burn itself up in the flame. Being too attached to a sound would be like a deer so attracted to the sound of a violin that he doesn't hear a hunter creeping in from behind. A strong attachment to a smell is like a snake that is attracted to the smell of musk—when it reaches the musk and touches it, it is killed. Attachment to taste is like a fish that rushes to eat a piece of meat that a fisherman throws in the water, not knowing that a hook is concealed in the tasty morsel. Attachment to touch is like an elephant who goes to wash in the cool water of a marsh on a hot day; once immersed in the muck, it slowly sinks and dies.

Likewise, among us there are driving forces of evil and driving forces of desire that ultimately bring an end to a person. Consider a person who goes to war for wealth and fame, attracted to the booty and the medals. He gets killed without any essence or meaning. There are many examples of attachments that you can see in your own environment.

Keep in mind that every strong pleasure has its downside. We consider eating and drinking an expression of pleasure or joy. We eat a variety of foods in order to satisfy our bodies, but with time you find that many of these foods can cause discomfort or disease, or even your death. If we celebrate by drinking beer, wine, or liquor, our spirit is high and it all feels enjoyable. However, ultimately too much drinking can rupture the liver and cause all kinds of diseases. We get labeled an alcoholic and can become estranged from our society.

You can see these kinds of things in your immediate environment. Each day you are so involved in samsaric actions that you create and multiply defilements every twenty-four hours. There is no time to even initiate a dharmic action. Worst yet is the consequence reaped in your next life that you cannot see, taking a rebirth in a place where you are not free and do not have eight freedoms, where you will forever be disengaged from Dharma. One of the requirements to practice Dharma is that you must turn away from samsara at some point. You must realize that building and performing samsaric actions lacks essence and is fruitless. If you turn away from samsara, your Dharmic practice will be clearer to you.

Within the four means of turning away from samsara, you must realize how precious your human life is. The preciousness of human life is indicated by the vast number of sentient beings in other realms, the present human beings who are practicing Dharma, and so on— again and again you are reminded of the preciousness of your own life and the circumstances that are present in your life, like having a lama, a teacher, the time to listen to his teaching, a desire to practice, and making time to practice that teaching. All these are precious and priceless when you compare your life with lives of beings in other samsaric realms.

This teaching on the four paths is not to soothe your mind or to instill a pleasurable sense in your mind, but to see the empty nature of samsara and the value of Dharma, to see samsara from a distance rather than being enslaved in samsara. There is no end to sorrow in your mind once you realize that, but you will see the preciousness of Dharma that is to end the suffering in a future life, and you will also be able to find the same opportunity to practice Dharma in the next form of life. Thus the teaching of four means of turning away from samsara is very important when you practice Dharma.

The text says, "The three worlds are as impermanent as the clouds of autumn." The meaning of that will be explained. It is very, very important to meditate on the impermanence of life prior to any practice of Dharma. If you meditate on impermanence due to death, it will bring the seed of practicing Dharma. Meditation on the teaching on impermanence is to remind you that when you are feeling lethargic in samsara, when you have no feeling and seem lifeless, when you are in that state it can remind you of death. If you think you are going to die immediately, you will seek a means to cure yourself, a means to stay away from death. When you realize that death can come at any moment, the need to turn to the Dharma will be clear to you. At death you are not sure of rebirth or the kind of rebirth. Or if you die due to the termination of karma, then you must seek a path to get a better rebirth in the next life. Meditation on impermanence should remind you to practice Dharma.

Meditation on impermanence and death can minimize your attachment to samsaric life. At present we are completely involved in promoting samsaric life: every hour is taken up with eating, sleeping, and enjoyments. On top of that, we want to acquire all the necessary and luxurious things. A person who is building a house or planning it for the future will try to make the house as permanent as possible, make it last forever. His orientation is like that of a person who thinks he is never going to die, so he tries to earn as much as possible and clings to this life. But when you realize that death can come at any moment, then the need to turn to the Dharma will be clear to you.

After death, all the things you have done will be left behind. You cannot take anything with you. They will be enjoyed by somebody else. When death comes to a person, there is no diversion. Yet you spent your time forgetting about Dharma in pursuit of samsaric goals. No one can avoid death. When Shakyamuni Buddha was living, many people died. Even when Guru Rinpoché was living, many people died. Death cannot be avoided by buddhas. They cannot say, "You don't die" or "You don't have to die." Even in the presence of a buddha or bodhisattva, the most powerful figures of the universe, death is common.

When Guru Rinpoché was visiting Tibet, King Tri Songdetsen's daughter died. When the grieving king asked the most powerful and enlightened Guru Rinpoché to revive his daughter from the dead, Guru Rinpoché somehow invoked her scattered, lost mind, and on her heart he wrote the syllable *Nri* and brought her back to life. However, later on she died and was reincarnated as one of the tertons. The fact is, she was revived from the dead but still died. Death is a fact that no one can avoid. Nobody can run away or hide from death.

You feed your body with the best food and wear the best clothes, or you appreciate the young bodies of beautiful girls. However, when you die your dead body rots and gets dirty. Others stay away from your body, they keep their distance. When you are dying, it's hard to find friends. Friends keep their distance because they are also facing the truth of their own death.

And so at the termination of one's karmic merits, a person or sentient being must die. If you cannot escape death and death is the one thing you must face, what do you do? You turn to Dharma.

Another way to meditate on impermanence is to remind yourself to think about all the enlightened beings, like our own great teacher Buddha Shakyamuni, Guru Rinpoché (Guru Padma Jungné), and the many other tertons, great lamas, and great siddhas of India.[12] Now ask, "Where are they?" They have attained full enlightenment and can perform any number of miraculous actions. They are above death. But still, where are they? We know through sacred books that these kinds of people lived and that they did such and such things and were in such and such places. We know their stories, but where actually are they? Such is the manifestation of impermanence. They found and attained enlightenment. They held power over death, power over the decaying body, but they also manifested impermanence.

Think that your body is like a worm. You are like a worm in Sikkimese ground. Nothing more than that. That is one way of meditating on impermanence. Another way to think about impermanence is to think about great beings. Consider this existence, samsara, which includes all six realms. One of the six realms is the gods' realm, which is considered to be prosperous, not having the suffering that other realms have. However, even the kings of the gods' realm do not live forever. They must also die. Since we don't see them, we have to believe that his realm also comes to an end in time. Now come down to earth. Read history, which will show you impermanence. Look at the Roman Empire. It was once powerful and rich, but now it's just a monument of stones.

Permanence cannot be bought with any amount of wealth. It cannot be fought for with arms and ammunition. Impermanence cannot be deceived by your intelligence. Impermanence is there. It pervades and cuts across everything. The examples in history are pervasive; you can easily find a prominent example of impermanence to meditate on. Likewise, newspaper accounts are replete with the rise and fall of the powerful and wealthy. Not even the greatest wealth and power can prevent impermanence and death. No one can avoid death.

Then look at your own life, your samsaric life. We are geared toward acquiring power, fame, and fortune. Yet those people who already achieved success, which we are trying to emulate, do not even have the power to avoid the fact of impermanence and their own death. So pursuing our samsaric goals is meaningless. Realizing that, one should then turn to Dharma.

Another way of meditating is by taking various examples in your immediate environment and meditating on impermanence. One natural fact is the change of seasons. In spring you feel lethargic, lie on the green grass, and smell beautiful flowers. Summer comes and everything is still green and the sun is hot. Fall comes and leaves change color and texture and begin to fall. The flowers that were beautiful in spring are gone. Winter comes and all the leaves are gone. Trees are bare and the ground is frozen.

One can think as well about the impermanence of even rocks and mountains—the very symbols of permanence. We say "as hard as a rock," or "firm as a mountain." Yet even they are not permanent. You have seen rocks broken up on the ground; eventually they turn to sand. The biggest rock, the hardest rock, can be split into two by lightning. You have seen the firmest mountain eroded by a river and leveled to the ground. All these examples, which you claim are landmarks of permanence, even these are destroyed. Then reflect on your life. See where the permanence is in your own life.

Mitakpa is a good term to know, a very expressive term meaning "impermanence." It also applies to human relationships. It has neither good nor bad connotations. It is not definite; it is not indefinite. In a relationship, your best friend could turn into your worst enemy, and your worst enemy could turn into your best friend. Take the example of marriage: At one time a husband and wife came together. They were the only two people who understood each other. Later they can turn into the two worst enemies.

Let's extend this domestic example to broader circumstances, to the relationship of one town to another town, one country to another country. At one time a country was the enemy of another country. And then few years later they became allies. Impermanence is also true for a country's status in the world, it's prestige and power. A good example is one of the European kingdoms, such as Great Britain. At one time its power extended throughout the world. Now time has passed, and its power is diminished. Instead, some other country that was almost unknown is growing in power. What is the determining factor? Mitakpa!

Likewise, a person whom you consider to be bad now can later turn into a good person. That also is mitakpa. You must have seen people who are very poor at the start of their lives but later became very rich, or people who start out in life very rich and end up very poor. The desire to acquire wealth is the same for both rich and poor. The poor person does not want to remain poor, he wants to be wealthy. A wealthy person never desires to be poor. That's not his goal. He wants more wealth. They both want wealth. The decisive factor is mitakpa. The downfall or rise is mitakpa.

A man who was once powerful is nobody now. A man who was not powerful becomes powerful now. You have seen how a person who was once nobody becomes the president of the United States. In this relationship the determining factor is mitakpa. Meditation on mitakpa must not be a fault-finding meditation. You are not trying to find fault in other people or in phenomena. Meditation gives you the chance to realize mitakpa itself. Unavoidable, unreachable mitakpa. It is imminent and present in all phases of life. Meditation on mitakpa will make you realize the indefinite and transient relationships of sentient beings.

Once there was an enlightened teacher, Phakpa Katayana (a disciple of Shakyamuni Buddha). One day he went to a village and saw a woman by a house, breastfeeding a baby in her lap. The woman was eating fish and threw the bones to a dog. When the dog ran to eat the bones, she picked up a stone and threw it to chase the dog away. The enlightened Katayana stopped for awhile and used his intuition to see the whole relationship. He found that the fish she was eating was the rebirth of her father who had died, the child she was holding was once her ardent enemy, and the dog she threw the stone at was her mother, who had also died. He remarked that the relationships of sentient beings in samsara are all as funny and absurd as this one.

And so I tell you about the impermanence of relationships in our immediate environment, and the impermanence of people in our environment, and the impermanence due to our previous lives. Realizing all this, and that you have no definite, permanent relationship, you must meditate earnestly on impermanence. Meditation on mitakpa should include an uncertain potential cause of death. We meditate on indefinite causes of death. How is that?

Take the food we eat. The real reason for eating is to further our living, to make our bodies strong. You always eat food with an intention of satisfying yourself, of obtaining a kind of oral satisfaction. However, food can poison us and cause many diseases. The very food that we consume to further our living can end our living. For example, we eat fish not to kill ourselves, but if you happen to eat fish carelessly and choke on the bones, you might die. People die of improper eating. So the cause of death is all around. Even in the games we play. We engage in sport for fun, not to kill ourselves, but it can cause our death. Take, for example, sailing. People sail on the ocean with a high spirit. But the boat could capsize, causing our death. All these things are what you consider life-supporting systems, but at the same time, they can cause your death.

In summary, the meditation on impermanence means turning toward the Dharma. Just meditating on impermanence is not enough. Just being depressed about the impermanence in samsara is not enough (when a situation does not go right or changes for the worse, you become depressed or even harm yourself). Once you realize impermanence, turn toward the Dharma. That is the alternative. If you don't meditate on this, anything I teach you is like teaching words to a parrot. If you teach a parrot, "It is wrong to do an adharmic action," it will hold onto a worm in its claw and repeat "It's wrong to do an adharmic action," then tear the worm apart.

Nevertheless, that does not stop me from giving you the teaching on impermanence. Whenever the teaching is received, one must experience it and try to meditate on it. Although it is very hard to achieve enlightenment, through meditation you can minimize defiling and poisoning your mind. That is an achievement. At the end of the day, all the fruits of your effort to minimize your poison and truly meditate on impermanence depend on you alone. I can teach, but I cannot force you to do it. I have shown you the way to meditate on impermanence, which is one of the most important aspects of Dharma.

I now want to explain the intention and dedication of the practice. These two aspects of Dharma are very important: the clarification of intention and the dedication of merit at the end. It is very important that you earn merit by listening and by experiencing the Dharma path, which must immediately be dedicated to the enlightenment of all sentient beings. If you do not do it immediately, then after your meditation and after performing dharmic action, any anger will destroy what you have done. Anger dissolves all you have done. So the clarification of intention and the dedication are the two most important aspects of practice. If you wonder what the thing that should be dedicated is, it is the merit you earned by listening to the teachings.

Now we come to the dedication of merit and dharmic action. How can this dedication be done? With anything you offer to the buddhas of ten directions, like a single flower you put on the altar or offering a lamp or prostrations. All of these are the offerings, but merits you earned through these offerings should immediately be dedicated to the enlightenment of all sentient beings.

The dedication is analogous to gift giving. If you wonder what the gift is, it is the product of virtuous action, including everything you do that originates from the bodhisattva intention. To whom do you dedicate or give the fruit of these virtuous actions? Take your present parents as the main recipient, and most important, dedicate to the people you do not like, people who are your enemies.

True Dharma is free from both attachment and aversion. True Dharma is free from any aversions like "I do not like that person" and "I must keep my distance." It is also free from attachments like "This is my friend. This is my son, my daughter, my dearest friends." True Dharma is free from both aversion and attachment. Taking the enemy you do not like and your parents of this life as an integral part, and including all sentient beings throughout the wide horizon of the sky, you dedicate your merit to them. Give your gift to them. That is the place to offer your gift.

THE DEDICATION

What is the manner of dedicating the fruits of virtuous action? If you do not know, look at how the buddhas and bodhisattvas dedicated, have been dedicating, and will dedicate. In the same manner, I will dedicate the fruits of virtuous actions for the enlightenment of all sentient beings, so they can reach the state of buddhahood. And the recitation will include how Kuntu Sangpo (the primordial Buddha) and Jampalyang (bodhisattva Manjushri) dedicated their merits to the enlightenment of all sentient beings. Likewise, I will dedicate my merits and fruits of virtuous actions for the enlightenment of all sentient beings. Those words will be included in the chanting.

The mind is our most important aspect, and speech and action are servants of mind. When you dedicate within your mind, it is same as chanting. That's important.

Questions and Answers

Q: When Rinpoché was talking about the destruction of this world and everyone being reborn in the second level of the gods' realm, does that mean reborn in the gods' realm regardless of one's karma?
A: Regardless of karma.

Q: Then what is the use of doing anything?
A: Do not misunderstand. Being born in the gods' realm is not an enlightenment. That is still the general product of karma. With the destruction of this samsaric existence, all sentient beings will be born in the form land. First the desire land, then the form land, then the no form land, the region without form. Below this formless realm, including the entire universe, is the wheel of samsaric existence. So being born from the lowest to the higher is not freedom from samsaric existence. The suffering will perpetuate there too. Like people born in America, some are born in the bad parts and some in good parts of the country. All are still within samasara.

Q: Rinpoché said if someone had a strong realization of impermanence without an understanding of Dharma, he would go crazy. What would be the best help for someone who sees impermanence and gets sad?
A: It is very important and favorable for a person if he has a realization of impermanence or is in touch with impermanence. Once he realizes impermanence, he grasps the fact of living. For us Buddhists, once we feel everything around us is impermanent and know we are under the law of impermanence, we understand we need to seek protection. Seeking protection for us Buddhists is to seek refuge in the three precious ones, Buddha, the Dharma, and the Sangha. These three precious ones taught the doctrines and disclosed Dharma to us.

KARMA: CAUSE AND RESULT

The Intention

It is important to formulate the intention before you receive the teaching. If you wonder why, the reason is the karmic relation—there is not a single sentient being who wasn't your parent.

All sentient beings desire happiness, but they do not know how to acquire happiness. They do not desire suffering, but they perpetuate actions that produce suffering. Once you realize the suffering of sentient beings, true compassion will be born in your mind. For those sentient beings who are far from gaining the great knowledge of what to acquire and what to abandon, you must formulate an intention: "I must endeavor to enlighten, and there is no other way but to enlighten them." Hearing these deep words of teaching on the meaning of Dharma, you must promise yourself, "I shall act according to Dharma and enlighten all sentient beings under the wide horizon of the sky." Likewise, you should also think, "I will receive this deep spiritual advice and meditate and practice accordingly so all sentient beings can attain enlightenment." If you can make your intention a bodhichitta intention, then the action of teacher giving a teaching and the response of a student listening to teaching turns into dharmic action, whatever Dharma you practice.

THE TEACHING

If, when his time comes, even a king should die,
his wealth and his friends and relatives shall not follow him;
wherever men go, wherever they remain,
karma like a shadow will follow them.

Prior to guru yoga we learn about the four turnings away from samsara. We have discussed how hard it is to obtain a precious human birth and impermanence, and we know how to meditate on impermanence.

We realize now that everything is impermanent, everything is changing, and that being depressed and feeling sorry and sad about this fact is not constructive. After being born, it is inevitable that one will eventually die, and death seems like a flame burning out or the evaporation of water. This is easy to conceive, but this is not the end, because inevitably after death you must take a rebirth. You are reborn after death. This death and rebirth, one after another after another, constitutes a wheel (*khorwa*), and it is analogous to a fly trapped in a bottle going around and around. The fly has nowhere else to go and must circle within that enclosure.

Depending on the result of your action, you might be born in the human realm, god realm, or jealous god realm. As a result of unvirtuous action, you might be reborn in a lower realm like the hell realm, hungry ghost realm, or animal realm.

Suffering and happiness alternate as products of one's own karma. There are circumstances in life that bring happiness; in other circumstances, one suffers and is filled with sorrow. This is true for beings in other realms as well. In the animal realm, a dog with a rich owner has an easy life. Another has to suffer and wander in search of food. Some birds have an easy time; others must hide from predators. It is the same for all animals.

Take the circumstances of your own life. Sometimes you are happy. Sometimes you are sad and upset. All these moods alternate continuously, they appear and disappear. This is because you are reaping the fruits of the seeds you have sown. You are reaping the fruit of past karma. Your sad circumstances and sufferings are the result of karma you have acquired. The good time you are having is likewise the product of karma. So a person always faces his karma.

There are three different karmas: virtuous karma, unvirtuous karma, and neutral karma. One produces these three kinds of karma. It is like throwing seeds on the ground—there is no way these seeds will disappear, they will produce a shoot. This is all a product of karma.

Realize that what you consider to be a small action can bring very significant results. Let's take the example of a seed. The seed of a tree is small and insignificant, so insignificant that if you leave it somewhere, it can easily be lost. But once you sow that seed, you will see the growth of a huge tree—quite a significant result from a seemingly small cause. Every action is like that; you must not take any of them for granted, you must not undermine any of your actions. Every action has a visible and definite result. Whatever it is, there is nothing that does not have a karmic result. Each action will produce significant karma. This is the teaching of karma and the result.

You must think very carefully. You must ponder these things, contemplate every action deeply. Take the example of killing an insect, which seems very insignificant when compared with other actions. You press your thumb on an insect and it's dead. But the consequence of that action is having to take rebirth five hundred times more than that insect, and that insect will kill you because in one lifetime you eliminated its life; five hundred times it will eliminate your life. In that way, the consequences are grave.

In the present, when people practice Dharma they feel nothing goes right for them. They complain that by practicing Dharma, they are estranged from society. All kinds of problems come up, nothing seems to go right, and nothing appears as it should be. But this is according to the samsaric point of view. From a dharmic point of view, it is much better to exhaust the bad karma you have accumulated from past lives so that the future becomes brighter. It is very important to exhaust the bad karma within one's sight and range. If you extinguish the karma that is passing by, you have a brighter future in terms of Dharma. When you perceive your life through Dharma, bad karma is not at all bad.

In this regard, the teachings on turning away from the wheel of existence are very important. Within the wheel of existence, action consists of conquering and subjugating your enemies and expanding your friendships, fame, and wealth. If you are devoted to these goals all the time, you will never have time to practice Dharma. That is why turning away from samsara is very important.

One does not turn away from samsara blindly. Rather, through Dharma, you realize there is no firm definition, no line drawn on who is your enemy and who is your friend. An enemy in another place, another rebirth, another circumstance, and another time could be your friend. The same applies to your friends, all of whom in other rebirths and circumstances could be your enemy. Realize that one cannot have confidence that a relationship will not change in this life; there is no permanence in a relationship. Such impermanence motivates us to turn away from samsaric relationships.

The same is true for the things we spend our lives and resources accumulating: none of these are inherently stable or beneficial. For example, we concentrate all our efforts on acquiring wealth. The goal, to acquire wealth, somehow justifies the means, so that we try to acquire riches by any and all means. However, achieving wealth is not the end of the matter. Having wealth comes with many worries. If you built a beautiful house, you might have to worry about protecting it from fire, and with any kind of wealth, you always worry that other people will take it away from you. You constantly worry about the wealth you possess. Even something essential, such as eating, is not absolutely good. Although we search for and consume nutritious food for our health, for strength and growth, food can also cause death or chronic disease.

Within relationships, if one continues to feel attachment and aversion, one is prone to insult and to criticize others, while at same time, one feels hurt if criticized by others. This is the process of samsara: in a relationship one praises one person and criticizes another, while simultaneously being criticized or praised. The aversion to insult and the attachment to praise can bring suffering.

When you see the faults of other people, you must realize it is the reflection of your own mind. The fault is not inherently in another person, it is the defiled perception of your own mind. Likewise, if someone criticizes you, there is no reason to get upset or seek revenge. Realize that this is the product of one's own karma, which cannot be affected by others. Realize because someone is labeling you negatively doesn't mean you're that bad person. If someone describes you as a bad person, you must see the empty nature of that statement. You must tell yourself, "That is not what I am going to be," and realize that the current negative situation is due to your own karma. By realizing these two aspects of karmic perception, you can be free from attachment and aversion, which can cause imbalance. Be free from seeing other people's faults by realizing that the perception is a product of your own karma. If you realize that whatever faults you see in others are faults of your own perception, you will not be affected by the suffering of attachment and aversion.

And that's how you should formulate your intention and thoughts. Orient your actions to realize that action within samsara is senseless and has no essence. Wherever you are born within six realms, it is infested with suffering. You must realize there is suffering in all these realms. If you do not, then you do not desire to hear the word of Dharma.

THE DEDICATION

We will now dedicate the merit of what we have taught and what we have learned to all sentient beings, thinking, "The merit accumulated by receiving the teachings, and the merit accumulated in the past, present, and future, I am distributing to all sentient beings for their happiness and for the attainment of buddhahood."

THE SUFFERING OF SAMSARA: THE SIX REALMS

THE INTENTION

I MUST ENDEAVOR to enlighten by receiving this spiritual advice and meditating and practicing according to Dharma so that all sentient beings, including my enemies, can be led to liberation and attain enlightenment.

THE TEACHING

Due to ignorance, craving, and becoming
in the realms of men, gods, and the three inferior spheres,
in all five realms beings revolve foolishly,
like the turning of a potter's wheel.

ANGER AND THE RESULTING EIGHT HOT HELLS

The wheel of existence encompasses six realms. The three lower realms (ngandro sum) are the hell, hungry ghost, and animal realms. The three upper realms (dedro) are the human, gods, and jealous gods realms.

Now for the hell realm, there are two kinds: the hot hell and the cold hell. The hot hell has eight strata. The common characteristic among all strata is that they are formed by the anger of sentient beings. The floors of the strata are burning iron—on top of the floor surfaces are fans of burning iron.

The karma produced through your anger, the fruit of harboring anger or manifesting anger constantly, is rebirth in the first stratum of hell called "Reborn" or "Revived Again" (Yang Su). There, the mere sight of other beings generates anger and rage. And when you grab anything or hold anything in your hand, it magically turns into weapon. So all sentient beings in this first stratum of hell grasp weapons and get into fights with one another, ultimately slaughtering one another. When they all die, a voice from the sky says, "Revive Again," and they all come back to life and the process of fighting and cutting one another repeats again and again. Realize this is caused by anger and that's why you must abstain from anger.

Below that first stratum is "Black Line" (Thik Nak). Here, sentient beings are held down by the officials of hell, who draw lines across their bodies: eight lines, sixteen lines, thirty-two lines. After the lines are drawn, the officials take a burning saw and hack each body along those lines. As they hack the upper part of the body, the being feels pain and suffering. Then as they hack the lower part of the body, the upper wound heals. They then hack the upper part as the lower part heals. This continues again and again. Such suffering goes on for many kalpas. The suffering is caused by constructing the mandalas without knowing their basic line foundation, painting deities without knowing the lines and geometrical graphics, drawing chorten,[13] drawing deities, and incorrectly setting up altars. The result is you are born in the second stratum of hell.

Below that is the third stratum of hell called "Dudjom." In that hell, there are mountains that look like animal heads, like lions, tigers, and rams. Sentient beings are born in between these mountains. Two mountains will ram into each other and press sentient beings almost to death. But there is no death. The mountains will pull back again, and the sentient beings will live. Then they will close in again and cause much pain and suffering. This process of intense pain and revival endures for many, many kalpas. Sentient beings are born in that hell because of catching and taking lives of an insect and rubbing it between your palms, or clapping your hands together to kill a flying mosquito. That's the same motion as the hills crushing beings. In Tibet we have lice, which we trap between two thumbs and kill. The fruit of that action is being born in this third stratum of hot hell.

Below that is the fourth stratum of hell called "Cry for Help" (Ngöbu). In this hell, all sentient beings are led to an iron house. When they enter, the door shuts automatically. Then the fire begins to heat up the house and it begins to burn. Sentient beings inside start burning and getting cooked. Realizing there is no way out, they cry out in pain for help. The awful cries can be heard outside of the iron house. This is the hell that comes from breaking vows by monks or practicing laypeople, and also by breaking the samaya, the ethics of tantra.

Below that is the fifth stratum of hell called "Louder Cry for Help" (Ngöbu Chenpo). In this realm, sentient beings see a big iron castle. They go inside to find some shade or comfort. Once inside, the fire starts burning intensely, two hundred times hotter than the fire in the "Cry for Help" stratum. The beings cry louder and scream at the top of their lungs for help. Being born there is due to drinking a lot. These are people who don't eat but instead drink alcohol.

Below that is the sixth stratum of hell called "Tsawai Hot." In this hell, officials throw sentient beings up in the air and skewer them on a trident, and they also thrust hot burning tridents into their mouths, their noses, and all their sense organs. The flames come out of every orifice and the burning sensations are intense. You suffer unbearable pain. Sometimes in this realm sentient beings are thrown into boiling water and cooked thoroughly. Your body and bones fall apart, but you still feel the pain. The torture is continual, and the suffering makes you believe that death would be a pleasant thing. However, until you exhaust your karma, there is no death. You suffer constantly for many kalpas. This hell is caused by not keeping an honest relationship with your own lama.

Below this is an even greater degree of hot hell, the seventh stratum, called "Rabtu Tsawai Nyalwa." The process is the same. The officials skewer the sentient being on the hot tridents. The only difference is that they wrap the sentient beings in burning iron blankets to intensify the pain and suffering. Also, sometimes beings are thrown into boiling hot water. The temperature is twice as high as in the tsawai hot stratum.

Below that is the eighth stratum, Narmé Nawa. *Narmé* means "the topmost suffering." In this realm, the fire will be blazing. Cries for help are heard, cries of suffering, cries of burning. You will not see their bodies because they are completely enveloped by the fire. You will see this ball of fire, and within that inferno the voices cry out. The cause of this suffering is betraying your tsawai lama, killing your father, killing your mother, causing disturbances in the Sangha, making things up that are untrue, creating false disturbances, and breaking or betraying your esoteric teachings.

All eight strata are known as "hot hells." The main cause of being born in any one of them is anger or taking the lives of sentient beings. The process of meditation involves experiencing all of this within one's meditation. Merely knowing the suffering described here intellectually will not help you, nor will visualizing someone else suffering, because you will not feel the same degree of suffering. Therefore it is important to visualize yourself born in one of these hells and to experience the suffering in your mind. Once you begin to experience the suffering, fear will come into your mind. Once you experience the suffering and fear, your mind will turn to Dharma and you will realize the true suffering of all sentient beings. Then the path of Dharma appears more clearly, and this will liberate you from all the suffering.

Once you realize the suffering of sentient beings in this realm of hot hells, true compassion will be born in your mind and the way to liberation from suffering will open before you. To illustrate, I'll tell you the story of Shakyamuni Buddha, who, prior to his enlightenment, was born in hell. He was born as Baksita, who pulled a chariot with a rope. At that time he had a friend called Karmarupa. They worked like a pair of horses, pulling a chariot with their human bodies. Then Baksida realized all the sentient beings there had to suffer. He knew how much, since he was suffering himself. As he looked around and saw all other beings suffering, as he realized this, from the depth of his mind he thought, "If all these sentient beings have to suffer, then I will suffer for them. I will drag the chariot myself." So he told one of the hell officials, "Since all sentient beings here suffer to this extent, I will suffer for them. I will take on their suffering. Please put all the chariot ropes on me and I will draw for them." The hell official said, "What are you talking about? All the sentient beings must exhaust their own karma." He then took a burning hammer and hit Baksita's head. Baksita instantly died and was reborn on the thirty-second floor of the gods' realm.

So by realizing there is suffering everywhere, and not getting drowned in that feeling of suffering, which is not constructive, you work toward Dharma, realizing there is even a way out of hell. That bohdisattva intention of Baksita liberated that sentient being out of hell to the thirty-second level of the gods' realm.

There is suffering all around us, but there is a path away from the suffering. You must not think the suffering itself is the inevitable dead end of life. You must see it as a chance and a path to liberation from suffering. It's analogous to the feeling when you are sick, "I want to die." If you are suffering from illness, you will get a doctor or take medicine and try to get well and survive rather than descending into discouragement and depression about feeling like death.

As another example of a path to enlightenment, let me tell you the story of a daughter of an Indian family. Actually, the child was not a daughter but was given a girl's name. The family had many sons who died one after another. Because death was so common in that family, they named their son as if he were a daughter. The tradition at that time was that if a child had died in a family, in order to protect the next male child, he was often given a female name, which is why this male child was named as a daughter of so and so.

Dzawai Pumo was the female name of this male child. When he grew up, he asked his mother what his caste class was. At that time in India, you worked according to the caste you were born into. His mother realized that if she told the truth, that he belonged to the caste of collectors of jewelry from shipwrecked vessels at the bottom of the ocean, then he would probably leave and die in a shipwreck himself. So she told him, "You belong to the tailor caste." So he joined the tailor caste for awhile. But soon they found out and excommunicated him, saying, "You do not belong to the tailor caste." When he was kicked out, he went back to his mother and said, "They told me I don't belong to that caste. What caste do I belong to?" His mother told him, "You belong to the caste of incense seller or incense maker." He went to the incense maker and was there for a short while. But they kicked him out, telling him he did not belong to that caste. He continued that way, going from one caste to another, and each time he got kicked out. Meanwhile, he provided a good living for his mother.

After he was excommunicated by all those castes, he finally asked his mother, "What caste do I really belong to?" Having no other alternative, his mother said, "You belong to the caste of jewelry collector. However, my son your great grandparents and many of your forebears died at sea in shipwrecks. Therefore, it is not possible for you to pursue that profession." However, he did not listen and arranged to ship out with the sailors. When he was ready to set sail, he asked his mother for permission to leave. His mother held onto his clothes, crying and begging him not to leave. When his mother started crying, he told her, "This is a great occasion, to be on a ship, on the ocean. This should be a celebration of joy rather than a time of sadness. Your crying and trying to stop me from collecting gems is a bad omen." So he kicked his mother and took off.

When he sailed the ocean, a wind called "unpredictable wind" came and wrecked his ship. But he held onto a plank and floated for awhile. Then a wave took him to a deserted island. He looked around and saw a beautiful house. When he opened the door, he saw four goddesses cleaning and preparing the throne for someone. He asked, "For whom are you preparing the place?" They said, "We are preparing for Dzawai Pumo." He replied, "Oh, that's me," and he climbed on the throne. For several years he stayed there and had a good time. But after the exhaustion of one's good karma, one must move on. So when his karma was exhausted, he said, "Well, I must move on." They said, "Please stay here. Do not go away." But when he insisted on going, they said, "Please don't go south. It is not good for you." However, he went south to be adventurous.

There he again saw another island with a beautiful house. He opened the door and looked inside. There were eight female offering deities, preparing the throne. He asked, "For whom are you preparing?" They said, "Dzawai Pumo, who is coming here." He replied, "Oh, that's me," and sat on the throne. He stayed there for several years and enjoyed his life.

On and on he went from one beautiful place to another, one group of goddesses to another. This was the product of the good karma, serving his mother while he was in samsara. Every time he left a place, he was advised not to go south, but he insisted on doing just that. At last he came to a castle. The top of the castle touched the highest point in the sky, and in front of the castle stood a huge guard with red eyes. He asked who lived inside and thought there might be another group of fairies. The door opened. So he walked in. When he entered, the door closed. He expected to find the fairies. Instead, he saw bunches of people and drills coming down from the ceiling. People were screaming and suffering because their brains were being drilled through.

When he asked what was happening, they said, "We are suffering as the consequence of kicking our mothers." Then he realized that he had also kicked his mother. He looked around to escape, but there was no place to go. He tried to find an exit but could not. A voice came down and said, "Those who are suffering, let them go. And those who are not, let them enter." Immediately after the voice spoke, a drill came down and started to drill his brain. He felt the terrible pain. He began to experience the suffering of his brain being drilled. With the intolerable suffering, he realized there were many others who were suffering because of the same karma, numerous sentient beings who committed the same kind of crime in samsara. Since all of them had to go through his kind of suffering, from the very kernel of his heart, he generated the bodhichitta (compassion) mind (*jangchup sem*). He then thought, "Let all the suffering of sentient beings who have to go through this suffering be upon me. Let me suffer for them from the depths of my heart." While experiencing that suffering, he formulated that intention. When that intention was formulated in his mind, the drill came off his head and disappeared. He then died and took a better rebirth.

This example is mainly to make you aware of the importance of bodhichitta, a very, very important intention. Bodhichitta, formulated in this way from the very kernel of your heart, is the path to enlightenment, the path of liberation from the suffering that surrounds us.

Now, since we are in samsara, circumstances will arise that cause us to be angry. When you become aware that you are getting angry or become aware of your originating anger, it is very important to catch yourself immediately and realize it, telling yourself, "I am angry." Also, in some sense, repent your anger, make a confession, and resolve to abstain from anger in the future. By doing that, the product of bad karma from anger can be absorbed. Suffering surrounds us like the ocean. However, at the same time there is a path that can lead us out of the suffering. The root of this path originates from bodhichitta from the depth of your heart.

You may be angry at your Dharma friends or have been angry at them. Realize it, admit it, and make resolution not to be angry in the future. Make such a resolution in front of Vajrasattva (this will be taught later).

COLD HELLS

Now we come to the eight cold hells, the stratum of hells that are extremely cold. One hell is a glacial ice surface where naked sentient beings wander in a snowstorm.

The first realm of this cold hell is called "Blister Hell" (Chu-wurchen). In this hell, sentient beings get blasted by the frigid snow storm and their bodies blister all over. Another realm is called "Broken Blisters." As the cold increases, these blisters burst, creating big wounds. Then in another realm the degree of coldness increases to such an extent that you cannot open your mouth. Everything in your body is frozen. "A chu" expresses the cold you feel, and you will be "achuing" without any real sensation of the cold because you are frozen. In another realm, the cold increases even more, to such a degree that one loses one's voice. One has to take a deep breath once in a while, but it's so cold that the pain is excruciating.

As the cold increases, at a certain temperature the color of your body will become blue, like the utpala flower, and the wounds covering your body break into four different directions. The wounds will crack like that flower, in different directions. Increases in coldness cause inflammation within the wounds, they turn red, and the wounds crack in eight different directions. Now in "the Big Padma" (Padma

Chenpo), all the wounds in the body will crack twelve times and six-teen times, like the cracking of the earth in a drought. Picture it like that, the wounds cracking four times, then eight, then twelve, then sixteen, and so on. Then the wounds turn dark red, and now the body itself begins to crack in many directions. In these cracks, worms with iron teeth will be born and begin to eat you through those cracks.

SHORT-LIVED HELL

The Short-Lived Hell (Nyetsik Nyalwa) has no defined space, and there is no defined suffering. The suffering can be anywhere and any kind. One example of this hell is a sentient being born between the cracks of rock. These beings start growing but cannot grow bigger because of the limited space in the rock. But the beings keep growing.

Some sentient beings will be born in the form of insects inside of a rock, a hard rock where there are no pores. When you break the rock you can see the worm inside. Some sentient beings are born in a glacier or in a frozen land, where a mind exists entirely restrained in a straitjacket. A birth can be of that nature. Some will be born in a tree and take the trees as their own bodies. Many sentient beings attach themselves to the door of a house, a pillar of the house, a mortar and pestle, or a broom. Their minds get attached to things and consider those things as their own bodies.

One historical example of this type of rebirth that actually occurred is told in the story of Murti, the great Indian Buddhist saint. With his foresight, he saw that his deceased mother was reborn in Nyet-sik Nyalwa, in Tibet, near Dankuk, Lingtsang. Just as I traveled to the United States without knowing the language, Murti traveled to Tibet. On the way his interpreter died, so he had to travel alone, not knowing the Tibetan language. He searched for the Tibetan family in Nyetsik Nyalwa where his mother was reborn and, being a great saint, he found them. He then worked as a shepherd, worked hard and for a long time. The owner of the flock was very happy and asked the great saint, "What do you want for your service?" Murti said, "I don't want anything. I just want your hearth. The owner was surprised. "You just want my hearth? No money or anything?" Murti affirmed, "I just want your hearth." So the owner said, "You can take our hearth." Murti then dismantled the hearth made out of stone and mud. He found a rock and cracked it open. There, he found the worm that was the rebirth of his mother. When he opened the rock, the worm died. He ground the rock and the dead body of the worm and made it into *tsa tsa*, a small stupa-like thing. To make it, clay with remnants of relatives or great lamas is put into a mold and dried. He made many *tsa tsa* to help the consciousness of his mother. Nowadays this is a very common Dharmic tradition.

Another example of the Short-Lived Hell is evident in the story told about an old house near Golok province. In that part of the world where I come from, people used wood to cook with and to heat the house. Every time they made fire in this particular house, they heard a strange voice coming out of the wall. So the house owner made a mark on the wall with charcoal. The next day they took the wall apart and looked inside. There they found a mound of silver. On top of the silver was a frog. When they dismantled the wall, the frog died. Later it was told that the frog was the rebirth of the previous owner of the house who died some time ago. Because he was attached to his wealth, he was born as a frog and came back to claim his wealth. The strength of his attachment caused him to take that kind of rebirth.

Nyetsik Nyalwa is commonly believed to happen all over. Because of that, people do not throw their hair into wet places. Sometimes when you cut your hair and throw it in a wet place, you will see the hair turn into a worm. In India it often happens that when people wash their bodies, a layer of skin comes off like dirt. When it falls on the ground, it turns into worms. Those examples are Nyetsik Nyalwa, attachment to one's body. The consciousness finds an object and assumes it as its body.

Another example happened in my time. This event was told to me: In Tibet, people carry a flint stone that they use like a match. Once, someone happened to drop his stone in a marshy land near the water. That stone turned into a frog. The iron part of it didn't change, but the rest assumed the shape of a frog. Because of strong attachment, one is liable to be born in this kind of realm, Nyetsik Nyalwa. Some sentient beings can get attached to a broom, thinking, "My body belongs to a broom." When we use such a broom, it's like using someone's body as a broom, and so they experience suffering. There are countless rebirths of that nature that have indescribable suffering. And that is called "Nyetsik Nyalwa."

RELATIVE HELL AND THE UTMOST HELL

The last teaching was on the consequences of rebirth in samsara, samsaric existence. We have discussed the eight hot hells and the eight cold hells and the suffering in the Short-Lived Hell. Now we will discuss Relative Hell, Nyekhor Nyalwa, near the four directions from Utmost Hell, Narmé Nyalwa. In one direction is the Bottomless Coal, Nima Mor Gayok, where the surface is a kind of ash but the bottom is live coal.

When a sentient being has suffered for long time in the utmost strata of a hell, when he begins to exhaust his bad karma, he will see a big shady area in the distance. He will feel the same desire as we would in a desert or when beaten down by extreme heat. In that circumstance, when we see a cool, shady place, we long to go there. So, having been tortured in the extreme heat, the suffering sentient being advances toward what looks to be a cool spot. However, when he reaches it he finds not shade but live coal underneath a thin layer of ash. Putting his left leg in the ash, his left leg burns to the bone. So he lifts his left leg out and the flesh grows back. But now the right leg is in the ash and is burning to the bone. So he lifts that leg out, but now the left leg is in the ash and burning, and so forth. He has to do this again and again, and although he desires to die, there is no death for a long time.

Now on the outskirts of the Utmost Hell there is a marshy land called "Marshy Land of Dead Bodies." Again, another sentient being who was suffering in the Utmost Hell and who nearly exhausted his karma sees a distant pond-like area. He longs to drink water and goes toward the pond. When he reaches the pond, however, he finds only marshland filled with dead human and animal bodies, decaying and smelling terribly. Automatically, with his karma, he is forced to enter, whereupon he is drowned in the putrid smell of dead bodies while worms with iron teeth start eating him. He has to suffer immeasurable pain for long time before he can begin to exhaust his karma. At that time he will come out of the marsh and see a beautiful green field. With joy he will go there. But the minute he touches the grass, what is there is only sharp spikes, and because of his karma, he has to go through that field of spikes. At each step, spikes pierce his foot and sharp pains run through his body. So he quickly lifts the foot, but has to make another step with the other foot, and so on and so forth. He has to suffer for a long time. After exhausting that karma, the sentient being escapes and sees a beautiful forest through which blows a wind. He heads to that forest and sees a bodhi tree waving in the wind. But when he reaches the tree, there are only iron pillars with knives for leaves. As the wind blows, the knife-leaves drop to his body, stabbing him from above and cutting him to pieces. Afterward his limbs will grow back but will be cut up and suffer the pain again and again. This cycle is continuous, there is no death, and he suffers.

The Utmost Hell is central and has four main branches, each of which has four subdivisions. In total there are sixteen divisions, or directions: north, east, west, south, northwest, northeast, etc. Between the main branches is the hell called "Shamari Dongpo," for those who have broken their vows as monastics. This hell is described as a huge tree in the form of a hill. When monastics take vows, one vow includes "not seeking the company of a man or a woman"—not having a husband and wife relationship or lover relationships. If a person breaks that vow and enters into such a relationship, they are born in this hell. The being born here will hear the lover's voice at the top of the tree. Wanting to be with the lover, the being rushes up the tree, but when he climbs, all the leaves are like knives pointed downward. Yet his desire is so strong that he climbs on and tears his body apart. When he reaches the top, he finds not his lover but only vultures and vicious birds who attack and peck his eyes out, tearing him apart. He will then hear the lover's voice at the bottom of the tree. And again he will rush down as the knife-leaves turn upward and cut him to pieces. When he comes down, a burning iron man is there to hug him, burning his body and brains and cutting him to pieces. Still there is no death.

In the discussion of the suffering in the hell realms there is also traditionally a detailed exposition on comparative time systems, in order to have a sense of the timescale in the hell realms. Without the books we cannot go into the details here, but one example, which we shall revisit in a later teaching, refers to fifty years of human life as equal to one day of the gods, in Tibetan, Gyalchen Deshi. Fifty nights in the god realm are equal to one night in the first floor of hell. So the time in hell could be immense.

THE HUNGRY GHOST REALM

We now turn to suffering in the realm of the hungry ghosts (*yidak*). Rebirth as a yidak is mainly rooted in greed, the emotion of greed. There are two categories of hungry ghost, one that is commonly found everywhere and another that can travel in space. One kind of yidak is called "Chi Dripa." For many hundreds of thousands and millions of years, as the mind of that yidak in a state of desire strives endlessly to find food, it will suffer with hunger. Sometimes that yidak sees water flowing in the distance. Since its legs are very tiny and its stomach is huge, it has a problem walking freely. Still it tries to get to the water because it is hungry and thirsty, and by trying hard it will at last reach the bank, but when it does, the water dries up and it finds only stones and rocks. Sometimes it will see fruit-bearing trees in the distance. In a state of starvation, it will try to get to the foot of the tree, but when it reaches the tree it finds the tree dried up and barren. Sometimes it sees lots of good, nutritious food, but when it approaches the food, guards with weapons chase it away. During the summer, even the rays of the moon are too hot for this yidak; during the winter, even the sun is too cold, so it suffers continually from the cold and the heat. These yidaks are called "Chi Dripa" and are the exterior defiled yidaks.

Then we come to the interior defiled yidaks. These yidaks have a throat as narrow as a needle. They usually don't get food, but with their karma, when they do, their mouths produce poison, which brings them much suffering, and they cannot swallow the food because their necks are so thin. Even against all odds, when this yidak with its karma does manage to swallow a little food, he is still not able to satisfy even a fraction of his hunger because his stomach is so large and because this tiny amount of food turns into flames and burns his stomach and his internal organs. He suffers a burning sensation internally. Whenever he desires to travel, because his stomach is as big as a whole country but his legs and arms are tiny, like flutes, he cannot move around freely. Those yidaks are called "Nang Ki Drip Pa Chen." Then there is a yidak called "Rulku Gyi Dripachen." Many worms and types of insects make nests on his body and eat him away. He faces immeasurable suffering and pain.

A long time ago a saint by the name of Nangwa Shedra went to the land of yidaks. When he got there, he found a beautiful house, inside of which a very beautiful woman adorned with precious jewels sat on a four-legged throne held by four yidaks. The woman offered food to the great saint and said to him, "When these yidaks ask for food, please do not give it to them," and then went away. As he ate, the yidaks approached him, saying, "Please give us something to eat." With a compassionate heart, he gave them something to eat, but when he gave food to the first yidak, it immediately turned into the silk husk of a corn. A food offering to the second yidak turned into a bowl of iron. The offering to the third yidak turned into the creature's own flesh. When he gave food to the fourth one, it turned into blood and pus.

When the beautiful lady returned, she found this great saint had given food to the four yidaks. She said to him, "I told you not to give food to these yidaks. Do not misunderstand me. I have more compassion for them than anybody else, but they have no karma to consume food." So the saint asked the lady, "How did this relationship occur?" She said, "One is a rebirth of my own husband. One is a rebirth of my own son. One is a rebirth of my daughter-in-law. One is a rebirth of my servant. People do not believe these relationships are possible, yet we have them because of karma. When we were born as human beings on Earth, we belonged to a very well-to-do family. One day Phakpa Katayana, a great saint, came to visit for alms." She felt devotion to the great saint and offered him alms. Then she told her husband to dedicate the merit with the sympathetic joy of giving charity to the great saint. "You must dedicate and make a great supplication." When she requested that of her husband, he got furious and said, "Why give food to that useless monk? It will be better to offer to the exterior gods (gods of the exterior sects). There is no point in offering to this monk. Instead give him cornsilk." When her husband got angry, she thought, "Maybe I should ask my son. He could originate kind thoughts for this offering. It would have boundless merits." When she approached her son, he also got angry and said, "What is the use of giving food to this monk? Instead he could have a bowl of iron." That's why when this great saint Nangwa Shedra gave the yidak food, it turned into a bowl of iron.

And one time in the life of this beautiful lady, her relatives prepared lots of good food for her and sent it to her through her daughter-in-law. On the way to her mother-in-law's house, the daughter-in-law ate all the good food and brought only bad food for her mother-in-law. When the lady saw the food, she asked, "Didn't you eat all the good food? Aren't you giving me the bad food?" The daughter-in-law replied, "I will never eat your food. I'd rather eat my own flesh than eat your food." As result she was reborn a yidak. When this great saint Nangwa Shedra gave her food, it turned into her own flesh.

In another instance, this lady sent food for her friend through her servant. The servant took the food and on the way consumed half of it. When the lady asked, "Did you eat half of the food?" the servant said, "I'd rather consume my own blood and pus than eat your food." As a result she was born in the realm of yidaks. When this great saint Nangwa Shedra gave her food, it turned into blood and pus.

If the husband and the son hadn't generated these bad feelings in the offering to the great saint, they would have been born on the thirty-second floor of the god realm. The main cause of being born in the yidak realm is greed. We will be born there because of our greed, or holding on to our wealth, or being stingy in making offerings to the enlightened gods and deities or to the great enlightened teachers and saints. When we hold onto our wealth and don't give charity to needy people, the ultimate result will be birth in the yidak realm.

As we saw, the root cause of being born in the hell realm is anger. If you are full of desire, you will be born in the human realm. If you are influenced by pride, you will be born in the god realm. If you are jealous, you will be born in Lhamayin, the jealous gods realm.

Once you know the result of your karmic action, you must be cautious about actualizing those karmas. We tend to think that many of our actions are small and insignificant. We imagine such things as a small karmic action, saying to ourselves, "I don't think it will produce any bad karma at all." But that is not correct. One time a monk took a vow to not terminate any birth. He was not allowed to cut trees or grass or terminate the birth of any living beings. Now at this monk's place there was a tree with a hanging branch whose leaves touched his head whenever he went to and fro. He would get annoyed, but he knew that he was not supposed to cut down the tree. However, he was preoccupied with the thought that these leaves were giving him trouble. So he decided, "I don't think cutting down this tree will result in any bad karma." And he cut it down. When the monk died, he took rebirth in the form of a naga called "Aili Dhama." A small tree grew on top of his head. Whenever the wind swayed the tree, it destroyed his brain and brought a lot of physical pain and suffering, but no death.

There is nothing insignificant in terms of karma. You should not consider that any action to be insignificant, or think, "Oh, this will not bring anything. Oh, this is a minute karma, so it doesn't matter." No matter how insignificant any action may look, they all have significance and will all bring significant karmic results. That's why you must be cautious in your actions. Insignificant actions brings significant results.

Think of the foolishness of those people who became yidaks. The gift had already been given by the lady of the house to the great saint. The only thing they needed to do was generate sympathetic joy and simply praise her action. Instead, they generated greed and anger unnecessarily, which resulted in the significant consequence of taking birth in the yidak realm and suffering for many eons. There is no insignificant action. There is no minor karma that will be all right. All actions you perform bring significant results.

Another karmic effect is that if you make a resolution to give to charity, or make a resolution to give something to somebody else, and then do not give, that's a sure means to be born in hell. When you have charitable thoughts in your mind and decide to give, or if you have a thought such as "I would like to give. I can afford to give," and then don't give, you will be born in the yidak realm.

In order to receive good karma, virtuous karma, it is important for you to compliment another person's generous action. For example, if X is giving something to someone, it is not necessary for you to give the same amount. In such instances, when a person is giving charity to help people, what one needs to do is meditate and generate sympathetic joy, having a thought in your mind like, "The donor is being so generous and has done such a great action," and generate a wishful thought like, "Let his action produce immeasurable good karma." This is called "Jesu Yirang." Je Su means "after." Yi Rang means to be content with others' actions. If you generate that state of joyful mind, even if you don't give a physical gift, you acquire the same karma as the person actually giving the gift.

On the other hand, if someone makes an offering to an alter and, instead of being appreciative, you come and start criticizing the offering, saying it is not complete or not properly done, or this is good or this is bad, and only bring out the faults, or if when somebody gives a gift to another person, you come along and say, "That is hopeless, that is not necessary, that is not useful," the result will be that for many, many lifetimes you will be born in a very deprived state of human life.

Now, as we mentioned earlier, one category of yidak is a space traveler. There are several kinds, like Tshen, Gyalpo, and Shindré. Tshen attach themselves to or find homes in rocks and mountains. Gyalpos were previously born as lamas, trapas (monks), and practicing laymen who meditated on wrathful deities. Not knowing the complete path, they attached themselves to the wrathful deities. It's called "kyé rim," visualizing oneself as a powerful wrathful deity and not knowing how to dissolve that visualization. Once you die, you are born as a Gyalpo, the spirits attached to the wrathful actions.

Shindré were people who were attached to their wealth. Even at the time of death, they thought only about their wealth and remained attached to their houses and material things. When they died, they were born as spirits, lingering around the house, attached to wealth and material things.

Another kind of yidak is called "Therang." They live in caves and have only one leg. They can carry off or control the mind or the soul of a person. Therang uses a weapon in this manner: There is a bone at an ankle joint that he takes out and burns in the fire to increase its size. He takes it and throws it at a being, killing the being. This type of rebirth makes you perpetually feel the need to harm somebody. You are possessed by the kind of greed that says, "Let me be better than others. I do not want to give anything away." You are always greedy and have a harmful mind, and because of such feelings you are born in this yidak realm.

In Tibet some groups of people go out as bandits. Sometimes they get killed and are born as yidaks. These yidaks have to die every seven days, repeating the experience of how they died the first time. For example, if a person got shot and died by a bullet, he would be born as yidak who has to experience that death again every seven days. People who commit suicide by jumping off a cliff or hanging themselves will be born in the yidak realm. Every seven days they have to commit suicide and go through that suffering again and again. Once this being is born as a yidak, the vicious circle begins. He says, "I would like to get away from this suffering. I would like to be transferred to the realms of other sentient beings." But when he tries to transfer, he cannot, and this creates anxiety that increases his suffering even more.

Sometimes it is possible for these yidaks to transfer their power to affect or possess other people. This has happened when a passing traveler stops by a house and suddenly someone in that house gets sick. In Sikkim, for example, it's common to witness people get sick very suddenly or even go crazy. These events are due to the yidak.

When these yidaks have successfully affected someone, powerful tantric practitioners, Ngakpas, are invited in to help dispel the yidak's power. These Ngakpas will make an offering by burning, and they will then burn the yidaks, mixing them up in the offering. Sometimes Ngakpas will put mantras in stones and throw them at the yidaks, hitting their bodies with the mantra power. This will cause wounds in the yidak's body and bring them more suffering. Sometimes yidaks are buried deep down in the earth by the power of these great Ngakpas. That's how yidaks get more suffering by affecting sentient beings.

Some of the country gods belong to the yidak realm. At one time a lama was taken through the country on horseback, or he felt like he was on a horse. He was taken to a place where he a saw a sick person whose body was covered with mustard seeds. This man's family lived in the land that had that kind of yidak spirit. So the lama did mantra and took the mustard seeds one by one out of the patient's body, curing him. This country god, Shidak, belonged to the yidak realm and offered the lama lots of wealth in return.

It is a very common phenomenon in parts of Tibet and the Himalayas for lay people to give their hearts and souls to country deities, or the family protecting gods, not knowing their origin. Many of these gods—family gods, country gods, land gods, and water gods—belong to the yidak family. You should not take refuge in them for your life, soul, and enlightenment, but you can be in harmony with them. They can help you do away with your present impediments and avoid circumstantial impediments. But if you try to take refuge in them, then your rebirth will be within their realm. Even though they are powerful, they are suffering sentient beings and you too could easily be part of them.

The great renowned Patrul Rinpoché has written about many such instances. Laypeople often gave everything to the country gods, and later on they themselves were reborn as one of them and suffered. Once, when a chief of the county died, he was reborn as a god of the yidak realm. Invited by the great lama, he came and identified himself as a rebirth of so and so, the deceased chief of the county. He told people, "If you don't behave, I have to take your life." He also said how much suffering he, as a reborn spirit, would have to go through if people didn't make offerings, like burning food in a fire. He and other yidaks smell the burned food and satisfy their hunger that way.

THE ANIMAL REALM

Now we will turn to the suffering of the animal realm. Most animals are in the ocean. Great numbers of rebirthed animals are ocean creatures of various types, mainly fish and conch and so forth, which are analogous to dregs of beer. Ocean animals prey on one another—a little fish gets eaten by big fish, and that big fish is eaten by a bigger fish.

There is said to be a huge fish in the ocean that is eaten up by small worms that attach their shells to his hide. This enormous fish lives by Mount Meru.[14] When the small worms eat inside of this big fish, they sometimes touch its heart, and it will tumble with pain, sometimes causing an earthquake. The lower regions of the ocean depths have no light at all, no daylight. Sentient beings there suffer enormously.

Animals living on land are called "Dündro Ketalwa." They include deer and birds of all kinds. They all suffer continuously. Take, for example, a grazing deer. It takes a bite of grass and looks up to see if someone is after it. Again it takes a bite and looks up, ready to bolt. Such animals have antlers, beautiful skins, and musk, but these attributes or qualities are the very cause of their death: people kill deer for their antlers, skin, and musk, causing them much suffering. Likewise, consider the oyster: the pearls they produce are believed to grow in the oyster's brain, so when a pearl, the life force of an oyster, is taken out, the oyster is killed. Or consider the fox, tiger, or lion, who are hunted down for their skin. Or elephants, killed for their tusks and bones. These body parts are essential for the survival of the animals but are the root causes of their death.

Take finally the example of domesticated animals who are quite free from predation but suffer just the same. You don't see too many horses being used in contemporary urban settings, but in parts of Tibet, horses are the main transportation, carrying loads from the valley to the mountains and back again. Iron bits are crammed into their mouths, by which they are made to turn left or right. Just imagine having a piece of iron in your mouth that is pulled back and forth, how painful that would be! That is the experience of a horse. There are yaks in the Himalayan region that are also used as beasts of burden. People put ropes through their noses. When a yak doesn't go in a certain direction, the master commands it by pulling the rope running through the nose, causing the yak great pain. These are some of the sufferings of domesticated animals. The root cause of being born in the animal realm is ignorance.

This concludes the teachings on the sufferings in the three lower realms: the hell realm, the hungry ghost realm, and the animal realm.

THE HUMAN REALM

We now come to suffering in the human realm. The human realm is typically described as a happy or joyous realm. However, it too is filled with suffering. Human beings go through the suffering of change—for example, the kind of change experienced by the senses that make you desire to be cold as soon as you feel too hot. Then when you go to a cold region and feel really cold, you desire to go to a warm or hot region. You continually want to change from one place or situation or set of conditions to another. And we have already discussed how food that we consume to live can cause sickness and disease, which means suffering.

People also suffer from wanting something they don't have—for example, people in America have cars but they like to walk for exercise. People in other parts of world would love to have cars, but have to walk. It is true that people who live in mansions sometimes want to live in a more modest or open space, while people who live in modest houses often have an intense desire to live in a mansion. When people do not have an alternative and believe they have no choice but to accept their current situation, they often live in misery. This is the suffering of wanting to change.

There is also suffering caused by attachment to a perception or a concept. You could be attached to the concept that your body or that human life always faces suffering. You suffer by believing in a concept that this existence is just suffering. We could say this is suffering over suffering—that is, suffering simply by the fact that evidently there is suffering. Suffering over suffering can also be understood in another sense: when there is suffering, people engage in or cause more suffering trying to cure that suffering. Take a blister, for example—that is already suffering. Then you try to cut it off and end up with a deeper wound or more blisters. Or your father dies in the morning and you suffer by being sad over his death. Then your mother dies in the evening and you have more sadness. Looking at it very carefully, a human life is not free from suffering.

Then there is the suffering of sickness, which is evident all around you in families and in hospitals. A young man has strength and endurance, but when he is sick he can't do anything. People who suffer for a long time do not really live but rather endure, unable to do whatever they used to enjoy doing. They are angry at people who take care of them and resist taking medicine. Caregivers sometimes wish for the sick person's death. It's too much of a problem and they think, "Why won't this person die?" Even the patient himself thinks, "If I have to suffer like this, it is better to die."

Then finally there is the suffering of death. You all know what that suffering is like. The dying person is attached to his family, his children, and his house. He does not want to die. But everyone who is born must die, though the time of death is never definite. It can come to anyone at any time. Being attached to one's wealth or to others makes it harder for a person to die.

People who are not close to anyone also suffer because they know the wealth they collected will be enjoyed by someone else. They will leave everything behind, even the very body they took care of for a long time. They now have a desire to be with their relatives and renew their friendships, but they cannot because they are in the process of dying. As they are dying, sometimes people reflect back and realize they were very mean, so they desire to do some dharmic action, but it's too late. The suffering of death is now unbearable.

Essentially there are four stages of suffering in human life: birth, old age, sickness, and death. When you are a baby, you are enclosed within the womb of your mother. There is no happiness there. When the mother consumes hot food, the child inside will get very hot. When she consumes cold food, the child shivers with the cold. At the same time, when the mother pushes herself against something, the child feels it's being pressed against two walls. The suffering in the womb depends on the actions of the mother. Then around the time of birth, a kind of wind will come and turn the baby around to prepare it to leave the womb. The baby feels a sensation like a very strong person is grabbing hold of its legs and throwing it against a wall. At the time of birth, the baby has a feeling of being churned or pressed through an iron hole, as if it were a rope being pulled through an iron hole. Once it is birthed, it feels like it is thrown in a bush of thorns. And when the umbilical cord is cut, it receives a pain as sharp as an arrow piercing through its heart. With that sort of pain, the child forgets all past incidents of its life. That's the time you are cut off from memories of past experiences.

Now imagine being old. As you age, all the organs of your body will deteriorate. Your sight will begin to dim. Your sense of hearing will begin to wane. Your body strength will weaken. You eventually lose your teeth and can no longer consume certain types of food. Sadly, you cannot eat whatever you wish. If you eat your fill, you'll have the sensation of discomfort or pain, but in any case, food will lose its taste. You will not be able to sleep; at night you will toss and turn in your bed. Then it's as if the days are like nights and the nights like days, no difference at all. Even the natural warmth of your body will diminish. You cannot wear light clothes because they won't keep you warm enough, but when you wear heavy clothes they will feel too heavy on your body.

It is possible that you were once well known. When you become old, however, you will be left behind. Your opinion will no longer be valuable; it won't carry any weight and you will be considered senile. Even within the family household, the younger generation will not listen to you. They will think you talk too much or do not make any sense. That's how you will be suffering.

* * *

This realization of suffering in all six realms is very important because we do not pay attention to it. We undermine the suffering. We do not consider suffering as one of our realizations. However, now you are aware of the suffering in all six realms. You realize the fruitlessness, devoid of essence, of rebirth and existence in the six realms.

Once you know all six realms have suffering, where should you turn, what should you do? That's when you must turn to Dharma. There is a path in the Dharma that says, "You will be liberated from all samsara in one body and one lifetime, and for sure in the next lifetime."

But ordinarily we are not aware of the suffering in the six realms and always live in the illusion of the happy human birth, praising how great human birth is and having romantic ideas about the six realms.

Thus we wander in illusion and do not make this path of liberation successful. So now you must bring all these sufferings to your own heart and mind and experience them in reality. Once you experience it in your mind as real, then you will begin to pursue the path to liberation.

THE DEDICATION

We will now chant the dedication. The dedication is to take all sentient beings, your parents, your enemies, and all other sentient beings on the earth, and by listening to Dharma and practicing it, by this virtue, may all sentient beings attain enlightenment. With that intention, please dedicate the merits and the virtuous karma you have just acquired.

Questions and Answers

Q: Do all physical objects have sentient beings trapped inside? They are in walls, in rocks?
A: No, not all rocks and trees. Some are trapped in that sense, but not all rocks have consciousness trapped in them.

Q: If anger is the primary cause of ending up in a hot hell, what is the primary cause for rebirth in a cold hell?
A: Anger is the fundamental root cause of rebirth in a hell realm, generally. Rebirths in various hells is determined by karma, so using coarse words or creating disturbances through false accusations results in rebirth in a certain type of hell.

Q: Rinpoché mentions the officials of hell. What types of beings reside in hell? Are they themselves suffering or not?

A: These officials don't physically exist. Their existence is a perceptual reflection of the sentient beings within the hell realm. They see it as it appears to them: officials are chasing them, beating them, and pushing them into fire.

Q: You say these hells are psychological states as well as real states?

A: Yes, the hells are your perception. These things are perceptions. However, if you perceive this as real, then it is real. If you perceive this as not real, then it is not real.

Q: How could someone suffer more by bearing the suffering of others?

A: You have to train yourself for bodhichitta. That's why that state of mind is very hard. It's almost inconceivable for us. Through meditation and inculcating bodhichitta in mind, then and only then can you originate this kind of honest intention; training not in any specific way, such as sitting down, but training the mind—for example, if you are wealthy, wishing somebody else to be wealthy like you; if you are happy, wishing somebody else to be happy. Within your own many daily circumstances and experiences, expand your mind to incorporate all other sentient beings.

Realize the importance of bodhichitta, the vast bodhi mind. That's why in the beginning of any practice or action, you are always reminded of the formulation of your bodhisattva intention, the dedication and formulation of intention. Realizing the indescribably suffering of countless sentient beings under the wide horizon of the sky, you formulate your bodhichitta intention and try and try. The time will come when there will be a spontaneous and honest response.

Q: Can you help other beings simply by wishing them to be liberated? Wishing from your heart for them to be healed? Or do you have to go through their hell, at least in your own experience, in order to start healing them?

A: Your question has two levels. The first level is the training of one's own intention. If your life is happy, wishing everyone to have equal happiness, or if you see other people happy, wishing all sentient beings to be as happy, that's the mind of helpfulness, the helpful mind. Or putting oneself in the situation of another's suffering, experiencing that suffering, and originating the sympathetic mind. The second level is how can one help? For example, if a sentient being is suffering, what can we do to alleviate the suffering? At this time, we are just digging the foundation. Such a level of helping others comes after the construction of the house. If you want to get a homeless person off the street and invite him to stay at your house rent free, you can do that after you have constructed a house. When you are first digging the foundation, the ability to train your mind to experience the suffering of those who are lower than you is very important. You are setting up a proper foundation. Once you attain enlightenment, then your compassionate heart is boundless in its power.

Q: Could Rinpoché talk about the jealous gods and also about the relative number of sentient beings? Are there many more sentient beings?

A: The number of sentient beings in the realms of hell is like the stars in the night compared with the number of sentient beings in the yidak realm, and so forth. Going up to the human realm and the god realm, sentient beings are fewer and fewer in number. The human realm has the least number of sentient beings. It is possible to count humans on Earth, but almost impossible to count the number of animals or insects. Look at the rays of sun and try to count the flies swarming together; it's impossible to count. The difference in number between humans and insects is vast.

If you compare people who are suffering and the people who are not suffering, the people who are suffering are greater in number. Among those people who are not suffering, who are practicing and acting according to the Dharma, there are not many. If we were able to calculate the numbers comparatively, the chart would be a pyramid shape, with insects and animals at the base in the lower realms and humans at the top in the human realm, those who act according to the Dharma being at the very top. As in Tibet, however, there are few people who practice Dharma. This is because of karma and not for any other reason. Human life has eighteen aspects of fortunate circumstances and opportunities and is called "the precious human life." But if you are not in accord with those circumstances, it is just an ordinary wasted human life.

Q: I work in a hospital where people are really sick. Did these people get possessed by the yidaks? How do you remove their suffering? What could I do?

A: It is very difficult to analyze crazy people under the influence of yidak. Their condition could be due to karmic or present circumstances. Such circumstances might have two causes: one is the yidaks and the other is the imbalance of the wind within one's own body. Four elements in the body should be in balance for a person to be healthy. But if there is an imbalance, the wind of the body gets into the life vein and a person can become mentally imbalanced and go crazy. It has to be viewed in those terms. It is very difficult to see the exact cause because there can be many, many causes.

Q: What can be done to alleviate their suffering?

A: It is possible to help them since you are a practitioner. Pray to the Three Precious Ones. Through their compassion and boundless power, suffering can be alleviated. And by your true practice of Dharma, at some time you will acquire the power to alleviate their suffering. In Tibet they say when a person is sick, it is possibly due to a karmic disease or it could be due to catching a disease or the effects of a spirit. If it is physical disease that is causing the imbalance, then medicine is given. If it is a spirit, they perform a ritual to help the sick person. If it is a karmic disease, the person is made to do a meditation or a special meditation to deal with that karmic imbalance.

Q: Breaking the samaya vows. What kind of conduct should we follow as practitioners and as Vajra brothers and sisters?
A: A detailed discussion on the samaya is not appropriate teaching at the present moment because we are doing Ngöndro. Not that it will come into a conflict with Ngöndro, but just that it is not in sequence. If you summarize the treatises on samaya, from the tantric point of view the honest and the ethical relationship requires perceiving all other men and women within the practice of esoteric teaching as your own brothers and sisters and, for the most part, you must perceive all practitioners as the manifestation of gods and goddesses. However, it seems it is very difficult to do those things at this moment or in the present situation. So the best you can do is to keep clear perception.

Why don't we get along? We don't get along because of the words we say to each other. We get attached to those words. Reading between the lines of what has been said and picking up certain vibes, something like that, which really does not have any substance. But you get attached to those perceived words and develop more attachment and aversion. If somebody says something, you think, "Oh, this person said something bad to me," and you get upset.

Once you are practitioners of the Dharma, the expanse of your mind should be broader than an ordinary person's. That's why you are taught about intention first. Intention is the means to broaden the space of your mind. So first you must think the space in your mind is broad. Even if you cannot visualize your Dharma brothers and sisters as real brothers and sisters or gods and goddesses, try to keep pure perception. Try to stay away from attachment and aversion, such as attachment to praise and aversion to criticism.

If everybody sees everybody's faults, they will not see wisdom. It's very easy to see faults: "This is not good. That's not right." But it is very rare that you see the wisdom of a certain person. Try to keep a clear perception or try to have no conception or presumption about anything. Try to expand your mind. Try to incorporate and try to accept this practice in your mind: "If that is so, it doesn't matter." Not just the words. Do it truly from your mind.

THE BODHISATTVA INTENTION

THE INTENTION

As WITH ALL the sequences of teachings, please formulate your intention while listening to the teaching. There isn't a single sentient being that has not been your parent. If you were to measure the ten directions of the sky, it would be limitless. Since the sky has no limits, it encompasses all sentient beings in all six realms, wherever they are.

THE TEACHING

All sentient beings, like our present parents, have been very kind to us. If you think about your parents, not only did they care for you during childhood but all through your life they tried to protect you from harm. They do not care for their own bodies but always worry about their children's safety. Their attitude is to give their children the best food and clothing they can provide. They kept you in their minds and in their compassionate hearts. With their loving hearts, they always cared for you. Such are our present parents.

There isn't a single sentient being who hasn't been your parent. We don't remember them, but in the past, when we had other lives, these parents have been as kind to us as our present parents. Parental love is not limited to human beings but is also found in animals. If you look at birds you'll see that a mother bird realizes her baby might be cold and sits on it to shelter it and keep it warm with its wings and body heat. And if you look at its feeding pattern, the mother bird flies far and brings food to its young in its beak, putting it into the open mouth of the baby. The smallest insects have this same kind of relationship. So the feeling and behavior of parental love is seen in other realms. Knowing that your parents have been so kind, you should realize all sentient beings are the same.

All sentient beings desire happiness. The source of happiness is Dharma but they do not know how to perform dharmic actions. Sentient beings do not desire suffering but do not know that the seed of suffering is adharmic actions. Sentient beings do not know the distinction between dharmic and adharmic actions. Even as they desire happiness, they perpetuate adharma, which is how they perpetuate suffering. There is a contradiction between desire and action. Knowing that all sentient beings live in contradictory desire, bring all these sentient beings into the realm of your mind and wish that they all be free from suffering. And thus, generate compassion.

Compassion is not just a speech: "Let sentient beings be free from suffering." It should come from the depth of your mind. Just showing compassion to your own relatives, your wife or husband, is not really compassion. Big compassion is visualizing all sentient beings under the wide horizon of the sky, and then thinking and desiring the liberation of all sentient beings from suffering. Big compassion is very different from limited compassion.

There are many different dharmic and adharmic actions. Originating compassion is one act of the Dharma, a frame of mind having the intention that all sentient beings be liberated from the suffering. Bodhichitta (compassion) is the formulation of that goal: "I shall practice the Dharma path and seek the enlightenment of all sentient beings." These two together, the intention and the practice, are bodhichitta.

Most sentient beings under the wide horizon of the sky do not know what to acquire and what to abandon. They do not know since they are under the influence of ignorance. They do not know how to acquire actions that are dharmic. All sentient beings are perturbed by the six defilements: desire, ignorance, egotism, jealousy, greed, and anger. They are like crazy people or blind people who cannot see what to acquire and what to abandon. Even if you are blind, if someone leads you, it is possible to travel outside of your containment. But if there is no one to guide you, you can't go outside, at least not without great danger. The teacher, like the tsawai lama, the main teacher, leads students to the path of the Dharma. If a person is blind and is on a top of a steep rock, he will fall. Likewise many sentient beings stagger unknowingly toward the precipice. A teacher is needed.

Bodhichitta is the formulation of the intention to practice this path: "I shall attain enlightenment in order to liberate all sentient beings who do not know what to abandon and what to acquire." Bodhisattva intention precedes all the practices. Within this path, the inculcation of compassion is very important. Since we do not meditate or inculcate compassion, we cannot really relate to other sentient beings in dharmic terms. That's why meditation on compassion involves looking at the suffering sentient beings, taking that suffering upon yourself, and experiencing the suffering within yourself. For example, if an animal is going to be killed, at that moment, put yourself in the body of that animal. What will you do if you are the one that is being killed? Take this kind of suffering within yourself, realize it, and generate compassion.

All these sufferings come about because of not knowing what to acquire—how to act according to the Dharma—and not knowing what should be abandoned, what should be left out, and what should not be acted out. Because sentient beings do not know Dharma, they act contradictory to the Dharma. The result is suffering. However practitioner must bring that suffering into himself and meditate on compassion.

If one can settle one's mind and see the suffering inside of oneself, then one will not venture to take another's life. It is always easier to take another's life if one does not know what it is like to be killed. This is why compassion is within the meditation and practice sequence. Our ability to realize the extent and depth of the suffering is limited. It is very important to know the nature of the suffering within the six realms and that there is no happiness within these realms. You cannot inculcate compassion just by looking around. We tend to think it is all right or it is bearable. We must be able to see and realize the full suffering that is inherent in the six realms. This is very important.

Usually we are plagued by suffering by speculating about what might happen. For example, "I must do something or I might die of starvation. I must do something or this bad thing might happen." But we forget that human beings, who are able to make a living most of the time, do not die of starvation. If you look at animals, who cannot manipulate the environment like human beings can, they can still survive by searching for food. In reality there is no need for worry of this nature. One can survive and maintain oneself and live modestly. Yet we have a tendency to speculate and to imagine what is not there. For example, once we get one kind of food, we look for something better or for variety. The same is true for shelter. You have a roof over your head, but that's not enough. You want to have a better, bigger house. That's how you get wrapped up in samsaric suffering.

The third kind of suffering, which is within the human realm and seems unbearable, is being sick or ill. But that is not unbearable compared to what is to come. For example, if you are in pain, the pain might last a year or two years, or one might die of the disease, but if you think that is the ultimate suffering, it is not. If it is true that one goes to heaven after one dies, then you will not have to worry about suffering, then it is well and fine. However, one does not know where one will go. Knowing that there is much harder suffering in other realms beyond your suffering in this life now, just knowing that, is the practice of the Dharma. Knowing the suffering in the six realms is very important.

How do you escape the suffering that is unknown yet is to come? To know Dharma is like practicing preventive medicine, or like a diagnosis and treatment of the disease. Take the example of small-pox. To prevent it you get a vaccination so you will not be sick with smallpox. Likewise, know Dharma and know ahead what unbearable sufferings there are in other realms. Compared with those sufferings, the suffering of the human realm is bearable and minor.

Knowing how to get away from and be liberated from the suffering in other realms is the medicine that is Dharma. If one practices Dharma, one can reach the realization of Padampa, who said, "My death is not ordinary death. My death is an enlightenment." You reach a point where you become comfortable to go on to the next life. But if you do not practice now, or to the extent that you are not comfortable going on to the next life, then at the time of death you will have to bear suffering, realizing, "Oh, I knew Dharma, but there was no chance for me to practice Dharma."

People who do not know anything about Dharma usually say, "Oh, I wish to die," or, "Let me die." They seem to desire death. This is because they do not know what is coming, what the wheel of existence is, or what the suffering will be like in the six realms. Not knowing that, they desire death. Not knowing the Dharma is like a person who sees a tiger and goes to pet it, thinking how beautiful the tiger is, but gets eaten. This thinking originates from ignorance, not knowing that a tiger can maul you and is a vicious animal, not an animal to pet. That's why it is very important to know what kind of suffering there is within the six realms, so that one does not take death so lightly.

If you wonder what the wheel of existence means, it is like a bee trapped inside of a vase. The bee will fly round and round in the vase, unable to escape. Likewise, all sentient beings of the six realms will be born from one realm to another realm, cycling endlessly and unable to escape. We might have earned enough karma to be born in the god realm or we might be born in a hell realm owing to bad karma. In either case, we will circle round and round without end.

THE DEDICATION

We now dedicate the merit of what we have taught and what we have learned to all sentient beings, for their happiness and for the attainment of buddhahood.

THE REALMS OF THE GODS AND THE JEALOUS GODS

The Intention

As we do every day, and before receiving the teaching, formulate the intention of liberation and the enlightenment of all sentient beings under the limitless horizon of the sky.

The Teaching on the Jealous Gods Realm

We now turn to the three upper realms. We begin by examining the realm of the jealous gods. The karma to be born in Lhamayin is jealousy. For example, you see a rich person and dislike him immediately because he has lots of wealth. Or being jealous of a person because of his high position, you immediately dislike and envy him.

Whatever status or wealth one receives is because of one's karma. A child who is old enough to recognize what wealth is will, from an early age, try to acquire it. All human beings, and even countries, try to acquire wealth. Some need to work hard for it, others don't. Some people's families acquired wealth in the past, but that wealth could disappear. All these are the product of karma. We tend to think there is something we can do to make ourselves wealthy. We believe that's within our power. However, in actuality, it is essentially the product of karma. So when a person is promoted to a high position or becomes

wealthy, being jealous of him will only result in rebirth in Lhamayin. Or when someone is promoted, doing your best to demote him
or bring him down to a lower level will cause rebirth in Lhamayin.
Or leaders who, instead of being selfless examples of good leader-
ship, try to pursue their own fame, take others' wealth, and defame
competitors—they will be born in Lhamayin. All feelings and actions
of this kind will result in rebirth in Lhamayin.

The region of Lhamayin resembles a god with a huge body and
vast wealth. Its location is the center of Mt. Meru, which stands on
a base, Ri Gyalpo Rirap, originating in the vast ocean. Because of
their common good karma, Lhamayins (Skt. asuras) sowed the seed
of a wish-fulfilling tree called "Phag Sam Shing." When one prays
for a substance or for anything at the tree, the wish will be granted.
The tree grows tall and the top rises into the realm of the gods. Its
fruits are in the realm of the gods, and the gods enjoy the fruits while
Lhamayins are left with the stems and the roots. Lhamayins feel jealous, knowing that the tree was planted in their region but the fruits
are reaped by the gods. They get very angry, don their armor and
weapons, and invade the realm of the gods.

Karma to be born in the realm of the gods comes by keeping the
strict ten dharmic actions. Once one is born in the god realm, one
does not have a feeling of anger. Since gods do not feel anger, they
have to go to the northern side of Mt. Meru. There is a spring there
where they wipe their faces with the water. After they wet their faces
and drink the spring water, anger originates in their minds and they
begin to have a feeling of anger. They also receive weapons in their
hands and now are led by the king of the gods, Lhayi Wangpo Gya-
jin Dewa (Indra). The bottom of his palace is the north star. Indra
leads the thirty-two warriors who ride on the heads of thirty-two
headed elephant. In this manner, they begin to fight back against
the Lhamayins. Gods can travel through space at seven human
heights above ground. They have miraculous power and can uproot

the mountain and throw it at Lhamayins. When the battle becomes heated, one can sometimes see the sun getting very red. That is a sign of the conflict.

If a god is decapitated, he will die, but injuries below the head, to the hands or legs or body, will not hurt him. Lhamayins, though, are like human beings; there are many places where they can be mortally wounded and die. When Lhamayins are killed, they fall into the ocean, which sometimes becomes red with their blood.

If human beings do lots of adharmic actions, the Lhamayins will win the war. When the gods lose, there is no rain on the earth and the crops become infested with bugs and and various insects and wither. When human beings do dharmic actions, the gods will be helped and will win the war and chase back the Lhamayins down to the golden base of Mt. Meru, to their own region. The gods also send their king, Tapsang Ri, to his palace, called "Drong khyer Sangsa." When the king of Lhamayin loses the war, he gets very angry and stamps his foot on the palace. Sometimes we get an earthquake.

So, the result of harboring jealousy is to be born in Lhamayin, which, as we have seen, is a life of perpetual brooding, jealousy, and battle. The counterpart of jealousy is the meditation on sympathetic joy. Seeing someone with a high position or great wealth, instead of being jealous, one must inculcate joy, thinking that if all sentient beings had that same wealth, how happy they would be. Let all sentient beings have the same position of authority. Let all the sentient beings have the same wealth. How happy everyone will be. The wrong way of thinking is, "How happy I will be if get that wealth." That is not a right intention, not a right meditation of joy. That's just jealousy, which will prevent you from wishing that all sentient beings the same power and wealth.

THE REALM OF THE GODS

We now come to the suffering of the gods. It is important to know that every action results in different karmic consequences. Practicing the ten dharmic actions—not killing, not stealing, not lying, and so forth—without bodhisattva intention or compassion results in rebirth in the god realm. Just pursuing these ten dharmic actions will result in birth in the god realm.

I will make a detailed presentation of karma and its results. For now I'll use as examples animals that we may observe daily around us. Some feral cats have to steal all their lives, they come out of hiding to steal food and then run away and hide in the bushes. Other domesticated cats are lazy and fat and are washed and brushed frequently. The same is true of dogs. Some are made to sleep in a bed and are given the best food, eating better than some human beings. Other dogs have to steal all their food or are chased and hit with stones or get their tails cut off. Look at horses. Some horses are born in the wrong place and have to suffer as beasts of burden, carrying things on their backs, while other horses are well cared for, brushed and groomed night and day by personal attendants who treat them better than they do other human beings. Many elephants in India have a tough time; they are chained and their noses are pierced, and people poke them and put pins in their heads. But the elephants in the god realm don't have to work as hard; they are ornamented and decorated, and all because of different karma. These observable facts are due to differences in karmic consequences.

In terms of joy or pleasure, the god realm is a superior state than the human realm. However, the realm of gods is not above the wheel of samsara. Gods love to while away their time. They love to play and they waste their time playing around. They do have the potential power of foresight, of knowing where they will be born after the god realm—if they make effort. Their eyes can see the whole Earth.

Their ears can hear all the noise and words spoken on Earth. They have foreknowledge and the power of knowing another's mind: gods can recognize your thoughts. However, the nature of their lives is to not concentrate or think about such things. They waste their time in a neutral position, whiling away their time.

The lower realm of gods, Gyalchen Deshi, includes the sun and moon. On one side of Mount Meru there are seven gold mountains. The outer one, the seventh, is called "Nyashin Dzin." Toward that side are the sun and the moon and the stars. These are all held up by the wind called "Lung Kola." Lung Kola has a round shape and holds the sun and the moon and the stars. That's why they are rotating. On top of that is the Heaven of Thirty-Three (Sungchu Tsasum, the terrestrial heaven). On top of that is the celestial heaven starting with Free from Combat (Tap Tral). On top of that is the Joyous Realm (Ganden). On top of that is Enjoying Emanation (Trulga). On top of that is Controlling Others' Emanation (Shentrul Wangché). The chief of that region is Garab Wangchuk. His influence manifests in us as laziness when we don't desire to do Dharma. Garab Wangchuk has five arrows. When a person is practicing or meditating, he shoots an arrow into them and makes the person drowsy or want to be quiet and daydream, not concentrate and study but think about other things. He makes you while away your time.

Garab Wangchuk caused lots of impediments when Shakyamuni Buddha was on the way to enlightenment. He told Shakyamuni Buddha, "There is no point in bearing hardship and practicing or being enlightened. Just don't get enlightened." When Buddha said, "I have gone beyond mundane life and obligations. I have sacrificed my life for other sentient beings. I endured many hardships for enlightenment." Garab Wangchuk said, "Well, you must bring a witness to verify what you have done." So Buddha called Sayi Lhamo, the Goddess of the Earth. The goddess rose up, showing half of her body above the ground, and said, "The alms the Buddha gave to other people, like eyes and hands, are countless; they are beyond measure." So then this king of gods was very embarrassed.

Gods of desire have luminous bodies that radiate light a long distance. It is not necessary for them to have the sun and the moon. They don't need external light to see because they radiate light from their own selves. The moon is in the region of the god called "Dawa," who owns the moon. The god of sun is called "Nyima."

Gods of desire cannot escape the unbearable suffering of death. When a god is about to die, the light disappears from his body. When the light disappears, he has a feeling of discomfort and suffering when he is with other gods. All gods wear flower garlands that never wither. But when the time comes for a god to die, the flower garland withers. The clothes these gods wear do not have body smells, but when a god is about to die, his clothes begin to have odor. The god's body does not perspire, but when a god is about to die, his body begins to perspire. These five signs of death will appear to the god, who then realizes it is time to die. Once he knows he is dying, he begins to open his consciousness and his ability to see. However, by the time he sees that his rebirth might be within the three lower realms, it is too late to correct the situation.

Other gods, all the young gods and goddesses, will avoid going near this dying god and will keep their distance. They will throw flowers to him and pray, "May you be born in the realm of the human. After earning good merits by ten dharmic actions, may you be born back into the god realm." So they pray for him but they all still ostracize him and keep him at a distance. Suddenly abandoned and left alone, he suffers unbearably. He cries and screams. With tears in his eyes, he looks toward the future rebirth and sees that he will be born in such and such a place. For seven days he will suffer: the unbearable suffering of being abandoned by other gods and the suffering of knowing he will be born in the lower realms. Seven days of the thirty-three stratum of the god realm is calculated as seven hundred years of human time. Within this time the god will suffer so much that his suffering will exceed the suffering in the hell realms.

WHEREVER YOU GO IN THE SIX REALMS, THERE IS SUFFERING

This now concludes the discussion of the suffering in all six realms. If you fall into any one of the six realms, including the realm of the gods, it is like falling into a ditch of fire where fire is everywhere. Or it's like falling onto the blades of a sharp weapon. Wherever you go in the six realms, there is suffering, nothing but suffering.

Now that you know the suffering involved in all six realms, bring these sufferings into your own mind and experience the suffering of each realm vividly in your mind. Realizing the suffering of six realms should not make you feel helpless. If one thinks, "If the suffering is everywhere, what can we do? It's better to do nothing." That's putting yourself into a disadvantaged position. How do you escape this suffering? To escape this suffering, be on the path of Dharma.

The practice of Dharma is like sowing a seed. When one sows a seed, the result all depends on what kind of seed was sowed. If you sow the seed of poison, you will grow a poisonous plant. If you sow the seed of medicine, you will grow a medicinal plant. Likewise, if you harbor the essence of Dharma and practice the Dharma, then the result will be above the suffering of the six realms. If your practice is contrary to the Dharma, it will continuously perpetuate the suffering of the six realms.

This portion of Ngöndro is very important before practicing guru yoga. Next, I will continue the talk on karma and its result. This will help you to realize what is the seed of being born in the wheel of samsaric existence and what is the seed of being liberated from the wheel of samsaric existence.

THE DEDICATION

As usual at the end of each teaching, one must dedicate the merit of listening to the teaching for the enlightenment of all sentient beings.

THE TEN DEFILEMENTS

THE INTENTION

As USUAL you must formulate the intention for the enlightenment of all sentient beings.

THE TEACHING

Now, AS we have been discussing, what is the real cause of being in samsara? Everything that happens does so because of the seed that was planted that results in a certain karmic consequence. Everything that happens, the happiness and the suffering, depends on your karma.

We can see that some families are happy and some are not. Within any single family, some members do better economically and professionally than other members, even the brothers and sisters within a family. Now consider your own environment. Many people desire success, and in that pursuit of that goal they become well educated. However, not all educated people attain the same goal or outcome. Some educated people do not find jobs, whereas some uneducated people do find jobs and become successful. It seems it doesn't necessarily depend on the profession or the training, but one's own karma. Even with two people working in the same type of job or profession, one person may do better than the other, become more successful, while the other person goes downhill personally and professionally.

Differences occur because of karma. One can directly observe karma by observing your own environment.

We may also consider something called "composed by karma." This phenomenon is shown in the patterns you see in nature. For example, in butterflies and bugs that are beautiful and perfect in their design, or the exquisite color and pattern of delicate flower petals. Such beauty and perfection cannot be produced artificially by people. Rather, it is produced by karma. These are all karmic results you can observe for yourself. There are also karmic results that are not within your sight of vision, such as the suffering of sentient beings in hell. But you begin to understand these sufferings due to karma if you have absolute trust in the Dharma.

We know about the wheel of samsaric existence and the suffering there, but the mere knowledge of it does not help. We must pursue a way so as not to be born within the wheel! It is like having a thorn in the path whenever you walk: you must uproot that thorn completely and destroy it in order to eliminate it. In the same way, the dedicated pursuit of Dharma can liberate and free you from being reborn in the six realms of suffering.

Now we must first understand what are the defilements that cause us to remain in the wheel of existence. There are ten kinds of defilements (nyönmong), and these are rooted in adharmic actions expressed through your body, speech, and mind: through your body, you can express adharmic actions in three ways; through your speech, you can express adharmic actions in four ways; through your mind, you can express adharmic in three ways, which give us ten kinds of possible defilements.

What are the three actions expressed through the body? These are: taking life, taking things not given to you, and adultery. There are many kinds of intentions that motivate one to take a life. Killing an enemy in wartime is taking a life based on anger. Killing wild animals is motivated by desire for their musk, meat, or fur. The motivation may be sheer ignorance, perpetuated by some religious traditions in their rituals—for example, when someone dies, an animal is killed in a ritual sacrifice so as to help the dead person, or so it is believed. The karmic consequence of such actions will cause a person to be reborn in the realms of hell called "Blackline" (Thik Nak) and "Revived Again" (Yangsu). Some are born in the Crushing Hell. Killing your own father, mother, or arahats[15] will result in rebirth in the lowest parts of the hell called the "Utmost Hell" (Narmé Nyalwa). There is no worse hell than that. The karmic consequences of such actions are boundless.

For an action to be completed in order to reap the karmic result of killing, it must have these components: an object, an intention or motivation, a weapon or means to kill, and the end result of the action itself. Having an object means knowing for sure that whatever you are going to kill possesses mind. After realizing the object to be killed, you formulate your intention to kill: "I would like to kill this being." Then one tries to materialize that intention—that is, to find the means to kill, to find a knife or arrow or guns—which is called *jolwa*. If you then kill and end a life, that is the end result.

For those who have taken monastic vows as monks or nuns, if they complete the first three components—having an object, intention, and the means to take a life—and then renounce the monastic vow before the act of killing, there will be a big difference in the karmic result. Also, within these four components, knowing the intention of one's mind is very important. For example, it could be an intention of a mercy killing so that the person does not suffer more, or the desire to feed sentient beings who are starving, or it could just be anger. Different intentions have different karmic consequences. If all those four components to taking a life are complete, then the karma is completely formulated with all its limbs. That concludes our discussion on the taking of life.

Now for the second defilement, taking what is not given to you.

There are three ways of taking things not given. First, if a leader's subject has an object the leader wants, the leader puts that person into a position in which he is forced to give up that object to the leader. Or the might of the army during war or conquest is used to take the defeated peoples' wealth by force. Second, one steals things without the knowledge or consent of the owner. Third, one cons other people into giving their money—for example, a businessman sells crummy goods but falsely claims that the quality is excellent and the buyer is getting a good deal. All of these are examples of taking what is not freely given.

Now for the third adharmic defilement, adultery. Having affairs with a man or woman who is married, or having affairs with someone who already has a relationship with another, is considered adultery. This completes the three karmic defilements of the body.

Now we turn to the four adharmic defilements of speech. The first is lying. Lying is fooling another person or saying what another person wants to hear in order to get something from them that they would otherwise not give to you freely. There are ordinary lies that people tell every day, often thoughtlessly, and there are big lies. The big lies are speaking against the Dharma—for example, saying, "Doing dharmic action has no good results," or "There is no happiness in the pure land," or "Buddha does not have wisdom," or "Whatever action you do, there is no consequence," and so forth. *Mé shindu nangwai dzun* is the lie of an imposter, or a preposterous lie—for example, telling other people, "I am a great lama. I can talk with the gods. I communicate with the gods. I am a siddhi. I have powers. I have the attainments." Saying any of these things to others is an adharmic defilement.

The second adharmic defilement of speech is causing misunderstanding between people or causing disturbances through one's speech. This is called "trama." For example, when two people are friends, a third person goes to one of the friends and says, "Well, you respect him and are nice to him, but he does this and that to you behind your back." This is intentionally causing misunderstanding or making ill feelings rise between two people who otherwise get along. The karmic result will be rebirth in the hell called "Loud Cry for Help in Hot Hell" (Ngöbu).

Trama has tremendous negative consequences when it causes misunderstandings and disturbances among sangha members or between the sangha and and the lama. Or when a person creates a disturbance or a misunderstanding between or within lineages of tantric practitioners, and between the teacher and the students—for example, telling your fellow students that your teacher is doing this and that to you, or going to the teacher and saying that some student is doing this and that. Another instance of trama is creating turmoil and misunderstanding among and between Dharma friends, making things up to create ill feelings. This kind of action has boundless negative karmic consequences, equal to the consequences of killing your parents and arhats. And as we have seen, big lies like speaking against the Dharma—for example, saying, "Dharma has no effect. Buddha has no wisdom. Dharmic action has no fruit. There is no consequence to adharmic action"—all have grave consequences. One will be burned in Nalyé, a hell that has no limits to suffering.

The third adharmic defilement of speech is rough speech. For example, seeing a blind person, instead of calling him by his name, you call out, "Hey, Blind!" Or, seeing a person who is deaf and cannot hear, instead of calling him by his name, "Joe," you shout, "Hey, Deaf!" These are examples of rough speech. Rough speech or harsh words also apply to situations where one knows a person has some faults and you emphasize those faults or drawbacks and make him pay for it. It can also include words or speech that cause anxiety and sadness in another person's mind.

The fourth adharmic defilement of speech is gossip. One talks constantly without saying anything meaningful. Or one sings without any need to or without any meaning to the song. Or one enjoys recounting something out of jealousy or anger, such as telling people how so and so was killed, or did this or that in the past, or going on about nonsense, saying things like "I said this. I did that. My grandfather did this," and so on. Meaningless talk, or *ngak kyel*, should be avoided, especially since it will hinder your practice—your ability to hear, ponder, and meditate. Your mind could get caught up in the meaningless recounting of trivia or historical events that have no connection to your practice. This kind of talk bewilders your mind and takes it away from the practice, causing great impediments. Those of you who have done Nyungné[16] know you have to take the vow of silence. All talk of a meaningless nature is thought to produce bad karma, so when meditating, it is necessary to take the vow of silence seriously to eliminate this kind of bad karma, which can have grave consequences. This concludes the four adharmic defilements of speech.

Now we come to the three adharmic defilements of mind. The first is called *napsem*, a state of mind in which one wants or covets something someone else has and finds a way to get it from him. The second is called *nöd sem*, the intention of harming other people out of jealousy and anger. If a person is prosperous or happy or wealthy, you formulate an intention to bring that person down or somehow to defame him or squelch him or cause him harm. The third is *lokta*, a closed-mindedness that thinks it can negate the effects of karma, believing that actions have no consequences or no karmic results.

In this vein there are philosophies, such as that of the eternalists, that profess that the Earth is made by some great being and is permanent and eternal. On the other hand, nihilists believe that after one dies, there is nothing, that everything ends, like the extinction of a fire or lamp. Then there are empiricists who say the complexity in nature, the roundness of a pea or the sharpness of a thorn or the beautiful color of a peacock, are all created randomly, by chance. All these philosophies are *lokta*. According to the Dharma, everything is formed and comes into being because of karma.

So these are the ten adharmic defilements of mind. They all carry the same consequences; however, taking lives or harboring contradictory or closed-minded views that negate karma and its effects have extreme consequences. These adharmic actions are like seeds that will grow in the future, which we call *geu*. Everything happens because of the karmic seed, the cause. Nothing happens by itself. When you think that something happens by itself, that's when you contradict Dharma and get locked in your closed mind. According to the Dharma, cause and effect are central and most important to understand. And the cause of all suffering is adharmic action, *chömin jawa*.

None of us desires suffering, but our desires and actions are contradictory. We desire happiness but we perpetuate adharmic actions. Hence it is important to realize that once you initiate a seed, a cause, there is definitely an effect. Any adharmic action will result in suffering. The cause is a seed that will grow to maturity and have a future result.

Now, what are the results of these adharmic actions and how do they manifest? There are four kinds of adharmic results: the ripening of the effects, the effects similar to their causes, the ripening experience that resembles its causes, and the karma of being born in an environment according to the karmic cause.

In the ripening of the effects (*namin gi drebu*), for example, anger, if acted out, will end in a rebirth in hell. Or acting with attachment and greed—in the sense that you have wealth but you can neither offer nor give alms and at the same time you cannot enjoy it—will facilitate your rebirth in the yidak realm. Or action under the influence of ignorance, not knowing what to acquire and what to abandon, will result in your rebirth in the animal realm.

The effects similar to their causes (*jepa gyuthun*) are explained in this manner: For example, in a previous life, a butcher always killed or was involved in taking lives, therefore now in this present life, he is likely to repeat the action of killing. Why? If you look at a kitten, from a very young age it likes to jump at things and clutch things with its paws and kill. Among people, it's the same. There are children who love to kill from a very early age. Some children will try to act like lama, try to meditate, try to do things by themselves from a very young age; they are oriented toward the act of Dharma. That is because in their last life they were practitioners. The result of past karma, where you stole all your life, is that you will take rebirth as a rat or a mouse that always steals, or a crow who is always stealing. As a karmic consequence of taking lives in a previous life, the person will continually take lives in his present and future lives until the end of samsara, without respite; this is *kyewo chipo drebu*. We can see how some people who have enough to eat and enough to wear still love to steal. Then there are those who are poor and can hardly make ends meet, but they do not steal at all (they are called "Shepa Gyutsen"). These effects are all the result of previous causes in past lives.

The ripening experience that resembles its causes (*nyongwar gyü tsen*) is seen in these examples: If in their past life a person took lots of lives, then the person in this life will have a short life, dying young, or suffer a chronic disease. Chronic disease or illness is seen in people who beat animals badly or threw stones at them in their past life. Illness is a result, and they are reaping the result of that karma. *Ngön gyi lé* means "karma from the previous life," which is different from karma due to "the immediate circumstances" (*tar kyi khyen*). Sickness, for example, could be a karmic disease, though it could also be caused by present behavior. For example, if you sit under the sun for long time it can give you a headache. That kind of illness is caused by not knowing the limitation of your body. Or one could fall ill because of possession by spirits that cause sickness. That is why divination is important in analyzing what kind of sickness one has, or what the attitude is, or the external influences of spirits, or the karmic influences. Within these three kinds of adharmic results, half are caused by your own karma. An external spirit influence might be due to having caused, at one time in your life, a certain pain to a kind spirit or being who is now in turn taking revenge.

In Tibet it is considered important to do a divination to find out what kind of sickness the ill person has. Medicine is not deemphasized, but at same time, the ritual to harmonize one's karma is done. Doctors are not commonly found in Tibet. Medicine is not considered to be the most important resource when one is sick. The most important aspect is to be able to do the appropriate rites and ceremonies, called *shabten*. If a family member is very seriously ill and the monastery is within distance, the family takes a few things there. Nomadic people will give animals to the monastery for purposes of healing. Farmers will take certain things to a monastery for the ceremony or rites for a sick person. I witnessed many circumstances where a patient got well immediately.

Now to return to the discussion of adharmic actions and their results. Being really poor is due to stealing, taking things without being given them, in your previous life. Similarly, people who took things from others by force or used force to intimidate others to give up their wealth might accumulate lots of wealth in their present life, but that wealth becomes the cause of their suffering—for example, their wealth is stolen or somehow they lose it all and they suffer the loss.

The result of adultery is also evident. Married people often do not get along and fight constantly. This is common among Dharma students present here. People often complain to me, "We don't seem to get along. What should we do?" There is no way to solve this disharmony. It is important to realize that it is the result of one's own past karma. If you get angry over the other person's faults, you get into a vicious circle, multiplying the bad karma. The best way to deal with that kind of situation is to first of all realize that whatever is happening is because of karma. Then deal with this karma with patience and tolerance. Realize, "It is my perception that is causing this turmoil in my mind. It is not inherent in my partner's behavior, but is a result of my karma." By practicing patience and tolerance, it is possible to eliminate the karma. And you can hope for a better situation in the future.

People may pick on someone's faults even though the person hasn't done anything wrong. When people accuse you even though you have done nothing wrong, a typical reaction is to fight back or try to prove your innocence, but in Dharma it is very important to realize that this is due to your karma. Trying to prove your innocence or argue back might simply perpetuate such karma. However, if you realize the person who is accusing you is doing so as a result of the past karma of your lying, take it onto yourself and meditate on patience and tolerance. Then that karma will be eliminated. With that understanding, be grateful for the accuser. Rather than fight back, instead feel the sincere joy in your heart, thinking, "I'm now being freed from the karma that I earned from past lives."

Misunderstandings and conflicts among people are the result of past karma. If a man has servants, the servants will try to deceive him. If he is a man of power, his subjects will try to revolt against him. Instead of trying to counteract the inevitable, it is of the utmost importance to realize that this is a result of karma and in order to eliminate the karma, one must act patiently and be tolerant of the situation rather than counteracting it and furthering the karma, which could bring worse consequences in the future.

When you hear unpleasant things or are the object of criticism or insult, it is important to realize that you are being insulted and criticized because of karma and that in order to eliminate this karma, one should not counterattack. According to the samsaric way of thinking, not responding in kind turns you into a person who has no self respect, or a person who does not believe in anything, or a person who is wishy-washy. But according to the Dharma, you are trying to eliminate bad karma so it will not affect you in the future. Instead of a counterattack, you try to develop the depth of tolerance, try to resolve this kind of karmic consequence and break the vicious cycle of cause and effect.

If one gossips or engages in meaningless chatter, the result will be that when you are trying to make a point, to say something important, people won't listen to you. They will say, "He is always saying such things. It doesn't mean anything." But if some other person says something, people will listen to him carefully. This is also the result of your karma. There is no way to correct the situation except from the depth of tolerance.

As a result of covetousness, whenever you would like to do certain things, they just don't go right. The result is always wrong. As a result of engaging in harmful thoughts, you experience a frightening situation where your life is in danger or a situation that is unpleasant. Harmful thoughts can result in harmful experiences and frightful and unpleasant situations. As a result of closed-mindedness that contradicts the Dharmic view, you are born into a tradition that harbors an adharmic philosophy and your mind is always in turmoil or disturbed.

Karmic rebirth in an environment or land that mirrors the cause, *wang kyi drebu*, is the power that influences you to be born in a vast desert where there is no means to grow anything for your sustenance. The result of taking lives is rebirth in a barren, rocky land that cannot be farmed and is filled with dangerous animals. The consequence of taking things without being given them results in rebirth in a land where crops will not grow well and people die of starvation. The result of adultery is rebirth in lands that are marshy and unpleasant to live in. The result of lying is living in an unstable land where floods wipe you out and are a danger to your life. The result of causing misunderstandings between people is in living in a land that is rough and very unpleasant. Using harsh words results in rebirth in a land where there are lots of stones, thorns, and bushes. The result of gossip and idle chatter is rebirth in a land that has opposite seasons: summer is cold, winter is hot, crops cannot grow in the proper season, and the land is virtually barren. The result of covetousness will be rebirth in a barren, fruitless land with an abundance of poisonous snakes and vicious animals that constantly threaten your life. The result of closed-mindedness that harbors the view that contradicts Dharma is rebirth in a land without any food. *Wang kyi drebu* is the power that causes you to be reborn in a land or a country that mirrors your adharmic action in a previous life.

THE DEDICATION

We end the teaching on the ten defilements by dedicating all the merit from listening to the Dharma for the enlightenment of all sentient beings.

Questions and Answers

Q: Rinpoché talked about two people doing the same job and one does better than the other financially. The question here seems to be, how does one know what is the right livelihood for oneself?
A: There is no way to know or recognize what is your right livelihood. All we know is the fact that you are a human being and certain circumstances appear in your life that are the products of your karma. Karma is sequential: first the experience, *nyongwa*, then the karmic result of that experience or action influences you to, for example, have a rebirth in a region of a certain quality. So a person may be born on

land that has thorn bushes. The quality of the land is bad enough, but on top of that he has thorns that scratch him all the time and hinder him from traveling back and forth. One can uproot the thorns, but the land is useless nonetheless. Such is the karmic result of using the coarse words when you were once a human being. You have earned or produced the karma of using coarse words.

CONTEMPLATING THE RESULT OF LIBERATION AND THE TEACHER AS GUIDE

The Intention

As USUAL you must formulate the intention of liberation and the enlightenment of all sentient beings under the vast horizon of the sky.

The Teaching on Contemplating the Result of Liberation

In our practice there are four turnings away from samsara: the preciousness of human life, the impermanence of human life, karmic results, and suffering in samsara. These are the four that we usually recite. However, in the preliminary practices of Longchen Nyingthik there are six, and that's why Patrul Rinpoche's *Words of My Perfect Teacher* has six practices instead of four. According to Ngöndro, the fifth is contemplating the result of liberation and the sixth is how to have a teacher.

Let us examine the fifth practice, contemplating the result of liberation. We all go from one life to another within the six samsaric realms, circling and circling, as if we are trapped within a wheel. Within those six realms, you are not free from suffering. We usually think that god realms are the best and the happiest realms, but we are aware that the suffering in a god realm can exceed the suffering in hell. The god realm is not above samsaric existence. At the extinction of that karma, one descends into the three lower realms and is trapped in a vicious circle. That is why we always have suffering.

Being in any of the six realms is analogous to roasting under the sun and getting scorched. Such is the suffering in samsara. Now if you wonder why you perform dharmic actions, it is to obtain liberation from the six realms of samsara. The experience of liberation from samsara is analogous to cooling off in the shade after getting roasted in the sun—feeling the coolness of the shade, the pleasure of it, and having an open feeling in your mind. Or we could say that suffering in samsara is like having to walk an extremely narrow path on a steep mountain, at the bottom of which is a raging river. If you slip, there is danger that you will fall into the torrent. You are in the middle of the path and cannot turn back, and there is no other way out. That is like existence in the wheel of samsara. However, once you have crossed that obstacle or that path, you come to a flat, beautiful land where you feel the stain is gone—it has finally left you and you feel liberated. Your mind is freer and happier.

Or we could say that suffering in samsara is like being in a den of poisonous snakes. Once you are in that enclosed, stifling space, you cannot step backward or forward. You must stand still because if you take one step, you will be bitten by the snakes. How does it feel to be liberated? It is like being in a beautiful garden with flowers blooming all around you, and your mind feeling its happiest.

It is essential for us to know the difference between suffering in samsara and liberation. The experience and consequence of samsara is suffering. The quality and the result of liberation is enlightenment. It is also important to know what liberation means, what freedom means. Because there are many paths, and they define freedom in different ways, one must be sure what freedom means. There is a freedom that liberates one from the lower realms, from the hell, animal, and preta (hungry ghost) realms, to rebirth in the higher realms, like the gods. That is one kind of freedom, but that is limited in quality and in duration. With the extinction of that karma, you will be born in samsara again. It is like buying a packet of seeds. All the seeds are similar, in that they are all seeds, but one must know what kinds of seeds will bear what types of fruits or plants.

If you ask what are the different kinds of liberation, there is one kind of liberation called "Nyenthö" (shravaka, "the Hearers") and another called "Rang Sangyé" (pratyekabuddha), two different practices with the same aim: liberation from samsara for oneself. These were practiced by Sharipu and Mongolana, the two closest disciples of Shakyamuni Buddha. They attained some state of accomplishment; however, they did not attain liberation from the intellectual obscurations (*shejai dripa*)—that is, grasping at mental objects with subject and object duality. Another kind of liberation is *sangyé*, ultimate buddhahood, the aim of attaining the fully enlightened or awakened state by complete abandonment of the obscurations and their habitual traces and by fully realizing ultimate reality. If you are not free from the intellectual obscurations (*shejai dripa*), then you cannot perform miraculous actions like the Buddha.

The power of the shravaka and pratyekabudda is limited in four ways. Once the Buddha attained complete enlightenment, he could see through time itself—that is, he could see many kalpas back into the past and many kalpas forward into the future, and he could see infinity itself. This power is not present in shravakas or pratyekabuddhas. Second, in terms of space, the Buddha could see all sentient beings at the same instant throughout all the places under the wide horizon of the sky. This power is not present in shravakas or pratyekabuddhas; those states cannot see what happened in a specific time in history or prehistory. Third, they can, to a certain extent, understand or realize how previous lives caused rebirths, though they cannot know to the extent the Buddha knows about the cause of rebirths or karmic results. Fourth, they have no power to know all of the Buddha, Dharma, or Sangha, whereas there is nothing the Buddha does not know. Shravakas and pratyekabuddhas are limited in these four ways because their intellectual obscurations have not been purified yet. If you attain the state of buddhahood, there is no more to be accomplished.

Now many people feel Dharma is Dharma. That's it. They do not think seriously of the beginning or the end—that is, what is the aim and the result of the practice. Many people come to me and say, "I like to do this. I like certain things and that's why I like to practice it." But it is very important to know what the result of the practice will be. So during meditation one must know what the point of the meditation is. It's not to be done just on a whim, "I like this." One must know the path and what the consequences will be, the result. That's why it's important for you to relate to the teacher, or find your teacher. Otherwise, you will not achieve the freedom or liberation you seek.

I'll explain with an example of very short, limited, and unsatisfactory "liberation." There are ten virtuous actions, which we are probably all aware of: not killing, not taking something not given to you, not committing an adultery, and so forth. These can be categorized as the path to liberation to be humans and gods. However, they are not included within the teachings on liberation because it is not the ultimate liberation. It is simply liberation or freedom in a comparative sense, liberated as a human being in the human realm. If one keeps up with these ten virtuous actions, with their karma, one can be born in the lower realm of gods, near to samsara, Gyalchen Deshi, where fifty days of human life is equal to one night of Gelchen Degé, the god realm closest to the samsaric realm. So you can have pleasurable existence for one kalpa. However, this existence will come to an end. We might say this is like being in a prison within a concentric structure. The inner prison is worse than the outer circle. It is all surrounded by a series of iron walls. The path of liberation from the human to the god realm is like being freed from the central prison to the outer ring of the iron wall. That is not freedom. It is just freedom from the inner circle of the prison to the outer circle of the prison. At any minute, a guard or custodian will come and take you back to the inner prison. True freedom is being liberated from that entirely. That is true liberation. You are freed from the central and the outer circles, not having to return to the previous existence.

Giving alms also accumulates merit to be born in the human realm or the god realm. For a moderate action, and depending on one's intention, one is reborn in a human realm with wealth. The optimum result is being born in a god realm, but again, this is not an absolute freedom. That is why everyone has to study. Everyone must grasp Dharma concepts gradually, check and understand them. Ask for spiritual instruction on the path of the attainment, the path of liberation. It is not possible just to get spiritual instruction right at this moment, whenever one wants; that is not the way it is done.

If you seek the path of enlightenment, there are two ways: the way of Sutra, or Hinayana, and the way of Tantra, or Mahayana. As for the Hinayana path, I have spoken on the ten virtuous actions: through those actions one can attain to a human realm and a god realm, and liberation or freedom in a comparative sense—as, for example, a human being in the human realm. However, it is not complete and absolute liberation. In this attainment of liberation or enlightenment of self, there are ten ways of understanding cause and effect relationships. In self-liberation, the path of the pratyekabuddha, a person attains a certain state of enlightenment through his own inquiry, having no teacher. If he does not have a teacher, how does he do it? Well, a person goes to a cremation ground and he sees a bone and asks, "How did this bone come about? This bone came about by the death of an old man and decay. How do death and decay come about? Through birth. How does birth come about?" and so on and so forth. He will build up his reasoning and face ignorance (*marikpa*, Skt. *avidyā*), complete darkness in terms of wisdom. He will originate the inquiry into *marikpa*. In doing so, he will come down to the level of bone itself.

The difference between the Hinayana path and the Mahayana is one of intention. In our tradition, Mahayana, we take bodhisattva vows first—the intention to attain liberation for the benefit of all sentient beings so that they are all liberated from their suffering in samsara. This becomes part of our mind. So the difference between Mahayana and Hinayana is bodhichitta, the bodhisattva mind. The value of bodhisattva intention is so vast that it cannot be analyzed or compared usefully with other intentions. It is vastly greater, for example, to a land with blind people who have a wish-granting gem that could give them everything they desire. Even that cannot equal the merits of the bodhisattva intention. The bodhisattva mind—bodhichitta—at one with the bodhisattva intention, is even much greater and more valuable than parental love. In our present existence on Earth, probably our best experience of love and compassion is our parents, knowing how much they care for their children. Yet parental love is much narrower than the bodhisattva mind that is one with the bodhisattva vow.

Such parental love may be categorized as desire, as attachment and aversion. The sense of "my children" originates from an attachment, so in general it cannot be categorized or analyzed as compassion, since it is just a feeling of helping one's own children. The bodhisattva mind (bodhichitta), however, considers all sentient beings under the vast horizon of the sky as one's own relatives and treats them as one's own parents or as one's own children. The scope of bodhichitta is vast, whereas the parental scope is much narrower. That's why they are not comparable.

Even the king of the gods cannot be considered a bodhisattva's equal. The king of the gods is the most revered among the gods—the most supreme, the most powerful, the wealthiest. However, he does not have the Bodhisattva intention, the view of incorporating all sentient beings under the vast horizon of the sky within the realm of his mind, like the bodhisattva does. That is why he cannot be compared with or be considered equal to a bodhisattva.

The bodhisattva is beyond any samsaric category of class, such as the monarch, the aristocracy, the Brahmin, or any of the lower classes, like fishermen and butchers who kill animals for other people. In the Dharma, these social labels do not mean anything. Certainly the bodhisattva will not be in any one of them. He is outside the four castes and, after taking refuge in the Three Precious Ones, he is inside the caste of the Enlightened One, the class of the Buddha.

The rarity of this bodhisattva manifestation is rarer than the rarest dream. It is possible to dream that the herd of animals is running through a hole in one's nose. One can also dream that one is riding on a galloping horse. However, one cannot imagine or dream of taking the bodhisattva vow.

One can see the expanse and the unlimited scope of the bodhisattva vows, unlimited in the sense that the bodhisattva considers all sentient beings under the wide horizon of the sky as his or her own parents. He or she relates to all these sentient beings as "my parents" in the same manner. It has nothing to do with giving someone a few things and thinking yourself as a bodhisattva. You cannot consider yourself a bodhisattva by giving some small amounts to a needy person. The relationship to all sentient beings and the reverence paid to each and every one of them is vast and equal. That is why the bodhisattva's actions are expansive and vast and his manifestation hard to visualize.

This is why it is important to know the differences in the attainment of freedom. If one desires to attain personal freedom through the Hinayana path, one can do so. If one wants to attain self-enlightenment, one can do so. However, one can also seek the supreme enlightenment of Buddha. The difference, as you are reminded again and again, is the intention. By adding the bodhisattva intention to the practice of the six transcending wisdoms, or paramitas, that are at the heart of Mahayana Buddhist practice—generosity (*dana*), discipline (*sila*), patience (*ksanti*), diligence (*virya*), meditation (*dhyana*), and wisdom (*prajna*)—one is on the path to the supreme enlightenment of the Buddha. In Mahayana practice self-realization is not enough. One takes the vow of serving all sentient beings throughout the wide horizon of the sky within the realm of one's own mind. That's why in our practice we clarify our intention first and then later dedicate to all sentient beings.

In the preliminary practices of Mahayana, you recite your intention one hundred thousand times. The recitation of your intention one hundred thousand times is done for you to be aware that it is a path to realization and does not end there. After reciting the intention one hundred thousand times, you might want to say, "I am now a bodhisattva," but that is not right, that is just the beginning of the practice. And we are reminded that there are many different paths and the intention of one's practice is very important.

THE TEACHER AS GUIDE

Let's now examine together how to find a teacher and how to relate to him or her as a guide. Although, as we have said, this is not included in the four common preliminary practices, it is mentioned in *The Words of My Perfect Teacher* and you may refer to it in future.

Once you are on the path of Dharma, it is virtually impossible to attain enlightenment by just reading books and scriptures or practicing without a teacher to guide your meditation. It is fine to be a good reader, but reading and speaking the words do not have much bearing on understanding the Dharma. Reading is not an end it itself in Dharma practice because you may understand the meaning of a word or a sentence, but rarely will you realize what it really says about enlightenment itself. For example, one can superficially grasp what *sangyé* means in the sense of knowing that *sang* means "waking" and *gyé* means "expanse"; this is a short, understandable definition, but the actual meaning goes much further, much deeper.

Understanding Dharma depends on one's intelligence, yet even intelligent people commonly say, "Oh, I can't understand that" in reference to Dharma. When people studying Dharma say, "Now it's becoming clearer and clearer," that is a sure sign that it is not clear. People often think that it is easy and all you have to do is translate or understand the words, or flip the words around, and say, "Now, it's coming to me." Then you know for sure the person is lying or is far away from really understanding. But if a person says, "Now I know how hard it is," or "Now I am beginning to know how hard it is," then that is the point where she is coming closer to attaining the meaning.

It is important to realize that I am stressing that point not just to express my own view but because it is said in the vinaya books for lamas and teachers: "There is no way to attain enlightenment without having a teacher." You cannot just read somewhere the simple meaning of *sangyé* and be awakened and go around saying, "I understand the whole thing." The depth of that one word is immeasurable, and you need the guidance and explanation and commentary of your teacher. There is not a single example of attaining enlightenment by just looking at a text, or by just looking at somebody recite some words, or by just thinking about it by oneself, or by glorifying someone else's attainment. There is not one single incidence where one obtained enlightenment by these means.

One can go crazy without a teacher's guidance when one tries to do a meditation in depth, saying, for example, "I want to clarify my vision," and pushing oneself to go deep in the attempt to see it. The more you push, the more different thoughts emerge to obstruct the vision, and there is a tendency for one to go crazy. If one is not careful, there are uncomfortable results when doing a meditation. Our mind rides the wind, and there are special channels the wind travels. The wind travels through one's body through psychic veins. If one is not careful, there is a chance you will displace the wind from its original position, or displace the mind in that sense, and the result is one could go crazy, go mad. Without taking refuge and without taking the guidance of your teacher, practicing Dharma has no conceivable desirable result.

Misguided Dharma practice is analogous to an uneducated person who sees a microphone and a tape recorder and thinks how great they are: the sound is trapped in that piece of thin film and suddenly it speaks again. Fascinated by this machine, he wants to build it and, in ignorance, not knowing what goes on inside, he tries and tries, but soon the time comes when he starts going crazy, believing it is impossible to build. In the same way, if you try to meditate by only reading a book or scriptures, you'd get only the same frustration and be well on your way to craziness.

You seek the guidance of your spiritual teacher or lama because there are no other people in this world who are more beneficial than your parents. Your mother carried you for nine months in her womb. When you were a helpless baby, your parents cared for you and reared you, holding you constantly in their minds with thoughts of how to help you, how to make you happy, how to do the right things. However, parental care is analogous to a mother cat killing a mouse and giving it to her kittens to play with. It is not that parents have a bad intention or have a bad motive to make you into a killer or bring you down to samsara, it is just that they do not know another way. Wishing you only the best possible things, your parents want you to know how to make friends or how to subjugate your enemies or how to make money or how to be successful in your life. The lessons they impart are not the result of bad intentions or bad motives. They don't intend to bring you down to samsara. Because they don't know another way, they think they are doing a great thing for you, as a cat or a tiger does instinctively for its young.

Being with your teacher or having entered into a relationship with your teacher is like being in a special forest in India where there are good-smelling trees. When you put an ordinary tree among those good-smelling trees, that ordinary tree also acquires a good smell. In the same way, seek the guidance of well-versed spiritual masters. Then wisdom or knowledge will grow like the ordinary tree acquiring the good smell of the fragrant trees.

Another point to be well aware of is the quality of the teacher. There are two kinds of teacher: one who teaches the path of the enlightenment and one who leads a person to the opposite way. For example, when the sun is beating down on you and you are very hot, you look into the distance and see a beautiful shadow underneath a tree. Right away you want to take refuge. So you go there. But when you get to the tree you realize there is not a shadow but a poisonous snake, and because you are so tired, you sit down and the poisonous snake bites you and ends your life. That can happen with a teacher who teaches the contrary path.

Before entering into the relationship, you must scrutinize and study the quality of the teacher. You must be good in judging the teacher. Once you enter the relationship, you must then always keep a pure perception of him. Here is an example of pure perception: One time Naropa was meditating. In his meditation one of the tutelary gods appeared and said, "Your karmic teacher is called 'Tilopa.'"[17] You must go and search for him in western India. Take teachings from him." So Naropa went in search of his teacher. He reached the country where Tilopa was supposed to be, and there he asked, "Have you seen Tilopa?" Nobody seemed to know who Tilopa was. At last one man said, "The man called 'Tilopa' is a beggar." If Naropa were an ordinary man, he would have said, "Oh, a beggar. I will not go see that beggar." But Naropa was a great practitioner and had a pure perception, so he asked the man to lead him to the beggar Tilopa. When Naropa got there, he saw broken walls and smoke rising behind them. He went in and saw a man sitting by a fire. The man had a bowl full of half dead and half live fish. He put each fish on the fire and snapped his fingers. Naropa got on his knees, prostrated, and said, "You are the great Tilopa. I would like to take teachings from you." Tilopa said, "What are you talking about? I am not the great Tilopa. I am a beggar. You can't say those things and prostrate." However, Naropa was persistent and at last Tilopa agreed to teach him. In the history of the mahasiddhas—*maha* meaning "great," *siddha* meaning "accomplished one"—the two of them were known as the great siddhas.

Our normal perception would have seen Tilopa as a beggar and a killer-fisherman. It is not that Tilopa couldn't find food or that he was economically deprived. He had taken the form of a beggar to help sentient beings. In essence he was a great enlightened teacher. There are as well eighty great siddhas of India. Saraha, who shot arrows, is well known. As is Shawa Ripa, so called because he was a deer hunter. Many siddhas were born into the lowest castes in India. Although it is our normal perception or the perception of students that they appear that way, in fact they have taken that sort of form only to help living beings.

Now here is an example of not having pure perception. During the time of Shakyamuni Buddha, the Buddha was served by one of his relatives, Legpe Karma, a monk. A time came when Legpe Karma said to the Buddha, "I don't see any difference between you and me. You have some kind of aura around you that I don't have. But other than that, I know as much as you do." The thing is, in that kind of situation, if you live with even the Buddha, you will begin to see his faults. So Legpe Karma continued, "I have served you for twenty-four years and I haven't seen any great qualities about you. So I'm taking off." And he left.

When the monk left, Ananda, who was one of his closest students, asked Buddha, "What will happen to Legpe Karma?" Buddha said, "He has only seven days to live. After he dies, he will be born a yidak, a hungry ghost." So Ananda went to Legpe Karma and said to him,

"Look, be very careful. The Enlightened One said you have seven days to live. After death, you will be born in the yidak realm." Legpe Karma said, "Oh, sometimes he lies. But sometimes lies come true. So maybe I will be careful." He then thought, "If I eat something, that will be the cause of my death. Maybe by food poisoning." So for seven days he fasted. On the seventh day he was still alive, and he thought to himself, "I am not dead. I can criticize his lies." At the end of the seventh day he was very thirsty, so he drank a little bit of water. That water became the cause of his death. After he died he was reborn in the yidak realm, a very bad rebirth in the flower garden.

These examples are for the practice of pure perception, to clean your perception. Be aware that if you live with your teacher and are too close to him in space or time, there is a tendency to see his faults. That is why keeping some distance from your teacher and practicing pure perception toward him are essential.

To have one common Vajra teacher is like brothers and sisters having the same father. To have one altar or mandala is like having one mother. Thus one should never cause conflict or misunderstanding among Vajra and Dharma friends. Be like the sash tied around your waist that holds your clothes. Compromise and accommodate, love one another, and show compassion for one another. That's how you should carry on the relationship.

In addition to accommodating others, one should have the ability to blend into a situation. In this regard, one should be like salt: you can put salt on any kind of food, it gives you the same taste. One should not speak harsh words to or use harsh language with one's friends. One should be able to tolerate any situation like a pillar that holds up everything on top of it, or like a roof beam. One should be tolerant and be patient in one's reactions to others. One must practice patience.

If a spiritual master or teacher is performing ceremonies or making ritual offerings to deities, actions that are geared to gain merit, students or disciples can help materially with money or by being helpful in body, speech, and mind. If you cannot do either, be happy and joyful in the situation or for the circumstances. If the teacher gains merit by performing the action, then everyone who helped in any of these ways will receive the same extent of virtue or merit.

That's how you should seek your guru or teacher, not forming judgments based on his physical appearance, or his position, or his disposition, or on rumors that may be circulating about him. This is the sixth teaching, which is not in our chanting practice.

This completes the teachings on the common preliminary practices, common to all paths. Next we will turn to the uncommon preliminary practices and intention.

THE DEDICATION

Now, as usual, in the realm of your mind, dedicate all the merit you have earned by listening to the teaching of the Dharma for the enlightenment of all sentient beings.

Shakyamuni Buddha

Guru Vajrasattva

Dorjé Naljorma

Guru Rinpoché Padmasambhava

Dorjé Naljorma

Refuge Tree Thangka

Key to the Refuge Tree

1. Kuntu Sangpo (Samantabhadra)
2. Dodrup Kunsang Shenphen (Jikmé Trinlé Öser)
3. Dorjé Sempa (Vajrasattva)
4. Do Khyentsé Yeshé Dorjé
5. Jikmé Gyalwa Nyugu
6. Jamyang Khyentsé Wangpo
7. Thupten Chökyi Dorjé
8. Dodrul Kargyi Dorjé
9. Gyalsé Shenphen Thayé
10. Gekong Khenpo Kunpal
11. Shri Singha
12. Yeshé Do (Jnanasutra)
13. Berotsana
14. Garab Dorjé (Prahevajra)
15. Padma Jungné (Padmasambhava)
16. Yeshé Tsogyal
17. Longchen Rabjam
18. Jikmé Lingpa
19. Jampal Shenyen (Manjusrimitra)
20. Vimalamitra
21. Tri Songdetsen
22. Dola Jikmé Kalsang
23. Jikmé Tempé Nyima
24. Jikmé Phuntshok Jungné
25. Yukhok Chatralwa
26. Apang Tertön
27. Patrul Jikmé Chökyi Wangpo
28. Khyentsé Chökyi Lodrö
29. Eight Bodhisattvas
30. Eight Arhats
31. Thukjé Chenpo (Avalokiteshvara)
32. Shinjé (Yamantaka)
33. Guru Rinpoché with Consort Yeshé Tsogyal
34. Tamdrin
35. Takhyung Barwa
36. Vajra Heruka
37. Chemchok Heruka
38. Buddhas of the Three Times
39. Yumka Dechen Gyalmo
40. Phurba
41. Sengdongma
42. Tsheringma
43. Gönpo Maning
44. Sadü
45. Mamo Ekasati
46. Tamchin Dorjé Lekpa
47. Lhamo Nganema
48. Yudrönma

PART 3

The Four Uncommon Preliminary Practices

TAKING REFUGE

THE INTENTION

OF THE NUMBERLESS sentient beings within the limitless boundaries of the sky, there is not a single one who has not been your parent. Like our present parents, they treated us with love and care. Bring these countless sentient beings under the vast horizons of the sky to the realm of your mind and generate boundless compassion. Think, "There is no other way to enlighten all sentient beings." That is the bodhisattva mind.

All sentient beings desire happiness. However, they do not know the seed or source of happiness that is virtuous dharmic action. All sentient beings want to avoid suffering. However, they perpetually create adharmic actions that perpetuate their suffering. Like blind men, these sentient beings have no light of wisdom. Make a resolution, "I will enlighten all sentient beings under the vast horizon of the sky. By listening to this teaching, I would like to experience the meaning and the essence of guru yoga and enlighten all sentient beings." That intention must precede listening to the teaching.

THE TEACHING ON TAKING REFUGE

In the actual Three Jewels and their essence, the three root sugatas;
in the nature of the channels, energy, and essence, bodhichitta;

in this mandala of the essence, nature, and compassion—
to these I go for refuge until the attainment of the bodhi essence.[18]
(Repeat 3 times)

We take refuge in the Three Precious Ones, or the Three Jewels—
the Buddha, Dharma, and Sangha. This is what differentiates Buddhists from other religions. At the present time, it is very important
to take refuge before practicing guru yoga. Taking refuge not only
precedes the practice of guru yoga but is a prerequisite for all the
practices you do. It is like the basic foundation of a house that must
be made before constructing the house. That foundation is taking
refuge, which you must do prior to taking the *wang* (the lama's empowerment to students), prior to vows, prior to any recitation, and
prior to any chanting.

To take refuge is to have faith and complete trust. Faith is one of
the eleven virtuous actions or dharmic manifestations. It is the state
of mind necessary for Dharma practice. Buddha gave a long treatise
or discourse on faith, emphasizing that faith must precede any kind
of dharmic practice. Faith depends on the state of mind. State of
mind is likewise related to karma: with the right state of mind, one
can analyze different karmic positions like good karma, bad karma,
and neutral karma.

There are three different kinds of faith. The first is called "the faith
of joy." When a person sees the statue of the Buddha, or Dharma
books, or chorten, or lamas, or monasteries, he sees them as manifestations of the Dharma and feels a joy at the sight of them. This is
called *dangwai depa.*

The second is the faith of wanting or yearning, *döpai depa.* Aware of
the suffering in all the realms, one yearns to be free from the wheel of
samsaric existences. Or, realizing suffering, a person yearns or desires
to be born in the god realm: knowing the happiness of the god realm
or maybe hearing of shravakas or pratyekabuddhas, or hearing of self-

enlightened Buddhas or the supreme state of buddhahood, she yearns for the achievement of all these qualities in order to be freed from the suffering of samsara. A person who realizes that Dharma is the seed and the cause of liberation pursues dharmic actions. He desires to abandon adharmic actions, knowing that adharmic actions will result in birth in the lower realms, infested with sufferings. The state of mind that knows cause and effect and acts to free itself from that is considered the faith of wanting or yearning. You all have this second type of faith, wanting to take refuge with the Three Precious Ones, wanting to abandon unvirtuous actions, and trying to do virtuous actions.

The third faith is absolute faith or trust, *yiché pai depa*. This originates when one knows the Three Jewels (the Buddha, Dharma, and Sangha), or *Könchok Sum*, which has extraordinary and supreme power. A person who has absolute faith is someone who has absolute confidence in the Three Jewels, realizing that through the power and grace of *Könchok Sum*, one is happy when one is suffering. Just praying, "Oh, *Könchok Sum*, help me," is considered to be mouthing empty words, without force. Instead one has to supplicate from the depth of one's heart and realize that happiness from suffering is due to the grace of *Könchok Sum*. The Three Jewels have absolute power.

Absolute faith is difficult to generate. It is very difficult even for us to have that kind of faith, the kind that brings tears just hearing the words *Könchok Sum*. This is the faith that vibrates through your whole body. My teacher, when he gave us a teaching about his teacher, the stories of his tsawai lama and the miraculous actions his lama performed, sometimes had tears in his eyes and the whole teaching had to be stopped for the rest of the day. That kind of faith.

Faith is like having fertile land where you can plant seeds and build a house. Without fertile land, there is no place to sow seeds and build your house. That is why faith is the vessel of Dharma, where the Dharma can be sowed. Faith is also like the seed you plant that brings forth the fruit of Dharma. Once you have faith in Dharma, the door to Dharma will open. Having faith is like opening a door. Entering the Dharma, you begin to realize the essence and the wisdom of the Dharma. Realizing its importance, you begin to practice Dharma. The ultimate result is enlightenment. If it is not the ultimate result, then it is like the seed that is sown that will subsequently bring about the fruit of enlightenment. If you do not have faith or trust, it is like having a burnt seed. If you sow the burnt seed, it will never grow.

Once one has faith that lasts day and night, it is like a wheel that goes around, a precious wheel. This is not an ordinary wheel. A long time ago, this wheel was used by the great kings to travel from one planet to another. If one imagined a planet, then one could be there with the help of this wheel. Faith is that kind of wheel. Having faith, you can devote yourself to Dharma night and day without tiring. Faith is like a precious wish-fulfilling gem. When it is placed in the banner (*gyaltsen*) and supplicated or worshiped, or an offering is made to it, this gem will provide people whatever they desire. That is faith, *depa*. Faith is also the immense accommodating space in which you can explore the depth of the Dharma in the vast expanse.

Faith is analogous to your feet, which help you travel from one place to another. But faith is the feet that travel the path to enlightenment. Having faith, your ability to abandon unvirtuous actions becomes more evident. Your ability to acquire virtuous actions and to act on them becomes easier. Understanding that essence, you realize the source of suffering is the negative merit created by unvirtuous actions and the path to liberation is by pursuing virtuous actions. Faith, like your feet, will lead you to materialize those desires for virtuous action.

Faith is also like a hand that grasps things that are Dharmic and will help all sentient beings on the path to enlightenment. Having this kind of faith, you will have the ability to seek the master, listen to the teachings, and get the spiritual instruction to pursue the path of enlightenment. This hand will extend toward all the great masters of the lineage and all the great teachers. As you practice, this hand will grow and blend the essence of the practice with your mind. In leaps and bounds your realization will increase, and thus you will be a realized one.

The Three Precious Ones, *Könchok Sum*, have unlimited power and grace, but they can only be brought to one's own mind through faith. The faith is the receiving part and the part that joins you to the boundless powers of Three Precious Ones. The compassionate power of *Könchok Sum* does not discriminate; there is no division into good and bad. However, the power you draw from *Könchok Sum* depends on the strength of your own faith. Only the strongest absolute faith can draw absolute compassion from *Könchok Sum*. If you have only a moderate faith in the Three Precious Ones, you draw the power of *Könchok Sum* at that level. If you have only minimum faith in *Könchok Sum*, you draw only the minimum compassionate power of *Könchok Sum*. If you do not have faith at all, then you cannot draw any power from *Könchok Sum*. It is like having an iron hook: to pick things up, there must be a ring to hook the object on to and pull toward yourself. In the same way, the extent of your faith in *Könchok Sum* will determine how much of the power of *Könchok Sum* you can draw toward yourself.

Right now you see many sentient beings in samsara. Buddhas visited our existence many countless numbers of times, so why are sentient beings still trapped in samsara? It is not that the buddhas did not try to teach sentient beings how to transcend samsara, but because sentient beings did not have faith or absolute trust in the buddhas. That's why sentient beings are now left in samsara. Gelong Legpe Karma was a cousin of the Enlightened One, Shakyamuni Buddha, and served him for twenty-four years. However, he never achieved transcendence. Buddha at that time had unlimited power that was entirely without attachment and aversion or discrimination, but Gelong Legpe Karma was not susceptible to his power. When your mind is not susceptible to the power of the Enlightened One, there is no way that you could give the Enlightened One a chance to transcend your consciousness or help you in any way.

Once you have faith, trust, and confidence, the compassionate power or grace and love of the Buddha will touch you. And once your faith is developed, you do not need Buddha to be physically near you. A long time ago there was an old woman called "A Woman Enlightened through Dog's Tooth" and her son, who used to go to Buddhagaya, India for trade. The Buddha lived in Buddhagaya. When her son traveled there, she used to ask him, "Please bring something from there so I can make a statue or symbol in the form of Buddhagaya to pray to or prostate to." But her son always forgot. Now when he was about to leave, she told him, "If you do not bring anything from India this time, I will commit suicide."

So her son went to India for trade and was coming back. When he was near the house, he remembered he forgot his mother's request. He realized she really meant it this time. So he thought, "I must lie. There is no way I can get away with doing nothing." He looked around and saw a dead dog on the side of road. He got off the horse and took out one of the dog's teeth. He wrapped the tooth in beautiful five-colored cloths. Then arriving home, when his mother asked if he brought some symbolic thing representing Buddha, he said, "Oh, yes. I have brought you this tooth of the Buddha, the best tooth of the Buddha." When he gave the tooth to his mother, she had absolute faith that it was the tooth of the Buddha. So she took it and made offerings and prostrations to it for the rest of her life. When she passed away, that tooth actually became the Buddha's tooth and produced many other relics. About the time of her death, a rainbow appeared over her tent. A great omen like that appeared. It is not that the dog's tooth had any power to create the miraculous manifestation, but simply the absolute faith of the old woman. She had no doubt that it was the tooth of the Buddha, and through her absolute faith and trust, she practiced. At the end, the dog's tooth really turned into the tooth of the Buddha, and she was touched by the compassionate power of all the buddhas.

Now you can see the difference. On the one hand we have Gelong Legpe Karma, the Buddha's cousin and physically near to him, but he could not transcend samsara and was not touched by the compassionate power of the Buddha. On the other hand we have this old woman with a dog's tooth who was influenced and touched by the compassionate power of the Buddha. This difference is also evident among a lama's students. Some students are better than others. It is also true of people who meditate on one particular deity (yidam). Some become enlightened and accomplished; some cannot achieve enlightenment. The differences depend on the strength of one's faith, trust, and devotion.

There is a land in southern Tibet called "Kong Bu," where lived a fool named Ben. One day he went on pilgrimage to Lhasa to see the statue of Jowo Rinpoché, one of the original statues of the Buddha. Upon arrival he saw there was no custodian at the temple, so he entered and saw the statue. In front were hundreds of lamps, tormas, and shalsi (food offerings). He thought (having never heard of dharmic consequences), "Oh, this Buddha eating this shalsi is very clever, keeping the butter melted and warm by the burning lamp." And then he thought, "Well, I'm hungry. So I'll eat the same way." He picked up the shalsi, dipped it in the melted butter, and ate it. When he was eating the shalsi, a dog took his shoes, which he had taken off before entering the temple, since they were unusually stinky. But he got them back. While eating, he had looked at the Jowo Rinpoché and saw the statue smiling. He said, "Oh, I ate your food, yet you are still smiling. You're a real good lama. Your lamps are extinguished by the wind, yet you are still smiling. I would like to give you my shoes for you to look after while I am gone. Look after my shoes, OK? I will circumambulate around you." So he put his shoes in front of the Jowo Rinpoché statue and went out to circumambulate the monastery. When the custodian of the monastery came in, he saw the rotten shoes in front of the altar. He was perturbed, thinking, "Food is here. No one should put shoes in front." He was about to pick the shoes up and throw them outside. At that moment, the statue spoke, "Kong Buben is the name of the person. He entrusted those shoes to me. Please don't throw them away."

When Kong Buben finished circumambulating, he came back and remarked, "Oh my shoes are not gone. You're really a good lama. You looked after my shoes, and I am also happy that you let me eat your food. Why don't you come to my place? I'll kill the biggest pig I have, and with the best wheat, I'll make chang beer. Please come to my house, OK?" Jowo Rinpoché said, "OK, I will come to your house."

Then Kong Bu Ben went back to his home and told his wife, "I invited Jowo Rinpoché to our house. He might come at any time. Look out for him." So she kept the watch. Usually she got water from the pond. One day she went to get water and saw the image or reflection of the statue in the water. She ran back home and said to her husband, "That must be your guest in the water." Kong Bu Ben hurried to the pond. He really did see the reflection of the statue in the water. He immediately thought, "Oh, my guest has fallen in the water. He must be drowning." So he jumped in and pulled the statue out and brought it toward his home. On the way, near to his home, the statue spoke, "I usually do not go to people's houses. I will not go any further." Then the statue disappeared in the rock.

Even now if one goes to that spot in Kong Bu, one can see the naturally created statue of Jowo Buddha in the rock. It's still there. And where there is a shadow or reflection in the water, you still can see the image in the water. If you cannot travel to Lhasa, you can go to Kong Bu and pay respects to the statue that naturally originated there; the merit is similar.

If you look at only the attitude of Kong Buben, that attitude itself created defilements. For example, dipping the shalsi in butter and eating the offering, and placing the smelly shoes in front of the statue. These are actions one may not do because they create so many obstacles and defilements. It is unvirtuous action. However, the strength of his faith left him with no doubt that the statue was a real buddha. Because of his absolute faith, the statue manifested as a real buddha whose compassion was expressed in that way. In order to be susceptible to the compassionate power of all the buddhas, you must have faith or trust or confidence in an absolute sense. Such absolute trust or faith is the prerequisite for the practice of any meditation.

The three basic aspects of seeking refuge—the differences in the way one seeks refuge, the place of refuge, and the way to seek refuge—all originate from one's intention. An ordinary person takes refuge by realizing the suffering in the three lower realms—the hell realm, the animal realm, and the yidak (hungry ghost) realm. Desiring to be born in the god and human realms, with that intention, he takes refuge with the Three Precious Ones. That is the intention of an ordinary person. The result of this kind of intention is not everlasting, but it results in immediate happiness that lasts for a very short time.

The intention of a moderate person is to be liberated from the wheel of existence. As it has been told, the wheel is comprised of six realms: three lower realms with their constant suffering and three upper realms, the realms of joy that do not last, such as the human realm, god realm, and jealous god realm. Realizing that suffering is present in all six realms, the moderate person swishes to be freed and seeks refuge with the Three Precious Ones. This is thinking about one's self, not about all beings.

The intention of the great person is to realize that, first of all, the vast expanse of the unlimited sky that covers the Earth and the planets is filled with sentient beings who are suffering. Realizing this, one seeks refuge to let all these sentient beings be freed from suffering. "Let all these sentient beings be free from suffering and attain enlightenment." At this time, the "I" or "me" concept does not come into play. The intention is to let all sentient beings who are suffering reach the state of enlightenment.

So there are three kinds of intentions. Since we take the path of the Great Vehicle, the Mahayana (the way of the bodhisattva, or Bodhisattvayana), for us the intention of the enlightenment of all sentient beings is necessary. The intention of the ordinary person has a very narrow perception and is limited in scope, seeking merely to be freed from the lower realm to the upper realm, thinking that will eliminate suffering. The upper realms are called "the realms of happiness," but they are not free from the suffering of samsaric existence, as, for example, in the desire for change: roasting under a hot sun, one wishes for cold, but in the cold one wants heat. And in the god realm one can enjoy oneself for many kalpas, but eventually one suffers. Gods can enjoy happiness within the immediacy of a certain time frame but in the long term and from a wider perspective their happiness is limited. The intention of the moderate person is also not enough. His realization is wider in scope than that of the ordinary person; he does realize that there is suffering throughout the wheel of existence. However, he is not concerned about other sentient beings who are suffering like himself. He is mainly concerned about himself, about liberating himself from suffering in the wheel of samsaric existence, disregarding others. Not caring about other sentient beings, the scope of his intention is limited. The result of this type of intention is Shravakayana (the way of the disciple) or Pratyekabuddhayana (the way of the self-enlightened buddha).

The way we go for refuge under the Three Precious Ones is to know that there is not a single sentient being under the wide horizon of the sky who has not been our parent. Like your present parents who have reared you, cared for you, and showed you love and compassion, these sentient beings, when they were once your parents, sacrificed for you. The number of these sentient beings is countless. It is not enough to be enlightened and leave all these benefactors behind, all these other sentient beings who have been kind to you in other forms of life. It is not enough for you alone to be enlightened. Therefore bring all these sentient beings in front of you in the realm of your mind and make the dedication to let all sentient beings be enlightened first.

The Dedication

As usual bring all the harmful spirits, peaceful spirits, neutral spirits, and different kinds of spirits, including all the sentient beings under the wide horizon of the sky, before you in your mind and dedicate the merit that you have earned by listening to the teaching, resolving to practice in order to facilitate the enlightenment of all sentient beings.

Questions and Answers

Q: Is it possible to develop the strength of your faith?
A: Yes, it is possible to develop the strength of your faith. It is similar to developing your writing or your recitation. If you have never written or used a pen, you cannot immediately write. But if you begin to practice writing, you can train yourself to write. If you never recited any text, you practice more and more and train your voice. Your mind is the same way. You cannot do higher meditation immediately without going through the lower steps and the ordinary types of meditation. You train your mind and get your mind into the practice of meditation. Faith is similar. Sometimes faith comes over us and there is trust, but sometimes it disappears. When there is a strong moment of faith, you have to perpetuate it gradually. There are people like

Kong Bu Ben whose faith just comes. His faith in the statue was very original, it just came. It can happen that way, the natural flow of the glow of faith. But you can also develop faith like you develop any kind of skill.

Q: What type of faith was Kong Bu Ben's?
A: Kong Bu Ben had a gifted faith, a natural, original glow. Some people love to paint, but they try and just can't do it. Some people don't know how to paint, never having trained, but are tuned to that kind of knowledge and can paint. Like people who never learned math, but once they are given some idea of how to do it, they immediately grasp it. Some are like us, and have to be trained gradually. Through intelligence, one has to be trained in faith, but the possibility of a natural glow of faith exists, which is a gift, though for others there is no glow at all and it may be attained only gradually through practice.

Some of you came to Dharma not knowing anything about Dharma, but still you came with a desire to practice. Your faith has grown just for Dharma. Some of you read Dharma books and were attracted by the concept of Dharma and came to practice. It is the same thing: one is spontaneous, one is a gradual process. Kong Bu Ben's faith is considered absolute faith, absolute trust. Ordinary people's faith is the faith that comes from liking or joy.

As for amulets and guards against the impediments and obstacles, lama gave you blessed strings and amulets. Their effect and their power depends on one's own awareness. It is known that in war, people who are fleeing from bullets, if they remember the lama's amulets are with them and visualize the lama, bullets will never hurt them. But if you forget, you could be harmed, anything can happen.

Q: I try to help others in my normal life. How is this any different from the intention Rinpoché talked about?
A: The intention I discussed is to practice the Dharma for the

enlightenment of all sentient beings. This is not an ordinary activity in your daily life, like eating food. Your intention to help others in your everyday life is good, but it lacks the bodhisattva intention to to dedicate Dharma practice for the enlightenment of all sentient beings.

THE MANNER OF TAKING REFUGE

THE INTENTION

As WE DO every day, please realize the limitless skies contain countless sentient beings. All these sentient beings desire happiness. However, they do not recognize the source of happiness, which is Dharma, and which is accomplished dharmic actions. They do not desire unhappiness or suffering. They do, however, perform adharmic actions that perpetuate bad karma. As well, they are ignorant of what to acquire and what to abandon. There is not a single sentient being who has not cared for us in one lifetime or other when they were our parents, and like our present parents, were kind to us. Now bring those countless sentient beings into the realm of your mind and make the resolution, "All these sentient beings, I will liberate them from the suffering of the samsara."

There are many paths to enlightenment. We are making a resolution to follow the path of guru yoga to lead all sentient beings to ultimate supreme enlightenment: "I will do this by recognizing the path and understanding and practicing the great guru yoga." That intention should be the motive for guru yoga practitioners.

THE TEACHING

Now we will talk about the manner of taking refuge. First, it is important to have the perception that the teacher giving the teaching is not an ordinary man. He should not be perceived as an ordinary person but as a supreme Kuntu Sangpo, or Dorjé Chang.[19] One must also see the place where one is taking teachings not as an ordinary place or building but as a transcended heavenly place. One must also transcend the ordinary perception of one's vajra friends, perceiving them not as ordinary men or women or as ordinary relationships but as gods and goddesses. This is the state of pure perception. It is the primordial state of all nature, all existence, and not anything recently created. Because of our own defiled perception, these things appear to us now as ordinary men and women and ordinary places. But the primordial state, the state of true and clear perception, has never been created and has always been there from beginningless time, just as the primordial state of water is water, though it turns to ice when influenced by cold and it changes back to water when heated by the sun.

Because of ignorance's influence, our perception is defiled. So while listening to the teaching, return to a state of primordial perception, or true perception of things, and the environment around you. Purify your perception, transcend, and see the teacher as an enlightened god and your vajra friends as gods and goddesses. See this region of the Earth as the land of the enlightened buddhas. This is what is described as a pure perception from the very beginning.

TAKING REFUGE IN THE BUDDHA-DHARMA-SANGHA

All sentient beings suffer perpetually in the wheel of samsaric existence. To be free from this suffering, sentient beings have to take refuge in Three Precious Ones. Taking refuge in the Three Precious Ones is analogous to traveling to a dangerous place and needing a guide and protector. In this situation, one must perceive the Buddha as a teacher who taught the doctrines, the Dharma as a path or experience, and the Sangha, or the community of monks, as those who are already on the path or are the practitioners. See them as your spiritual friends who might guide you in practice. See Buddha as your teacher, Dharma as your path, and Sangha as your spiritual friends. In this manner, you take refuge according to Mahayana tradition.

TAKING REFUGE IN LAMA-YIDAM-KHANDRO

In esoteric or tantric teaching, taking refuge is quite similar to the Mahayana tradition, but different terms are used and have different meanings. Instead of Buddha, Dharma, and Sangha, the terms "Lama," "Yidam," and "Khandro" are used (these are the "Three Root Sugatas," the essence of the Three Jewels). As we have said, the liturgies on these are the main course of training in tantric practice. According to the tantric tradition, one must perceive one's lama as the collected manifestation of all the buddhas, and one must offer one's body, speech, and mind in the service of the lama.

You may wonder how the lama is the collection of all the buddhas. He is the collection of all the buddhas because of the Buddha's compassionate heart. The rays emitting from the compassionate heart touch all the sentient beings. However because of the thickness of bad karma, sentient beings are not able to perceive their true nature. So the Buddha said, "At the end of the time, I will appear as a teacher, as a lama to the sentient beings."

We are currently in the kalpa where Buddha is represented in the form of the lama, the body of the lama. That is why the lama should be revered or perceived as the essence of Kuntu Sangpo, or Dorjé Chang (the dharmakaya manifestations of the primordial Buddha); or as Dorjé Sempa, the Vajrasattva Buddha of Purification, the esoteric aspect of the bodhisattva Samantabhadra (in sambhogakaya manifestation), all of them representing the ideal guru. They must be served with respect and revered through the body, speech, and mind.

Also, you must rely on the yidam (the tutelary deity). There are many yidam gods, such as Tamdrin. There are many khandro (female deities), one of whom is Yeshé Tsogyal (the queen of the Tibetan King Tri Songdetsen, who invited Guru Rinpoché to Tibet), and so forth. Through tantric practice, one must take them as one's spiritual friends. With their help, you shall practice the path and attain enlightenment. This is the meaning of lama, yidam, and khandro according to the tantric tradition.

TAKING REFUGE IN TSA-LUNG-THIKLÉ

In the tantric tradition there is another way take refuge: by the path itself—*tsa*, *lung*, and *thiklé*. *Tsa* refers to the channels and arteries of the vajra body. *Lung* refers to the energy moments—breathing, or air. *Thiklé* is the vital essence of the vajra body. Each are one of the three esoteric means of physical training to attain the union of great bliss and emptiness.

When you are practicing according to the terton Dorjé Nyingpo's terma teachings in the esoteric tantric tradition, you rely on *tsa* as the tulku (nirmanakaya manifestation). You try to purify and see the true tulku manifestation of all the *thiklé*. Then there is the wind practice called the *lungkhor jang*. It is involved with the breathing energy of your body, which is the sambhogakaya manifestation. Third is *thiklé*, which spreads all over *tsa*, which leads to the dharmakaya manifestation. Realizing the path and taking refuge in Dorjé Nyingpo's teaching can lead to the supreme state of enlightenment.

There is another way of seeking refuge. Within the enlightened gods realm, one practices to obtain the power of omniscience. So there are different traditions for seeking refuge.

DIFFERENT WAYS OF TAKING REFUGE

It is important to understand that there are different ways of taking refuge, according to different traditions, such as the Mahayana, the general tantric, and the Dzokchen traditions, although the essence of the practice is the same.

The first line in the taking refuge verse is:

> *In the actual Three Jewels and their essence, the three root sugatas;*
> (*Könchok sum ngo deshek tsawasum*)

Könchok Sum is the Buddha, Dharma, and Sangha. *Tsawasum* is the lama, or guru; the yidam, or titulary deity; and the khandro, or female deity: the three root sugatas. They are included in the esoteric tantric teaching and are the omniscience of enlightened gods. The liturgies on these are the main training for tantric practitioners.

The next line in taking refuge is:

> *In the nature of the channels, energy, and essence, bodhichitta;*
> (*Tsalung thiklé rangshin jangchup sem*)

As we have discussed, this includes taking refuge according to Dorjé Nyingpo's terma teachings.

The third line in taking refuge is:

> *In this mandala of the essence, nature, and compassion—*
> (*Ngowo rangshin thukjé kyilkhor la—*)

This includes taking refuge according to the Geluk Dorjé Kyabdro tradition, which is the Dzokchen way, the very essence of the vajra nature tradition.

The last line in taking refuge is:

> *To these I go for refuge, until the attainment of the bodhi essence.*
> (*Janchup nyingpo bardu kyabsu chi*)

This is the resolution that one will take refuge until one attains supreme enlightenment. The nature or essence of taking refuge is called "the resolution of taking refuge."

So you see there are different ways of taking refuge, but all converge into one resolution: taking refuge until one is enlightened. As a short summary version of taking refuge, just have absolute confidence in the Three Precious Ones. Have complete faith that these Three Precious Ones have the power to liberate all sentient beings from samsara. Knowing the absolute power of the Three Precious Ones, you declare, "I go to seek refuge." Practicing the short summary version of taking refuge, this is how one must think.

How to Supplicate the Enlightened Ones

We will now discuss in detail the ways to supplicate to the collection of all the enlightened ones for aid. In reciting the taking refuge lines, first visualize the place you are staying or practicing as an absolute state of heaven: beautiful, without fault, attractive to the mind, not made of ordinary objects perceived through your mundane perception but of highly precious gems. Everything around you is precious. The place is like the surface of a mirror, really smooth and beautiful. It does not have steep rocks or ant hills and so on. It is adorned with all kinds of ornaments that are attractive to one's mind.

At the center of this most perfect and beautiful heaven, visualize a tree that has five branches, abundant with fruits and leaves. The four branches extend out to four directions of the horizons, and the fifth is at the center. All the leaves of the tree spread out and their surfaces are decorated with bells, rosary beads, and ornaments like scarves. On top of the central branch is a throne held by eight lions. On top of the throne is a lotus (see the refuge thangka below), and in its kernel, the sun. On top of that sun is the moon. On top of that, visualize Guru Rinpoché, the manifestation of your tsawai lama, the collection of the

Refuge Tree

essence of all the buddhas. Visualize Guru Rinpoché as having one face, two hands, and two feet. In his right hand he holds a vajra of five spokes. On the left hand by his lap is the skull vase filled with amrita nectar that gives everlasting life. Guru Rinpoché's color is white with a reddish hue. He is wearing the lotus hat and a wide-sleeved robe. He is with his consort, Yeshé Tsogyal, whose right hand holds a knife, her other hand holding the skull vase (*thöpa*). This tree is in front of you. All these images are in front of you, facing toward you.

There are different ways of visualizing the appearance of the different deities. All these forms or appearances are not contradictory to one another but are different manifestations and appearances of one essence. The Guru appears with his consort in this collection of all the deities, but in the next section of guru yoga (the actual practice), he does not. There, he appears with a trident, which symbolizes the presence of his consort.

Above the crown of Guru Rinpoché, starting from the top, is Kuntu Sangpo, Dorjé Sempa, Garab Dorjé, and so forth. They have to be visualized just above the crown of Guru Rinpoché, not touching it. You must do the meditation with a spacious feeling. Many people complain, "I just cannot put Guru Rinpoché on top of my head. He keeps slipping," or "These lamas just cannot sit in that space. There is nothing for them to hang onto." So I say, just meditate spaciously because the figures can be there.

This is just a simple visualization. When it gets into involved meditation of the visualization, *kyé rim*, then you have to visualize certain deities in your eyes, nose, and in each cell of your body. You visualize each deity in each cell of your body. Inside of the heart of each deity is the sun and the moon seed with whatever letter there is, and another mantra going around it. Inside that, there is another deity and so forth. There are many, many different sets, converging like that. At such a point, people complain, "I can't fit one deity in another one. It doesn't really sit on my head. It keeps slipping down all the time."

Complaints like that rise if you don't meditate spaciously. That is why you must not visualize strenuously, but be relaxed and do it spaciously.

If you can perfect the visualization, it is possible all three spheres can be visualized in one sesame seed. The inner circle of the Guru is surrounded by tutelary deities (yidams): Dorjé Phurba, Shinjé, Tamdrin, Guru Drakpo, and other yidams. On the outskirts of that is Khandroma, Sengdongma, and Kurukulé. The front branch is Shakya Thupa surrounded by 1,021 buddhas of bright kalpas.[20]

These buddhas are multicolored. Shakyamuni Buddha is yellow but all other buddhas are multicolored and are complete with all the signs of the buddhas. For example, the wheel underneath the sole, and the crown on the head, all manifestations, are complete with thirty-two signs, like the Lord Buddha but in different colors.

On the right branch are the bodhisattvas: Jampalyang, Chakna Dorjé, and Chenrezik.[21] Consider them as embodying many countless bodhisattvas. Their ornaments are five-jewel crowns on the head and finery like bracelets, anklets, and clothes. Dorjé Sempa is thus ornamented. All of them are standing up and all are multicolored. On the left branch are the main arahats Shariputra and Mongolana, the two supreme disciples of wisdom and miracles of the Buddha who embody numerous other arahats, shravakas, and pratyekabuddhas. When you see the Lord Buddha's picture, most of the time you see these two disciples standing on each side. The colors of their bodies are white and they wear monk's robes. In their right hand they carry a monk's stick, which is used to make noise to drive away insects when they are walking. When they go to a house, they announce their presence. In their other hand they have an alms bowl.

The back branch figures will have books. Visualize those books. They're rectangular Tibetan books, stacked on top of each other, with tags of bright letters for the titles facing toward you. They are arranged in sequence, according to the lineage and the path, like all the books of the Dzokchen tradition. All the books are pointed or directed toward you, so you can see the titles in bright letters and you can also hear the noise of vowels and consonants of the Dharma: *ali* and *kali*, thirty consonant sounds vibrating.

Around this tree are the male protective deities, facing outward to all the impediments that will come to your practice. These deities will stop the impediments that want to disturb your practice. Gönpo (Skt. Mahakala) is one of the main Dharmapalas, the protectors of Dharma. All the female protective deities are turned inward to protect and preserve your dharmic attainments so that the attainments will not escape outside.

Then the visualization: You must think that these deities are looking with their compassionate hearts toward sentient beings to enlighten them. Like the expert captain of a ship, they help sentient beings reach the supreme state of enlightenment. You must also visualize your present father on Guru Rinpoché's right side and your present mother on his left side. All sentient beings are equally important as the mother and father, but at this time you visualize your own present mother and father.

Now in front of you, visualize your present enemies, people you don't like or have conflicts with, or the spirits that are hindering you or causing you discomfort. So you have your father and mother on either side of Guru Rinpoché, and your enemies and any hindering spirits in front. After visualizing those, visualize all the sentient beings of the six realms, more numerous than people in the market. Visualize all sentient beings together. Now with humility, bring your hands together in prayer and go down to the floor and do a prostration. With humility in your body posture, and with humility in your speech, recite the taking refuge lines:

> In the actual Three Jewels and their essence, the three root
>   sugatas;
> in the nature of the channels, energy, and essence, bodhichitta;

in this mandala of the essence, nature, and compassion—
to these I go for refuge until the attainment of the bodhi essence.

And in the humility of your mind, you must have full confidence in the power of the Three Precious Ones (or their manifestations).

Now from your mind, supplicate for all sentient beings of the six realms who are suffering, for all of us, including the good days and bad days. Knowing that only the *Könchok Sum* (the Buddha, Dharma, Sangha) and the *Tsawasum* (the three root sugatas—the lama, yidam, and khandro) have the power to liberate all sentient beings in the ocean of suffering, think, "I go to these manifestations to seek refuge until all sentient beings attain the supreme enlightenment."

The thangkas are used to aid one's meditation. I just described the refuge thangka. Use this refuge thangka if you are engaging in detailed visualization. You could look at the thangka and examine it, and then close your eyes and try to see the whole picture. When the image starts to fade away, revive it by looking at the thangka, and so forth, and practice visualization in that manner.

The thangkas are manifestations of the deities, the enlightened gods that you are meditating on. In recent times, thangkas have been turned into posters or pictures to decorate your walls—beautiful pictures that do not have any meaning. It used to be you kept a thangka of your yidam privately. No one would ever show anyone else a thangka, saying, "Oh, come and look at my thangka, my yidam." They would never say, "You know who my yidam is?" or brag about it. This will be discussed when I talks about the samayas, the ethics of tantric practice. Thangkas have significant meanings that we do not fully know at this time.

So that was the detailed explanation of how you can meditate on the taking refuge lines. There are people who cannot do the detailed version. It depends on the person's nature. If you can do the detailed version, know Guru Rinpoché well. Behold the essence of Guru

Rinpoché as your own lama. With the manifestation of Guru Rinpoché facing you, visualize your father and mother on his right and left, your enemies in front, and include all sentient beings of the six realms. Aspire to give their hearts, their lives, and their confidence to Guru Rinpoché. Put all in his hands. Say in your mind, "There is no place else to seek refuge for liberation from samsara except in you, Guru Rinpoché." You must make such supplication from the very depths of your heart, as the very kernel of your faith, not as mere words of an empty ritual speech.

The meaning of the taking refuge chant is vast. I have given you the meaning that will aid you in the meditation. He doesn't see any point of going on to analyze all the different meanings now, but it is important to know at least the details that are necessary to aid your own meditation.

You might wonder why it is important to visualize your present parents and your enemies. The visual presence of your enemy is very, very important, as are your parents on each side of Guru Rinpoché. This is because the difference between Mahayana and Hinayana practices lies in the intention or motivation. Hinayana intention is self-liberation: "Let me be enlightened." Mahayana intention is: "There are countless sentient beings in the vast horizon of the sky who are equally and perpetually suffering like me. Let all these sentient beings be freed and attain the supreme state of enlightenment." There is a vast difference between mundane action and dharmic interaction. In mundane, day-to-day life, we attach ourselves to our friends and people we like and show aversion or displeasure toward the people we do not like. This is absolutely and definitely contrary to the Dharma.

When you are practicing Dharma, at some level you must attain equanimity, an even-mindedness in relationships. That is why visualizing the presence of an enemy before you is important, because you must at some point realize that there isn't a single sentient being who has not been kind to you and that they have all entered a special binding relationship with you. That's why attachment and aversion in a samsaric relationship should be evened out in the Dharma relationship.

According to the Mahayana tradition, there are six perfections. The third one is the perfection of patience and tolerance. I like to use both terms, "patience" and "tolerance." This is very important. If we have a crop about to be harvested and there is a hailstorm, those crops will be destroyed. In the same way, anger and rage ruin whatever good karma or dharmic result you produced with a dharmic action. So meditation on patience and tolerance is the most important practice in the Mahayana tradition.

What is it like to practice patience and tolerance? We know from our own experience that life continually presents us with thorny obstacles and hardships, as if we were walking barefoot on a rocky road. Now if you wanted to cover all those obstacles with a smooth protective surface that is like leather, you would have to have leather as vast as the earth. That is impossible. Instead, you cover your own feet with leather, so that wherever you walk it is smooth, as if you had covered the whole earth with leather. Practicing patience and tolerance is like protecting the soles of your feet with leather. Then you can walk anywhere and the rocks and the thorns will not hurt you.

In the same way, you continually see faults and create enemies. You created all those negative things through your perceptions of the external world, but when patience and tolerance have been inculcated in you and have matured, these perceptions will have no effect on you. Patience and tolerance shields you from and protects you against habitual false perceptions. Let the perceptions run their course, knowing they cannot harm you, until they disappear.

When someone is trying to evoke anger in you, it is an opportunity for you to practice patience and tolerance. At such a time, you must ask yourself, "Who is this great person who is facilitating my practice of patience?" He could be an enemy or an evil spirit that can cause you harm, but realize these two manifestations are providing you with an important chance to practice patience and tolerance. It is important to realize that all these sentient beings do not know what to acquire and what to abandon, and that this causes many problems. The practice of patience and tolerance is a practical aid to your own life, whereas typical reactivity to perceived obstacles and enemies only harms you.

When someone says something bad about you, you attach so much importance to that flowing wind and then generate anger and fight against the insult. This applies as well to the people of a nation who feel insulted as a nation and react with rage. We convert a flowing wind of speech to a real entity, make it into something that's really attacking us, and then get caught up in the whole thing and engage in a fight that could end our lives. Instead we should realize that the words are just speech whose nature is simply a passing wind, and that getting angry reaps the fruit of bad karma. Once we realize this, the perpetuation of arrogance and the vicious circle of reactivity seems absurd. We attain this realization through the perfection of *söpa*, the practice of patience and tolerance. Of course, the perfection of *söpa* is very difficult.

When Buddha was a yogi of patience and meditating on patience on his way to supreme enlightenment, a king asked him, "What are you doing, yogi? What kind of yogi are you? What kind of mendicant are you?" Buddha replied, "I am mendicant of patience." The king shot back, "Oh, are you the mendicant of patience?" and cut off the Buddha's hand. "Are you still patient? Are you still tolerant?" Buddha responded, "Yes, I am still meditating on my toleration." So the king cut off another hand, and so on, chopping off all of the Buddha's limbs. But the strength of the Buddha's tolerance and endurance was so great that instead of blood, milk started to flow out of his body.

For us, such a degree of tolerance is very difficult to attain. However, practicing patience and tolerance at an everyday level is doable.

We put so much value on the words that are like a fleeting wind, reacting to them in a manner that merely reaps our own bad karma. There is no sense or logic to putting your life on the line just because you are insulted. So in the presence of an enemy or a person who is acting against you, it is very important to practice patience and tolerance. As the Buddha did, use it as a chance to examine and perfect patience and tolerance. In the same way, be grateful to the enemy as the person who is providing you with a chance to practice.

There are many great examples in history of victims turning to the Dharma after being attacked and plundered by the enemy. Those victims understood the transient nature of their wealth. The result of wealth is bewilderment and more desires and entanglements. If you have $100,000, you want to make more, and then even more. Once you have established a small business, you try to expand it quickly. But by taking it all away from you by force or by using every means to make you lose your accumulated wealth, the so-called enemy can show you that the wealth and possessions you try to increase in leaps and bounds has no essence at all and can be easily taken from you. You can be shown this harsh reality by so-called enemies or by spirits that affect you negatively. I'll relate just one instance of a spirit helping a person turn to Dharma. Gelong Mahapalmo was a great nun who became very ill due to the influence of the nagas. She was ostracized and not allowed to sit with or live with other people. Because of this she meditated on Chenrezik and obtained enlightenment. Likewise, the spirits can aid you on the path to enlightenment. Enemies and spirits of this nature are equal in greatness. Like your revered parents, they can help you.

Dharma is the path to supreme enlightenment and different circumstances can appear in your life to aid you on that path. One could be sickness. Knowing that the sickness is the result of one's own karma, it is good to be sick in this lifetime. There is a chance to revive from sickness and expend the karma, rather than dying and having to experience unresolved karmic consequences in the next form of life, where it could be quite heavy and grave. That is why you should feel happy when you are sick. Generate the intention: "Through my sickness, may all the sicknesses of all sentient beings be alleviated." In sickness, practice with such intention and chanting. Most of all do not get depressed. Do not feel sorrow or pity yourself, saying, "Oh, I am hopeless. I caught this disease. Now I am sick and depressed." Dharma is an ability to turn any situation and graft it into the path, an ability to take any circumstance and make it into a path to enlightenment.

You should now be able to see the importance of your so-called enemies and the evil spirits. No matter the situation, always consider the karmic result, even in routine annoyances or worries, like aging. Getting old is a fact of life, but many still feel bad about getting old, as if aging were the enemy. Once one is born, getting old is inevitable, as is death. Realize the karmic effect and the result, which will give you support and guidance. So turn to Dharma and practice. This will make your life meaningful.

While taking refuge and while generating and practicing bodhichitta, visualize all the enlightened Buddhas and the deities. When traveling, it is good to visualize them on your right shoulder. While sitting or staying in place, visualize them in front of you. While eating a meal, visualize them in the center of your throat and generate the intention that the food is an offering to the gods with whom you are going to take refuge. While sleeping, visualize a lotus in the center of your heart, and on the lotus, visualize all the deities. Thus they will give you the blessing of the realization. This concludes the taking refuge teaching.

THE DEDICATION

As usual we dedicate the merit we earned by teaching and receiving the teaching for the enlightenment of all sentient beings throughout the vast horizon of the sky.

Questions and Answers

Q: We take refuge with the Buddha, Dharma, and Sangha, and with Lama, Yidam, and Khandro, but what is the "mandala of the essence, nature, and compassion?"

A: The Dzokchen way of taking refuge is to have full and absolute confidence in the path itself. The path will lead you to the ultimate state of enlightenment. There are two different kinds of paths. The Dorjé Nyingpo (vajra essence) refuge is to purify all the defilements of the tsa, lung, thiklé—the three esoteric means of physical training to attain the union of great bliss and emptiness. Having confidence in purifying them as three kayas: tsa as tulku (nirmanakaya), lung as long ku (sambhogakaya), and thiklé as chö ku (dharmakaya); purifying them and having absolute confidence in that purification process. The Geluk Dorjé refuge is taking refuge in the mandala of the essence (*ngowo*), nature (*rangshin*), and compassion (*thukjé*). We have absolute confidence that by treading either path, all sentient beings will be enlightened and liberated from samsaric suffering and attain the all-encompassing omniscient state of the Buddha's. The Dzokchen path is to have absolute confidence on that path.

Q: Visualizing Orgyen Dorjé Chang in refuge, is his hand raised?

A: Like this, raised.

Q: Do we combine these two paths you just described or do we choose one or the other path?

A: These are two separate paths. In general it is very difficult to take all the paths. It is important to have one path to lead to ultimate enlightenment.

Q: Guru yoga opens the door to both of the paths? Where is Dorjé Naljorma in the refuge visualization?

A: Dorjé Naljorma is not in the refuge taking. If you think it is necessary to have Dorjé Naljorma, then it is OK to include her in the circle of khandroma (female deities) within the refuge tree thangka.

DEVELOPING BODHICHITTA

The Intention

As you do before every teaching, please formulate your intention and pray.

The Teaching

Ho! Deceived by myriad appearances, like the reflection of the moon in water,
sentient beings wander through the cyclic [samsaric] chain of lives.
In order for them to be at ease in the luminescent sphere of self-awareness,
I shall develop bodhichitta by contemplating the four boundless attitudes.
(Repeat 3 times)

Today is the teaching on how to originate bodhichitta. The Mahayana tradition is based on bodhichitta. Bodhichitta is its most salient feature and is therefore the most important aspect of meditation. When we take refuge in the Three Precious Ones, we take vows. In the Mahayana tradition we take the bodhichitta vow. Whatever is done regarding recitation, in chanting or in meditation, all these must proceed by first taking refuge and clarifying your bodhichitta. One must train one's mind accordingly. Within the sequence of our practice, after taking refuge we formulate bodhichitta with four boundless states of mind. The mind or the intelligence of a person can be trained to proceed toward the purified paths. At the present time, our intelligence or mind is in an impure state. With perseverance, this mind can be trained to travel the path to enlightenment.

THE FOUR BOUNDLESS STATES OF MIND

According to the sequence, first you must meditate on or inculcate love, followed by compassion, then sympathetic joy, and finally equanimity or even-mindedness. In our tradition, we meditate first on equanimity. The reason is that meditation on love and compassion prior to equanimity is enormously difficult. It is easier to first meditate on equanimity and then on love and compassion.

Equanimity
Equanimity (*tang nyom*), or even-mindedness, is defined as contrary to the feeling of attachment or partiality to those whom you like, and the feeling of anger or aversion toward those whom you do not like, your enemies in particular. Even-mindedness is the state of mind that does not have these attachments and aversions. In front of oneself, all sentient beings are equal. There are no objects of aversion and attachment. Thus the state of equanimity is achieved by placing all sentient beings in a relationship of equality, all having the same status.

The way to meditate on equanimity is to be aware of instinctive reactions of attachment or aversion. For example, notice that you tend to act toward your relatives—your parents, children, siblings, and even friends—in a loving manner or with attachment. However, you dislike and act with hostility toward your enemies or people with whom you have personal conflicts. Avoid these aspects of aversion and attachments. One must even it out to achieve a state of equanimity.

If you think carefully and deeply, you might have interacted with these people in a previous life. It is possible that the enemy you are so hostile to right now could have been your dear one in a past life—perhaps your parent, or best friend, or your own child. It is also true that those people whom you care for and are attached to could have been your enemies or adversaries in a previous life who caused you much suffering. To give you an example, the Tibetan King Tri Songdetsen had a daughter, Princess Pema Sal, who lived during the time of Guru Rinpoché. At the age of seventeen she died in the presence of Guru Rinpoché. The king asked Guru Rinpoché, "This daughter, was she reborn as my daughter as the result of good karma? Was she in some way related to me in my previous life? Why did she die at the age of seventeen? What was the significance of her meeting you and me at this juncture?" Guru Rinpoché said to the king, "This princess was born as your daughter not because of the purity of our karma, not because of virtuous karma, but because at one time you, Tri Songdetsen, and I, Bodhisatto, were born as brothers in a low-caste family. The princess was born as a bee at the time we were trying to construct a chorten."[22] The bee was attracted to his arm and somehow stung him, and he, without realizing it, brushed the bee off and killed it. As a result, she was born as Tri Songdetsen's daughter, causing the king grief.

The king was an incarnation of Manjushri, the great bodhisattva who had boundless power. Even he had to face the consequence of karma. If such a great incarnate had to face the consequences of his karma, there is no question about us facing the consequences of our karma. The kind of relationship just described originates from remnant bad karma. Your present enemy could have been your parent in a past life who was beneficial and kind to you. Remember the example I related earlier about the karmic consequences for the husband and son who generated bad feelings in the wife's offering to the great saint Phakpa Katayana when they should have dedicated the merit of her generosity with the sympathetic joy of giving charity to the great saint.

Even though we hold onto feelings of hostility against our enemies or have the feeling somebody is acting against us, that will not prevent the situation from changing. For example, if you do not respond to your enemy's hostility in kind but tolerate him and try to act in a loving manner, it is possible that this enemy could turn into your best friend. We see this in the common conflicts between families. Two families are often brought together in reconciliation by a marriage, after which they could become close. These examples show that being kind or helping your enemy, rather than taking vengeance, could turn the enemy into your friend at some point. But disappointment may happen as well. We see this all the time. A person is attached to her relatives or friends, thinking and expecting friendship and a reciprocal relationship of help and kindness. She enters into the relationship but it does not last; relationships are not everlasting. In close friendships, where we expect solidarity, it is quite possible that these friends could betray you. So your expectations and your attachments to your best friends and your relatives can bring lots of suffering. We see this even in parental relationships. Parents try their best to please their children, providing food, the best education, and so forth, but the children grow up and have conflicts with their parents and try to hurt them. Sometimes parents are even killed by their children. Through these examples please realize that there are no definite, lasting relationships, no relationships that do not change. This was also true in previous lives. Realize the ever-changing nature of relationships in our human society.

Keep in mind also that one must face the consequences, or reap the fruits, of one's action. If you produce an unvirtuous karmic result, it is you who will experience it and not anyone else; the consequence cannot be shared or passed on to others. You will have to face the consequences of that action, if not in this lifetime then for sure in the next.

From a social or societal point of view, an enemy is an object at which you express your anger or rage. However, in the dharmic point of view, an enemy brings about the circumstances for you to perfect your patience and tolerance. Having an enemy is important for the turn to Dharma. So when a greedy person who hoards his wealth, never making an offering to the buddhas and bodhisattvas, gets robbed by a thief, that provides a chance a to get a glimpse of the impermanence and essencelessness of his wealth. Thus, the thief provides a chance for him to turn to Dharma. Turning to Dharma means heading toward the path to everlasting happiness.

Since "my side" and "the other side" are not too different, "my side" can be "his side," and "his side" can be "my side." Since there are no definite boundaries or divisions between these two sides, the best thing is to realize that both sides are beneficial and one must be kind to both. Therefore treat both sides as equal and see it as one side rather than having two opposing extremes or entities.

Inculcating this kind of feeling, you begin to notice that there is less of a feeling of animosity, or if there is somebody out there who is hostile toward you, have less of a feeling that you need to protect yourself. You then begin to feel the two opposing sides you formerly created are now seem normal and neutral. This equanimity is not the boundless kind, but rather equanimity on a very small scale.

Boundless equanimity is the state of considering all sentient beings under the vast horizon of the sky as evenly and equally important, including my side, his side, and the neutral side. Include all sides, all sentient beings, and enter all these equal relationships in the great vast compassion, feeling that these sentient beings have no other way to find happiness. Practicing this kind of equanimity, make a resolution: "I will find the path to happiness for all these sentient beings." Include them all in the wide realm of compassion. At that point, one can call the experience "the boundless state of mind of equanimity." Such a state of mind can be reached by training your mind again and again until you realize this state.

Love

Bring all sentient beings into the state of equanimity, then generate love. Love is contrary to your wish for the well-being of your relatives, to your wish to harm to your enemy, and to any neutral position, or the apathetic position of being neutral. Love is contrary to all of these. Generating boundless love is to wish well-being, happiness, and peace for all sentient beings in the vast realm of equanimity. The true love that one must inculcate in oneself is like a parent's tolerant love toward a child. When a child throws a temper tantrum, he will throw things at his mother, pull her hair, and try to tear her lips apart. He will do everything possible he can think of to express his anger, but the mother somehow tolerates it all and has patience. She tries hard to please the child by giving him good food or toys and not minding what he has done to her. She undermines all the things that are done to her and generates enduring, endless love for the child who acts this way. That is the example of love. Now expand this kind of love in degree and in scope, and include all sentient beings under the vast horizon of the sky.

One must realize that all these beings seek happiness. However, they do not know what to acquire and what to abandon. The source of happiness is dharmic action, but they do not know this source. Instead, they perpetuate adharmic actions that create suffering. Their actions are contrary to their desires. Thus all sentient beings suffer constantly, and you have to meditate on compassion with the desire that there is no other way but to bring happiness to all sentient beings. This kind of feeling is contrary to "May my friends be happy," or "May others be unhappy," or "I don't care one way or the other about those people I am not related to." Eliminating these limiting and harmful views, you generate the feeling of love without any restriction, characteristics, or partiality. Bring about the search for happiness for all living beings. Inculcate in yourself again and again this kind of love for the well-being of all sentient beings without a thought of partiality.

Now, how do you express love? Love is expressed through body, speech, and mind. Love expressed through the eyes looks at any living being with a kind of appreciativeness or in a compassionate manner, which is contrary to an angry look. Look at the thangka of Vajrasattva (in Session 14, "The Vajrasattva Purification"). His eyes, and the eyes of his consort, are half closed. It's not because they can't open their eyes but because their eyes convey a compassionate, appreciative look for all living beings. Their eyes express appreciation and praise the attractiveness of living beings. So don't open your eyes wide with anger. (There are thangka paintings of wrathful vajra deities where you see wide-open eyes rolling with wrath; this is to protect the Dharma and is contrary to this Vajrasattva image of gentle, slightly open eyes.)

As for people who look at others with anger, that could result in negative karma. Once, long ago, there was a person who looked at other people in jealousy and anger. Later in the next life he was born as a yidak under the stone hearth of a family and had to eat leftover food. If you look at the bodhisattva with the eyes of anger, you will be born in hell directly. One must be aware, while taking the bodhisattva vows, that there are also physical dispositions one must abide by. The main bodhisattva attitude is not to offend the other person. As in old times when there was no running water and someone had to pour water as you washed your hands, you would try to wash gently so as not to splash water on that person. When you sat, you sat in such manner so as not to extend your leg into another's place and offend them; intrusion into another's space would be offensive. One has to learn polite physical attitudes.

Polite physical attitudes include not spitting. You are not supposed to spit everywhere. In the old days they used to chew nuts to get rid of their mouth odor, but they covered the spit with soil. If you see a beautiful meadow or lawn, don't disturb anything. Try to keep it as clean as possible. Don't throw garbage everywhere. When you are taking care of old or sick people, your attitude should be polite. When you are holding an old person, there must be gentleness in your hands or your grip, and you should lift him gently. These are some of the appropriate physical attitudes one much learn. They are the expressions of love through your body.

What are the expressions of love through speech? You should try not to create disturbance in another's mind by telling lies or by insulting, scolding, or cursing him. Instead talk to him in a straightforward manner and with complete sincerity. Try not to disturb his mind. From the mind you must supplicate or pray that in this lifetime and in future lives you will be the agent that brings happiness to all sentient beings, that you will be a provider of happiness to all sentient beings. You must inculcate this feeling in yourself by repeating it to yourself again and again.

The point of bringing your meditative level to love is to realize that within your environment there are people who are lower or higher, wealthier or poorer, than you. There are servants living in your house, and dogs and cats as well. All these beings are karmically related to you. Because of their past karma, they were born in a position lower than you and have to exhaust their karma. So rather than chasing away a stray dog that comes to your door, you must generate sincere love for it. Especially those who are less privileged than you, wish for their happiness and always treat them as equals.

One way to further virtuous karma is to be especially kind to those who have traveled long distances. Also, express love to those who are underprivileged. Express your love to old people, to your parents, to sick people who have been ill for a long time. If you express sincere love through body, speech, and mind, the virtuous karma will increase by leaps and bounds. Expressing love for your parents is extremely important. From the time you were a helpless baby you were cared for and brought up to be a responsible human being. Yet when parents begin to get old, young people get impatient with them. They will not listen to their words and will try to undermine what they say. Gradually the elderly are ostracized and begin to feel sad. This kind of sadness in one's parents will bring lots of unvirtuous karma. Even Buddha, after being enlightened, acted to repay his mother's kindness by giving her the teaching of Dharma. His mother was then born in the thirty-second realm of the gods.

It is important to help your parents and look after them when they get old. It is very important that you provide them with food and clothing. Always speak softly and politely in order to make them happy. One of the most important services you can provide for your parents is to gradually turn their mind to Dharma. This tradition is still present in the Himalayas. When parents get old, they are provided with ample time to practice Dharma. When you provide food and clothing, you provide an immediate happiness: freedom from their worries about subsistence. Now if you can turn their mind to Dharma, they will proceed to the path of everlasting happiness. This is the most important service you can provide to your aging parents who are nearing death.

Bring your aging parents, bring a person who has traveled long distances, bring the person who has been sick for long time, bring these people and all sentient beings to the realm of your mind and generate love without any partiality. Doing that is the origination of the boundless state of love.

Compassion

Compassion will develop when you take on the suffering of other sentient beings. For example, if a fish is about to be killed, try to put yourself in the position of that fish and realize the suffering the fish has to go through. Once you realize the creature's suffering, you will not want to take lives. Taking lives comes about when one does not realize the suffering that beings go through.

Likewise, if you see sentient beings suffering with pain and sickness, put yourself in the position of the suffering beings and realize how much pain they are enduring. After realizing the pain, realize the number of sentient beings in existence—there are countless numbers of sentient beings who are suffering in the same way. Now realize in your mind that all these suffering sentient beings are like your present parents. They have been kind to you in a former life, so they are as important as your present parents. Therefore make a resolution: "I shall take the path of enlightenment so I can liberate them from suffering." Doing so will generate compassion. This is one way to meditate on compassion.

If you have sincere and boundless compassion, you are immune to the effects of evil spirits and free from them. Take the example of Milarepa.[23] When he was meditating in Chungrung Dzong, the king of spirits, Binayaka, came with five other evil spirits to harm him. Milarepa was not shaken by them, but he acted like he was afraid. He prayed to his lama, yidam, and khandro, but that didn't help. He recited many mantras of wrathful deities and invoked the power of their wrath, and that didn't help. At last he remembered the teaching of his own lama, that the spirits are the embodied or defiled perception of one's own mind. There is nothing out there interacting with you. Rather, it is one's own perception that one is interacting with. By realizing this, he developed boundless compassion toward these evil spirits and they were subjugated.

The boundless compassion state of mind is contrary to wishing happiness for oneself, unhappiness for the other side, or having the neutral position of "I don't care." It is a resolution to bring happiness to all sentient beings under the vast horizon of the sky.

Sympathetic Joy

Sympathetic joy is contrary to jealousy. Jealousy is perpetually present in human society. Think of someone who has wealth and power, such a king or an aristocrat who has all the worldly things. Usually one has the feeling, "He is superior to me in wealth and position. I must compete with him in order to be equal to or be better than him." Feeling jealousy, people will compete to win, and if they cannot win, they will try to bring the other person down. This feeling of jealousy and envy counteracts any feeling of joy.

Realize this, and now take your poor friends and poor relatives. Wish them to be as happy or as wealthy or in the same position as the most privileged person in your society. After you're able to achieve that state of sympathetic joy for your friends and relatives, bring the people with whom you have no contact, the people in a neutral zone, to your mind. Then begin to wish for their well-being and welfare to be the same quality as a person whom you think is in the topmost position in samsara. Once you achieve such sympathetic joy for neutral people, you must consider those people whom you do not like, your enemies. Realize that these enemies were once your parents who were kind to you, like your present parents. Wish for their well-being to be the same as that top person in worldly samsara. Thus you should begin to reconsider your jealous thoughts about wealthy people. Rather than wishing their downfall, wish them more prosperity. And wish the prosperity to spread throughout society to everyone.

If one is jealous of people who are wealthy and privileged or people who are not pestered by sickness and get to live long lives, and if one perpetuates the feeling of jealousy and envy toward these people, one produces the karma to be born in the jealous gods realm as a lhamayin (Skt. asura). Instead, try to generate sympathetic joy toward these people, and wish that all sentient beings reach the same level of prosperity and be equally happy and privileged. Wish that these prosperous people be firmly secure in their wealth, and wish them to be more generous in giving.

*   *   *

This concludes the teaching on the four boundless states of mind. They are very important seeds to have in one's mind to bring about the complete manifestation of bodhisattva. You can summarize the lesson by saying that all these boundless states of mind are included in one mind that is broad and helpful.

Normally we have a jealous mind or one that bears resentments. We think, "I wish to be better than he is." Against a person who is wealthy, we think, "I wish for his downfall," and so forth. Normally when we are happy, we do not wish for the happiness of others. When we see others happy, we only wish to be as happy as they are. Or when we develop ourselves and are in a better position, we want still more. The minute we see someone advancing, we begin to feel competitive and think, "Somebody is trying to catch up with me," and we wish for their downfall.

The way we bring better karma in such circumstances is to have a broader mind. Once, long ago, there lived a mother and a daughter who had to cross a river. They held hands as they crossed through the rapids. The mother thought: "I do not want my daughter to be carried away. I'd rather be carried away than her. It would be all right. I wouldn't mind." The daughter thought, "If my mother is saved and I am carried away by the rapids, it will be all right." Both mother and daughter had good thoughts toward each other but both got carried away by the rapids and died. However, because of their kind and generous thoughts of helping each other, both were born in the god realm of Tshangpa. If you are like that, if you have good thoughts and a good mind, then the path and the land will also be good.

It is important to meditate on the four boundless states of mind, again and again, until they are fully inculcated in your mind, because that is the root of bodhichitta.

THE DEDICATION

Now, as usual, we bring all sentient beings into the realm of our mind and dedicate all the merit that we might have earned through teaching and listening for the enlightenment of all sentient beings.

SESSION 12

THREE TYPES OF BODHICHITTA

The Intention

As USUAL, formulate your intention, realizing that in the vast expanse of the sky there are countless numbers of sentient beings who all desire happiness. These sentient beings do not know how to generate the source of happiness that is the Dharma. They do not desire suffering but do not know that the source of their unhappiness is any adharmic act. Not knowing the origin of suffering, under the influence of ignorance, they perpetuate adharmic actions. You must resolve to enlighten these sentient beings, all of whom were once your parents in the past. Say to yourself, "I will listen to the teaching of guru yoga. In order to practice this deep path, I shall listen to the words of the lama and experience the meaning of the words so I can lead all sentient beings to the supreme enlightenment. And I shall make this intention clear."

As I indicated earlier, you must see the teaching spot not as an ordinary place but as a heavenly place. Do not perceive the teacher as an ordinary human being, made of flesh and bones, but as Samanta-bhadra or Vajrasattva. And pray with intention that these vajra friends are not ordinary persons. Through pure perception, perceive them as gods and goddesses. Pure perception is primordial and originates from beginningless time. It is not something made up right now.

It is very important to clarify and formulate the intention because the intention determines whether the karmic consequence will be positive, negative, or neutral. Intention is like the seed. If you plant the seed of a poisonous plant, the fruit or plant will be poisonous. If you plant the seed of a medicinal plant, the fruit or plant will be medicinal. The intention determines which way the karma will move. Virtuous karma is produced by virtuous, or good, intention. Any act that is performed with good intention produces virtuous karma, and vice versa, unvirtuous karma is produced by unvirtuous or unclear intention. Neutral karma is produced by leaning neither to positive or negative intention. Thus, clarifying one's intention before listening to the teaching or doing the practice is prerequisite to any kind of practice.

In the Mahayana tradition, anyone receiving teachings must clarify their bodhisattva intention and generate bodhichitta. In Hinayana, the bodhisattva intention is missing. When you practice Mahayana, as we do, bodhichitta is the main foundation that eliminates the self-oriented goal. That's why when you receive teachings, you must originate bodhichitta. Because you are asked to clarify the bodhisattva intention when you receive teachings and and when you practice, there is this verse in our practice:

> *Ho! Deceived by myriad appearances, like the reflection of the*
> *moon in water,*
> *sentient beings wander through the cyclic [samsaric] chain*
> *of lives.*
> *In order for them to be at ease in the luminescent sphere of*
> *self-awareness,*
> *I shall develop bodhichitta by contemplating the four boundless*
> *attitudes.*

This bodhisattva intention is difficult to practice without knowing the meaning, so the meaning has to be expounded.

THE TEACHING

Today's teaching is on these different kinds of bodhichitta intention: the king's intention, the captain's intention, and the shepherd's intention. The king's intention is to know that he himself must first have power so that he can help his subjects. If he is a powerful king, his subjects will be protected and powerful. Thus he looks to increase his power in order to help his subjects. His dharmic thinking is, "I must attain enlightenment first. If I am not enlightened, I cannot help other sentient beings. In order to help other sentient beings, I will be enlightened first and I will then enlighten all sentient beings." The captain's intention is that of a person who steers a boat and wishes all the passengers to cross the ocean with him. It is defined as wishing all sentient beings under the wide horizon of the sky to be enlightened with oneself, together in one moment. The shepherd's intention is like the shepherd who first looks for grassland and water, and then drives his flocks there, defending them from predators all the day. The shepherd gives importance to others first. He wants all sentient beings to be enlightened first and himself last.

Thus we have three different ways to formulate our intentions to pursue enlightenment. Now, according to the particular path you practice, there will be different levels of intentions, which are done in sequence, one after the other. When you enter the door of the Dharma, at that time there is generally one intention, although it has different names at different levels—for example, devotional and aspirational intention (*semkyé*), or the generation of intention (*möpé chöpé semkyé*). The first seven levels are called "completely pristine and noble intention" (*lhaksam namdak*). Above the seventh level are the eighth and ninth attainments, which are "pure" (*dakpa*). Such higher levels are called "perfectly matured and fully ripened intention" (*rnam parsmin pai sems byed*). The tenth level of attainment is the intention of Buddha, the enlightenment. It is called "the intention that has abandoned the two defilements": emotional defilement (*nyönmong pai dripa*) and sublime obscuration of transcended mind (*shejai dripa*).

In essence these bodhichitta intentions are all one; the differences lie in the stages of one's attainment. The generation of intention can be relative or absolute. Relative bodhichitta can be either the goal formation, which is aspirational—the bodhisattva formulates his intention to enlighten all sentient beings (*mönpa jangchup semkyé*)— or the actual practice of that goal (*jukpa jangchup semkyé*). The former is like the intention to go some place and beginning to make travel plans. The latter is similar to the acts you perform after you formulate your plans to go some place, such as securing the means of transportation and preparing food and clothing and various necessities. Then once a bodhisattva formulates an intention to enlighten all sentient beings, he begins the actual practice of Dharma by pursuing the six paramitas: generosity, ethics, patience and tolerance, diligence, concentration, and wisdom. Through the perfection of these six transcended perfections, he pursues the enlightenment of all sentient beings. Relative bodhichitta intention is vast and should be practiced in depth. One must train one's mind toward this kind of intention. When one attains the six transcended perfections (also called "being in the path of sight or view" or "seeing"), one realizes the absolute meaning of emptiness and sees the real manifestation of all the buddhas.

Relative bodhichitta is obtained by a monk making a vow of bodhichitta. It is ordained by the teacher and includes, as we have said, the goal formation and the actual practice. If you take this kind of vow with a teacher or lama, or with altar objects that are manifested buddhas, or through your practice, you must then practice the intention every moment of your life. Doing so will increase the capacity of the intention.

Absolute bodhichitta is not attained through practicing any rituals.

It is called "the intention that is meaningful in itself" (*döndam jang-chup sem*). Absolute bodhichitta is attained from the meditation or the experiential meditation on the intention only. If one tries hard, making the utmost effort and not wasting any time, meditating and experiencing this intention, then one will attain absolute bodhichitta.

In our practice, we take refuge from the collection of the buddhas, bodhisattvas, and lamas. After that we think, meditate, understand, and experience bodhichitta by clarifying the intention and doing 500,000 recitations in the preliminary practice.

In the visualization during the bodhichitta vow, the same image is used as when taking refuge: the tree with five branches in front with all the buddhas and bodhisattvas (see the Refuge Tree thangka). In those boundless skies are sentient beings from beginningless time, all of whom have once been your parents. Like the parents of your present life, they treated you with compassion and love, giving you the best food and clothing possible. They worried about your welfare until you could look after your own life. These leftover sentient beings, as numberless as drops of water in the ocean, are those who have not been transcended by the countless buddhas of the past. They are lost in the darkness, not knowing where the path is or where they are going. Under the influence of complete ignorance, they wander, not knowing what to acquire and what to abandon. Because they lack knowledge, they emphasize work and worldly samsaric goals for their children. They think that working, whether farming or business, can provide them with lasting happiness. If their children perform Dharma, parents worry they will have no source of income, will not be like normal human beings, and will face all sorts of suffering. Thus they try to push their children to make friends, conquer enemies, and build fame and wealth.

They are not aware of what the path is and what the path is not. However, one must not be mistaken about their intentions. Parents have, in every possible way, good intentions. They mean to help and look out for the welfare of their children, but it is like a moth that sees the burning lamp as the place of refuge, or a place to play in, or the object to play with. The moth flies round and round and eventually burns itself up in the flame, ending its life. Ordinary parents are passionately attached to the wrong thing, like fish that are so attached to the bait they will swallow the hook, or like deer that can't help rubbing their bodies against a tree to rid themselves of flies, too intent to see that hunters have placed a trap there to catch and kill him. Samsara is the pursuit of attachments to the senses—to sound, smell, taste, and feeling or touch. Samsaric traps are like honey on the sharpest edge of the sword: licking the honey will cut your tongue in two.

There are sentient beings who seem to know what to acquire and what to abandon. However, they are not able to materialize or practice what they know, unlike past buddhas and bodhisattvas who practiced day and night without rest and attained supreme enlightenment. There are people who know the path, yet are not able to practice what they know. Their position is similar to sentient beings who do not know the path at all. Realize that there are countless sentient beings ignorant of the path, or who know the path but do not practice. They go round and around within the wheel of samsara, the vicious circle of being born and dying in different realms.

The past buddhas and bodhisattvas were not able to transcend these sentient beings. One must realize all these sentient beings were once my parents who showed me compassion. So what is the point of my getting enlightened first when I see all other sentient beings suffering constantly? Thus, taking after the great buddhas and bodhisattvas of the past who have dedicated their lives to enlighten all sentient beings, I will follow the same path by supplementing their strength to enlighten all sentient beings, not leaving a single one under the vast horizon of the sky unenlightened.

Like that, we must formulate our intention and practice guru yoga.

We formulate our intention in chanting the bodhichitta lines that
begin:

> *Ho! Deceived by myriad appearances, like the reflection of the*
> *moon in water,*
> *(Ho natshok nangwa chudé dzunré gi)*

Ho na tshok means variety, many. *Nang wa* means sight, or object seen,
all the phenomena and sentient beings on this planet. *Chude dzun re
gi* means the reflection of the moon. It is not the real moon in the sky
but the reflection of the moon in the water. That moon in the water
has no essence. Because of this, all sentient beings wander in the six
realms without any freedom. Like prayer beads on a string, they are
caught in samsara—when you pull one bead, another bead follows.
In that way, they will go around and around in a circle without any
freedom.

The third line means to rest in ease within the supreme
enlightenment:

> *In order for them to be at ease in the luminescent sphere of*
> *self-awareness,*
> *(Rangrik ösal yingsu ngalso chir)*

These are general Buddhist terms, but in accord with Dzokchen.

Now the fourth and last line means making the four boundless
states of mind, which are compassion, sympathetic joy, loving kindness, and equanimity, my second nature:

> *I shall develop bodhichitta by contemplating the four boundless*
> *attitudes.*
> *(Tshé mé shiyi ngang né semkyé do)*

Developing these states of mind as the seeds of the bodhisattva intention, the formulation and the practice of that goal, you decide, "I will generate the bodhisattva intention." The bodhisattva intention is to walk the path in order to enlighten all sentient beings under the wide horizon of the sky.

PRACTICING THE INTENTION

Now let us turn to the actual practice of the bodhisattva intention that is the vow and resolution of that intention. We have predictable ways of relating to others in our daily life. We try to make ourselves famous, to be an expert, or wealthy, or be the best at something. We wish for the well-being of our relatives and friends, are indifferent to many other people, not caring whether they are up or down, and we wish those we don't like to be at the bottom or at least not equal to us.

When you meditate on equanimity, or the equality of oneself and others, bring all sentient beings into the realm of your mind. In practicing equanimity, or even-mindedness, first of all realize that all sentient beings have been attached to their sense of self from the very beginning of existence. However, that self really doesn't exist. There is no inherent self. But we get attached to that concept of "self" or "I" and become the owner of that ownerless object, making claims like "I, myself," "this is mine," or "these are my things."

Because we possess such a sense of self and are so attached to it, we suffer at the slightest change. We find it hard to tolerate heat or cold or changes in temperature. Our obsession to protect our body is boundless and beyond reason. We can't even abide an insect bite. If you think about it, a mosquito's sucking a drop of your blood will likely not eliminate your life. Yet when a small insect bites you, you slam it. You act like the insect encroached on your rights. Instead of flicking it off, you make sure you squash it. That act of eliminating the insect, smearing it off from the face of the earth, might seem very small to you, but the karmic effect is like a landslide, resulting in your rebirth in the Hell of Dudjom. The insect was merely trying to fill its tiny stomach. You have the power to tolerate the bite and give the tiny amount of blood, after which it will fly away. So instead of killing the insect, practice patience and tolerance for the feeling that it is out to get you.

This realization of the insect's harmlessness originates from an understanding of what to acquire and what to abandon. There isn't one sentient being who has not been your parent or related to you in a special manner in one lifetime or other. But these sentient beings wander in the vicious circle of samsara, not knowing Dharma, not able to differentiate the real path versus the non-path, or what to acquire and what to abandon. So generate compassion toward these sentient beings, thinking, "Oh, they do not know what they are doing, but I know the path. At least I know the consequence of this action. So I will try to generate patience and tolerance."

You must remind yourself of the resolution you made in the practice of Mahayana that you will enlighten all sentient beings. Taking this resolution for bodhisattva mind, harming any sentient being is not possible. Acting in anger might justify your feeling that something is out to get you, but it is not an action in keeping with your bodhisattva vows. Such intolerant action will bring you rebirth in the Hell of Dudjom for a very long time. So you must resolve to see yourself and all other sentient beings as equal.

The next resolution is to interchange the position (*dakshen jewa*). When you see sentient beings suffering from hunger, poverty, and any other manner of suffering, formulate your intention with your breath. When you exhale, think of all the happiness and prosperity you have and let that be transferred to all the suffering sentient beings. It's like taking off your coat to give it to a poor person in the the winter. As you exhale, give your sense of prosperity to the sentient being who is suffering. When you inhale, make an intention that all those suffering due to disease and other illnesses that plague sentient beings "be onto me." With every inhale and exhale, you begin to take on the misery and suffering of others and give them your prosperity and happiness. You begin with one sentient being that is within your sight, and then increase the number by two, three, four, and so on, until you let all sentient beings under the vast horizons of the sky receive all the wealth and happiness you have. With every inhale and exhale, think, "I shall take all the suffering of sentient beings onto myself." In interchanging the position, you wish someone else to be in your good position and yourself to be in someone else's negative position. If by practicing you make this intention part of your mind, then the many defilements you have accumulated over the eons will be purified and you will be freed from the three lower realms.

As I mentioned earlier, when the Lord Buddha was born in hell, this kind of intention was truly born within him. He and his friend Karmarupa were pulling a chariot in hell. Karmarupa was very weak, suffering from exhaustion. The Lord Buddha immediately thought, "Instead of my friend suffering, I will take up his position." So he went up to the official of hell and told him, "Look, let Karmarupa go. Put that chariot rope on my head. I will pull. I would like him to be free." The official of hell said, "All sentient beings must exhaust their own karma. Who are you to take on the karma of some other person?" He took the burning hammer and hit the Buddha on his head. Dying there, he was reborn in god's realm. That is the result of being freed from the three lower realms.

Sentient beings in hell are always beaten by these officials with a hammer or get hacked to pieces, and so they desire death, but there is no death. Yet in this case the Buddha died in hell and was reborn in god's realm because of his true feeling of this kind of intention.

In the present day, it is evident that people think of themselves only. They are driven by individual self-centered goals: "Let me the best. I don't care about someone else." Every "I" action is geared to one's individual goal for fame and winning. In the process, others are ignored or overlooked or eliminated. But lamas of long time ago said, "Once you are a practitioner of Dharma, then you must act contrary to samsaric goals. You should not think of 'me' and 'my goals,' or 'What can I get? What's in it for me? Is there a profit for me?' You must give the profit to others. You must take the loss and take a humble position. That is the practice. You must think, 'I am the practitioner of the Dharma. I am a Chopa. I don't really need all these things. It will be all right to give all the profits and the best things to others. I will just take the humblest position.' One must bear this kind of intention when one is a practitioner." So said the lamas. The byproduct of meditation on this kind of intention is that there will not be any impediments of sickness and disease in your life. And you will avoid obstacles created by evil spirits, ghosts, giants, or whatever, which some people can see and some cannot. When you see these evil spirits in body form, instead of getting scared, thinking about their wrath or about what you can do to eradicate them, begin to strengthen bodhichitta. That will subjugate all evil forces. This is the immediate byproduct of bodhichitta, but in the long run, this kind of intention is at the root of enlightenment.

Understanding the formation of karma and the consequences of adharmic samsaric actions is very hard. So listen to the teaching, where it is expounded in detail, carefully and understand the teaching in the whole context. Doing otherwise will be very dangerous. For example, if you generate the bodhisattva intention just to avoid and eliminate impediments, such as sickness or evil forces or bad encounters, this is not dharmic intention. Such intention is for a selfish goal; it is not the root intention of supreme enlightenment.

The real goal of the bodhisattva intention is the enlightenment of all sentient beings. Being immune from evil forces and disease is simply the byproduct of bodhichitta meditation. But, again, know that one cannot use this method just to achieve immunity from disease or evil spirits. This story is an example of what will happen. Long ago there was a man who found a sparrow with a broken leg. With true intention, he tried to heal the bird's broken foot and eventually the bird got well and flew away. Then later it came back with a seed and gave it to the man. He planted the seed and soon turnips came up. When he cut opened one turnip, he found gold, a miraculous production of gold. He took the fold and put in on the altar. The next day there was another batch of turnips with gold inside, and so on. One day his friend came by and asked, "Hey, how did you get all the gold? How did you get the seed of this kind of turnip?" The man replied, "Well, I came home one day and found a sparrow with a broken leg. I tried to heal it. When it got well, he flew away and came back with the seed. So I planted it. Since then these turnips have been giving me gold." This guy thought, "Oh, wow. This is great. I will do the same." So he went home and found a stone. He threw the stone at a sparrow and broke its leg. Then he started to heal the sparrow. When it got well, the sparrow flew away. Sure enough it came back with a seed. He planted it, and soon turnips came up. He cautiously opened one, but instead of gold, he found a baby. The baby came out and started to eat everything. In fact, the baby emptied out the house. That kind of thing might happen if you deviate from the intended path.

After the resolution to interchange positions, the third resolution is to meditate for others to be in better state than yourself. This is like wishing other sentient beings to be happier than yourself. The virtuous karma is earned by knowing what the source of happiness is, which is Dharma, performing dharmic actions, and acquiring the merits. One should think: "Let all the virtuous karma be dedicated. Let all that karma be materialized for the benefit of sentient beings other than myself. I do not care if I am sick. I do not care if I wander within the wheel of samsara. I do not care if I am in born in the lower realms. But let all other sentient beings be enlightened and let them be able to reap the fruit I sow." When you inculcate in yourself this kind of intention, you take the suffering from others onto yourself as real.

During the time of Jowo Buddha, Lama Jangchub Naljor, a practitioner of compassion, was giving a teaching. A dog strayed into the room. A man listening to the teaching picked up a stone and hit the dog to chase it away. When the dog was hit, the lama exclaimed in pain, "Aya ya!" and then fell from his seat. People were baffled and said, "How can the lama feel pain when the dog got hit? That's impossible. The dog got hit and the lama falls off his seat. That's ridiculous. The lama must have made that up. He's just acting." But the lama took off his shirt. Sure enough, he had a big bump on his back. It was as if the man threw the stone at the lama rather than at the dog. In reality, by the power of his compassion, the lama took the injury for the dog. There was no question about it. He had a big red bump on his back.

During the time of Lama Dharma Rakshita, a Hinayana practitioner who knew about Mahayana and practiced great compassion, there was another incident. In the community where the lama lived, there was a really sick person. The doctor said that he must eat human flesh to be cured. This great saint then said, "If it will benefit you, then take the meat from my body." So he cut a piece off his thigh and gave it to the sick person. The sick person ate the flesh and was cured. However, the lama suffered from extreme pain, unable to sleep for days and nights. He had been meditating on the realization of emptiness, but had not achieved full realization. One day as he slept a little, he had a dream. In the dream a white person appeared and said, "If you are to obtain the supreme enlightenment, you must go through this hardship. What you are doing is the best." He then spat on the wound of the lama, rubbed it in, and disappeared. Upon awakening, the lama found his wound healed. The person who appeared in the dream was Chenrezik, Avalokiteshvara.

Once the Lord Buddha was born as the king Padma in India. At that time there was a big epidemic and people were dying. The king gathered all the doctors and asked the cure for the disease. The doctors suggested that the meat of the rohu fish would be the cure. Rohu was not available at the time, so one day, during a holiday of making offerings to the buddhas and bodhisattvas, the king decided to make a resolution. He wished that after his death he be born in the lake in the form of rohu. So he prayed and supplicated, then jumped off from his high palace wall into the lake. Upon his death he was instantly reborn as a rohu fish. He was a fish, but he had a human voice that cried out, "I am the fish called rohu. Eat me and you will be cured." And people came and start filleting the fish. As one side got cut, the other side grew back, and so forth. At last when the epidemic was controlled, he told the people, "I am the incarnation of your king, Padma. I gave up my life to be born as a rohu fish in order to cure you. To reciprocate my action and kindness, you must all practice Dharma. You must practice what to acquire and what to abandon." Thus, through his sacrifice, many sentient beings at that time were liberated from samsara.

These are some aspects of the resolution and the formulation of the bodhichitta goal with kingly intention, captain's intention, and shepherd's intention. You must consider and formulate your intention again and again toward this path.

THE DEDICATION

As usual the merit we earn from listening to my teaching and from my giving the teaching should be dedicated to the enlightenment of all sentient beings under the wide horizon of the sky. Like Manjushri and Samantabhadra, who always dedicated the merits to the enlightenment of all sentient beings in the past, present, and the future, we will dedicate our merit for the enlightenment of all sentient beings.

ACTUALIZING THE BODHISATTVA GOAL THROUGH THE SIX PARAMITAS

THE INTENTION

As USUAL you are requested to formulate your intention, which is pristine in nature and has a motivation that your present parents, your enemies, and all sentient beings under the wide horizon of the sky be led to liberation.

THE TEACHING

The intention and the goal has been taught. Now we will discuss actualizing, or materializing, and sustaining the goal through the six perfections, or paramitas: generosity, ethics, patience and tolerance, diligence, wisdom, and concentration.

Generosity

As we have learned, there are six paramitas that we practice on the path. The first one is generosity, or almsgiving, which has several aspects. The first is giving material things (*sangsang gi jinpa*). It doesn't matter whether the object that is given is big or small, the merit depends on one's intention. For example, sometimes in practices or in ceremonies, yidaks are given a food offering and water—a little bit of water is put on the plate . The offering looks simple and modest, but its meaning is vast. Such alms are given through the recitation of the mantras and the power of samadhi, of the lama's great concentrated meditation, which turn the modest offering into every necessity the yidaks might need—food, clothing, and so on. The power of mantra and meditation turns what is to our perception an insignificant object into a valuable gift, so that countless numbers of yidaks, like sands on the beach of Ganges River, will be helped.

One can also give an offering through burning, either a white or a red offering. A white offering is fried barley flour (*tsampa*) blended with different kinds of incense and dried things that have not been touched by any kind of substance related to meat. The sweets and so on are burned in a fire and given to yidaks. The red offering is wheat flour mixed with lard and burned in a fire. These offerings are given while chanting. The yidak is helped and fed through the burnt smell.

After giving food to a yidak, it is then proper to give the gift of Dharma. The gift of Dharma means that one will not do any adharmic action but will perpetuate dharmic actions with virtuous merits. By doing so, one will pacify these yidaks, who are prone to harm other people. They begin to realize their rebirth as a yidak is caused by their karma, which might be a consequence of taking lives or bearing anger and greed in their minds. So whenever a gift is given through samadhi or concentrated meditation, these yidaks, being satisfied with whatever gifts they receive from lamas, in turn help the Dharma and abandon the act of harming and taking other sentient beings' lives. They might even generate a bodhisattva mind, which is their gift of protecting human beings. In the long run, such giving becomes an aid to one's own enlightenment.

These are all gifts in a small degree. The greater gift is to give things that have special meaning for you, like a horse or an elephant, things that you really care for, or an object that has rarity and is precious and special to you. Above that level of gift, the highest degree of almsgiving or gifting is to give up your own life, your own body or limbs, for the sake of others, in one way or another, as in the example of the king who gave up his life to be reborn as a rohu fish to be eaten by the people as curative medicine. There are many such sacrifices in the history of bodhisattvas: A king, seeing a tigress with cubs dying of hunger, gave up his life to feed the cubs. Nagarjuna gave his head to a prince.[24] It is not possible for us to go to that level of sacrifice; however, know that the gift of your life without attachment is the greatest almsgiving.

There is also the almsgiving of protection. If an animal is fleeing from a predator or if an animal is ready to be killed by a butcher, to be able to release that animal from death is the almsgiving of protection. In Tibet most of the animals killed are sheep. So people will buy a sheep from a butcher and release it to a safe place. This could have an immediate beneficial result, and to be healed from a sickness, you would do such almsgiving under a lama's prescription. In the long run, you are contributing to the enlightenment of all living beings. Buddha said, "If you harm sentient beings you are harming me. If you are helping sentient beings, you are helping me. I manifest my body for the well-being of all sentient beings." Giving protection to any sentient being is the supreme almsgiving.

There is not a single sentient being who does not consider its life precious. Consider the smallest insect: if you happen to touch it, it will run away in order to protect its own life. The biggest animals, elephants and tigers, also run away from threats in order to protect their lives. If we do not consider their lives precious, then we will cause great suffering to these sentient beings. In Tibet there are Dharma laws that protect sentient beings living in the water. One may not catch fish and eat them, and there is also a law that prohibits playing with fish; one must revere their lives. There are also Dharma laws that protect woodland animals in monastic preserves. These animals are the ornaments of the protective deities of the land. So if you kill an animal, you are in some way depriving the protective god of that area. In turn, it might cause you harm and create catastrophes. Not harming these wild animals, which are the ornaments of the protective gods, is almsgiving that helps to keep the serenity of the land. When they are happy, these guardian gods provide good, fertile circumstances for one to practice Dharma. Ultimately, the almsgiving of protection is a dharmic action that in the long run contributes toward enlightenment.

Ethics

The second paramita is moral ethics. There are ten moral dharmic actions one must keep: three through the body (no killing, no stealing, no adultery), four through speech (no lying, no rough speech, not causing misunderstandings, no idle speech), and three through mind (not coveting, having no intention of harming others, and not harboring wrong views, such as not believing in karma or holding on to the philosophical extremes of eternalism or nihilism). Knowing the ten ethical precepts, you must observe them and stand by them. Not knowing means not knowing what to acquire that is dharmic and what to abandon that is adharmic.

One should try to accumulate dharmic actions to whatever degree or expense one can. The smallest action can be as valuable as a big action. It is said one can attain virtuous karma merely through speech and action. For example, coming to a temple or statue or any manifestation of the Buddha, you have a choice to go to the left or right of it. If you feel joy and think, "If I have to go by it, I'd go around it keeping the statue on my right side as a sign of humility," then even that action becomes a virtuous action. If you say, "So what? The path is the same distance. I don't care," and go to the left of it, then you could create unvirtuous karma for yourself unknowingly. Common things or events in one's life can result in virtuous or unvirtuous karma. In Tibet there is a tradition of carving mantras or statues and piling them on the roadside. At the sight of them, people take off their hats and show respect. This is not a hardship, and merely by thinking, "Oh, that is the manifestation of the Buddha. I must pay homage," will bring virtuous karma. Or seeing in the distance a person wearing a maroon robe, thinking this is a lama or a practitioner and taking off your hat in respect will earn virtuous karma.

Another ethical precept is to always dedicate whatever merit you have earned to all sentient beings. During your meditation, whatever action you have done that is dharmic, dedicate the merit for the enlightenment of all sentient beings.

Patience and Tolerance

The third paramita, patience and tolerance, is threefold in aspect. First, it tolerates false accusations. If another person deprives you of wealth and possessions, spreads the rumor that you are a bad person, and tries every means to arouse anger in you or cause you suffering, that is said to be harm from others. The paramita of patience and tolerance is to not to counteract such attacks with anger. Rather, one must counteract harmful actions with compassion and love. Think these accusations and bad things are due to the result of one's past karma, and in return express love and compassion to the person trying to harm you.

Second, it is able to bear hardship. We do not have the endurance to bear hardship. When the Dharma teaching is longer than you can handle, you get tired. When you practice longer than usual, you get tired and impatient, hoping it will end soon. If you are doing a samsaric task, you will go out there whether it's raining or burning hot, but when it comes to meditation or Dharma practice, you soon get tired or sleepy. So you must be able to bear discomfort when you practice Dharma.

Third, do not be afraid of realization. People who have not heard of or who do not understand the concept of "emptiness" or who have not had the experience of emptiness have a tendency to be scared of that kind of experience. One of the important moral codes is to not be scared of any kind of dharmic experience.

Diligence

Diligence is very important. If you don't have diligence, whatever you know won't help. So use diligence to gain experience in applying what you have learned and have meditated on. Maintain the continuity of learning and meditating on the teachings.

There is a Tibetan proverb that says, "Diligent people can turn even a mountain into dust because they are very diligent about their work." If they start something, they will finish it. They can even flatten a mountain if they set out to do it. The proverb continues, "The intellectuals go empty-handed at the time of death." They know so much, but they don't practice meditation or hold an experience in their hearts. So when they die, although they know so many things, they don't have much experience or feeling and will die empty-handed. In the same way, you know enough about how to meditate and practice, now use diligence to meditate on what you know.

Concentration

The fifth paramita, concentration, has two aspects. One is the place of the gathering, the community. The other is one's mind, which often gets absorbed or consumed by external things. It is almost impossible to obtain the perfection of single-pointed concentration if the hustle and bustle of the city intrudes on your consciousness. Therefore you must go away from the community and find a solitary place. The solitude of the mind depends on physical solitude. And when one is in the physical solitude of a forest or away from the noise of the city, one must try to make the mind conform to that solitude and not wander.

If one's mind is not in harmony with that physical solitude, then it is like a bird in a cage that is deprived of its freedom.

There are two reasons why one may not be able to leave the distractions of a community for a place of solitude. One is attachment to one's wealth and the other is attachment to one's relatives or immediate family. To counteract this attachment, realize that all phenomena end in separation. We tend to run away from this fact and get attached. Now one must pay attention to the reality that "Whatever comes together ends in separation."

Consider your own life, complete with parents, children, relatives, and friends. One day, all these people will go away in different directions. Right now the most important and visible thing to you is your body. You tend to believe that you are one with your body. You see your body as you. However, after death, the flesh-and-bone body will quickly disintegrate, burned to ashes in fire, buried under soil, or thrown into the ocean, and the mind or the consciousness will travel within the six realms and take rebirth. Even common phenomena called "body," which you are so attached to, come together only for a moment and must end in separation.

There is no essence to any kind of temporary gathering except suffering. Yet practicing Dharma to the very end is eternal happiness. But you get so involved with and attached to yourselves, your families, your houses, and your wealth. That wealth is a collection of defilements. You must go beyond those and into solitude. Be on the path of the Dharma to bring about ever-existing happiness.

Why is wealth a product of defilements? Once you begin to have wealth, you make friends, whom you try to appreciate, and you make enemies, whom you fear could cause you harm. Having a hundred dollars, you try to increase that amount, going from a hundred to two hundred to three hundred dollars and beyond. The sky is the limit. You devote all your time to building your wealth or growing your business. Then comes the problem of protecting or investing great

202 : LIBERATION FROM SAMSARA

wealth. Not only is wealth the product of all kinds of defilements, it is also the cause of suffering. You waste your life trying to protect, preserve, and pass it on. Then your life comes to an end.

The only thing you really need to eat is your usual daily fare. Regardless of all the food you have, you wouldn't be able to eat more than what you can eat at one meal. You need clothing, but you wouldn't be able to wear more than what you can wear at one time. You waste your time protecting that wealth even though you only need a bowl of rice or one yard of cloth. So having vast wealth just causes suffering.

Immersed in the business of earning wealth, there is no chance for you to think about the next life. The truth and the idea of a next life disappear from your thoughts. And then you begin to risk your life, traveling from one place to another. That kind of risk is more evident in Tibet, where people have to cross rivers to go from one place to another on business. On the return trip, the river has risen and one cannot cross safely, though one must cross. At night when there are no lights and you have to go after your cattle, you can fall or come across vicious animals. Even traveling by car means taking a risk, because people are killed in auto accidents. Yet all these risks are downplayed which can end one's life.

In order to earn wealth two things have to be undermined. One is Dharma, when you begin to think, "Well, it will be all right if I don't have enough time to practice Dharma. I will keep making money." Another is the moral codes that must be broken to get money, when you say to yourself, "Well, money is more important than the codes. I have to keep up with friends." Remember that there soon comes a time when your friends turn into your enemies, so and so forth.

At this moment you should reflect by thinking: "Why am I so busy and have no time?" Realize it is because you are working or doing business for your family to earn money. Because of that, Dharma becomes secondary or the activity begins to undermine your efforts in

Dharma. Therefore to become rich, one undermines the importance of Dharma practice and breaks the moral codes and ethics. However, that wealth will not provide eternal happiness. You cannot transfer your wealth to your next lifetime. The wealth you have earned by hard work goes to somebody else. It will be taken away by people you do not like and it will be enjoyed by other people.

When you begin to get old, some of your children will feel bad and will miss you when you are gone. Then there are others who will think, "Well, if he dies there will be lots of money for us," and they get impatient for you to die and feel happy that you will be leaving this world. That is what you will get from the glorious wealth you have built.

According to the Dharma tradition in Tibet, if a child is to be a monk or a Dharma practitioner and the parents die, their wealth is divided into two portions: one portion is given to those involved in samsara and the other to charity or the monastery for the merit of the late parents. If they only had one son who happens to be a monk or priest, then all the wealth will be given to charity or the monastery for the dharmic action to bring about good karma for the consciousness of the late parents. In poor families with lots of relatives or children, any remaining assets are divided equally among the children and the parents. When the father dies, half the wealth is given away to charity or for a Dharma action in the name of the father, and the other half is divided among the mother and the children.

Therefore you must realize now that accumulating great wealth, possibly by undermining Dharma practice and breaking moral and ethical codes, brings about suffering and wastes your precious human life. Attachment to one's own immediate family or friends also brings suffering. Close personal relationships have ups and downs and betrayals. Because of attachments, even those whom you always helped may not return your kindness or might even reciprocate in an unpleasant manner. There are people who only look after their own well-being, always thinking, "Let me be the best" and undermining others. When a friend becomes lower in position or rank, they will even ignore this friend's existence.

Your attachment to your family could start various defilements. For example, in an agricultural society, in order to feed your family you have to cut down trees or plow land and sow seeds. All these activities involve taking the lives of other sentient beings. So once you begin to expand your family, you will expand adharmic actions or defilements.

As a practitioner of the Dharma, I want you to be aware of the essencelessness of samsaric activity so that you can formulate in your thoughts and practice some detachment from these phenomena and activities. In samsara, one can be totally involved in earning wealth, making friends, or expanding one's power and knowledge to make things better, all of which can bewilder your mind. How much effort should we put into these endeavors? How much should we get involved in this samsaric world for the sake of mundane ends? The essence or the end result for samsaric efforts is very little. Even if you attained the greatest wealth and are a billionaire, your subsistence will be the same as what a poor man needs. Even if you have billions, you cannot eat ten meals a day. You eat three times a day, which even a poor man does. The pursuit of wealth becomes contrary to the Dharma, yet it is Dharma practice that leads to the attainment of supreme enlightenment.

Involvement in samsara breeds enemies of various kinds, both personal enemies and enemies of the country. You will want to eliminate enemies, but this is a false thought. One can never eliminate enemies. There will always be enemies, one after another. Just as there is no end in making friends. You always make more friends and have more and more relatives. There is no end to it. There is never a moment where you can say, "Once I am finished with this, I am going to stop." Once one project is finished, another project starts, another activity pops up, and so forth. You are always busy doing something. There is a saying, "There is no end to samsaric action. But if you leave it, it will end."

When I am in Sikkim there are many things I have to do. The best thing is to wake up to the officious day, and off I go. I leave samsaric things and go. Once we leave it, it will end. Otherwise your life with its mundane activities will go on and on, and the practice of Dharma will be less and less. It is not that you should abandon everything, but it is important that your perception comes into line with the knowledge of the essencelessness of attachment to samsara and its adharmic result. That is how you must begin to see it in your own life.

How do you get away from these kinds of attachments? There are two ways. The first is to leave your own home and go where you don't know anybody. Then you don't have to be concerned about someone else's well-being or harbor ill feelings for your enemies. You are a stranger and don't know anybody. You don't have to be concerned with relatives or get upset at your ill-wishing enemies and so forth. What kind of place should you go to? Generally the place should be without people or community. The ideal place to live is a cave. The caves in India are so bad you begin to lose the power of your body. Many monks have tried to live in these caves, which was the tradition in Tibet, and they had problems. I don't know how the caves are here, but go to the caves and live there. Then you don't have to worry about repairing a house. With a cave you don't have to do anything. You will be a loser in terms of eating good food or wearing good clothes or talking a lot with your friends. You will lose out on all those things. The best friends you will find are wild animals or deer. Find friendship with the animals in the woods. The great saint Milarepa said that in the cave, "where there are no people and where there is no deviation due to a sad mind, the mind blends into one with the constant thoughts of lamas of the three times. The mind is never detached from the worship of the Three Precious Ones."

When you go into this kind of solitude, you will automatically have an aversion to samsaric activities. You will begin to have transcended pure perception and then the concentration of your meditation. Far away from the community, where your mind can be attracted to different things, your attention is more concentrated and is detached from your friends and relatives who want to talk and communicate and have agreements or disagreements and become friends or enemies. This does not happen in an isolated cave with woodland animals, trees, and nature around. Shivala said, "The wild animals do not use abusive language. Nor do the trees. Let me have the chance to be in that place to practice meditation." The leaves will flutter in the wind and make sounds, but that sound does not convey any kind of value judgment, as you would get from people. This sound will deepen your meditation. Your mind will naturally open up. That is evident even now.

When people in the city go to the countryside, they naturally feel happier and more open. There is nothing special about the things in nature. The road is a road. Trees are trees. However, somehow nature opens your mind. And for food, you don't have to be picky. Find whatever is edible. Even water seems to be enough here, which is far from the case while living in a community.

In a solitary place your meditation will naturally become stronger. This is because there is nothing to do. You don't have to clean the house or anything like that. You begin to fall back on the practice of meditation. You feel it's now time for meditation and you do it. You push yourself a little, then a little bit more, and so on, so your meditation becomes stronger and clearer. But in a community, one day you shut off the phone and sit and meditate, but the next day there is something to be done and you find it necessary to attend to this or that. As a result, what you have gained or experienced yesterday is forgotten and gone. That is why a place away from a community is better for meditation.

Within the place of solitude, every action one performs becomes dharmic action. Not persevering in the practice of meditation, it will still begin to grow naturally into meditation. At the same time you begin to experience compassion and love. In the woods you will see wild animals and interact with them and begin to feel compassion and love for them. When you go into deep meditation, woodland animals will feel you are harmless and will begin to circle around you and come and stay with you. They feel and are affected by the power of the meditator's compassion.

In cities or in communities, one has to consciously contrive to control the mind. It's like imprisoning the mind, thinking, "I am losing my mind. I have to pull it back. It seems like it's going away, so pull it back." All these hard things you have to do to maintain meditative concentration. But in solitude, the mind begins to conform to the meditative level naturally. You even begin to hear the very different tones of wind. The wind can blow in a special tone. It has a noise, a very special noise. When I hear that, my heart begins to feel the sense of impermanence, and the intention to practice comes over me. These kinds of sounds in nature can stimulate different kinds of responses in you too. Even if a person is angry and upset in a community or city, going to an open space, in solitude, lessens his anger.

Once you reach a place of solitude, how do you meditate? You sit in the lotus position. Your body has to be straight and the neck bent forward a little, your eyes concentrating on the tip of your nose. This is the position of the meditation body. When your body is straight, your psychic veins are straight. When the veins and arteries are straight, the wind will flow freely. And when the wind flows freely and straight in the psychic veins, your mind becomes stable. Mind is generally unstable because the wind in your body is obstructed. Bring all these circumstances and positions together to begin to meditate.

There are many different ways of meditating. Whichever path you take, you can begin to perfect the concentration. Go to a place of solitude and practice guru yoga. Through this path, you will begin to attain the perfection of concentrated meditation, the stable mind.

Wisdom

Now we come to the sixth paramita, wisdom, or *prajna*. There is the wisdom of hearing, of pondering, and of meditation or contemplation. The primary wisdom of hearing (*thöpai sherab*) is the ability to understand what your lama taught. Not mistaking any meaning or any word, understand the exact meaning and exact word as clearly as the lama taught. The primary wisdom of pondering or thinking just that. When one hears the teacher's words and leaves them in memory, files the teaching away, so to speak, one will not remember clearly or will not remember to apply the teachings to one's life. But when one listens to the teachings and begins to ponder the meaning, clarifying one's doubts and questions in the attempt to get at the meaning, that is pondering the Dharma taught by the teacher in solitude. That is the primary wisdom of pondering.

After acquiring the primary wisdom of pondering the teaching, it is time to experience the teaching—that is, to acquire the wisdom of meditation. We don't have all the eighty thousand paths that the Buddha taught, but just think of the Kangyur collection of one hundred or two hundred volumes. Just imagine all the questions you can ask! There is no end to the teaching, nor is there an end to inquiry. You can unintentionally spend your entire life asking endless questions, trying to clarify every meaning. But you must at some point say, "Now I will stop pondering. Now it is time for me to experience the teaching I have heard." And then you must head toward the cave. If you don't, the cave will be just as empty as you are.

Now that is the detailed explanation of the paramitas. Certain teachings are connected to certain practices and in practice there are many different paths. When they are summarized and when the core is understood, they are all included in the realization of emptiness and great compassion. If you have the realization of emptiness together with great compassion, all the aspects of the six paramitas are complete. If you have realized emptiness, or void (or openness, as H. V. Guenther translates in Longchenpa's *Kindly Bent to Ease Us*), you have overcome all the defilements.

The medicine called *karpo chikthup* can cure any kind of disease. Similarly, if you have a true understanding of emptiness, you will have no attachments to external and internal phenomena. If you are not influenced by attachments and aversions, manifested by favoring your relatives and friends, and you avoid attacking your enemies or people you dislike, then you have completed the vow of ethics and kept the moral sense that is one of the six paramitas.

When you realize there is no self, then through emptiness you realize there is no I. Then there is no anger. Once there is no anger, you perfected patience and tolerance. When you persevere and understand the real meaning of emptiness, then the perfection of diligence and perseverance will grow by itself. When you meditate on emptiness, your mind will not be bewildered or be attracted by objects. When no objects distract you, that becomes the complete concentrated meditation. Once you have understood emptiness, that completes the primary wisdom.

Now the realization of emptiness and great compassion must be rooted in bodhichitta. As we have said, the difference between Mahayana and Hinayana is the presence or nonpresence of bodhichitta. The basic root path or the foundation of the path gets stabilized if you understand these three: bodhichitta, emptiness, and great compassion. The main foundation of Dharma is bodhichitta. Bodhichitta is the base and the offshoots are compassion and emptiness. Those are the three main things.

THE DEDICATION

Now as usual please dedicate all the merit from listening to this teaching and give the merit of this teaching to the enlightenment of all sentient beings under the wide horizon of the sky.

Questions and Answers

Q: You mentioned three foundations of Dharma. One of them is great compassion. How does great compassion differ from normal compassion?

A: At root there is no difference. Compassion says, "Let all sentient beings under the wide horizon of the sky be enlightened." And there is no other choice but to enlighten them. The only difference is in training: how much you realize or the degree of realization.

Q: I have a family and I feel responsibility for my wife and children, and for others. The question is, how does one overcome attachments to children and family?

A: Mahayana teaching is geared so people have to absolutely abandon samsaric existence and go into retreat to Dharma. Our teaching says you must leave and go. Since everyone has families, it is not possible to do that. However, it is important to see your attachment and know that your feelings and responsibilities are not only to your family and your children but to all sentient beings under the wide horizon of the sky. To enlighten them is your responsibility too. Narrowing down your responsibility to just your family is pure attachment. Your responsibility is to all sentient beings, including your children and your family. Tantric practice is like the lotus that is attached to the mud it grows in. The lotus is not tainted by the muddy water and it blooms, immaculate in color. In the same way, when you persevere in the meditation process and meditate more, it is for the enlightenment of all sentient beings, including your family, and samsaric things will not taint you.

Q: How may one find an oath that allows one to enlighten as many suffering sentient beings as possible?
A: There are many oaths to accomplish that goal. Guru yoga is one path that brings about the enlightenment of all sentient beings. Bodhichitta is the foundation of this path.

Q: What is transcended pure perception and how do we achieve it?
A: Solitude is conducive to the practice of transcended pure perception (*taknang*). It is achieved sort of spontaneously in solitude. Transcended pure perception is not pure in the material sense, but pure in the sense that you perceive all your Dharma friends not as ordinary human beings but as enlightened gods and goddesses. You see your lama as the real physical manifestation of Buddha.

Q: Is a vision of a yidam transcended pure perception or an actual sight?
A: This is the materialization of transcended pure perception. In the practice of transcended pure perception, when you see the fault of your friend, you realize this is due to impure perception. You recognize that this is not a correct perception and begin to correct it. In pure perception, you see the Dharma friend as an enlightened being, as a god or goddess. You begin to mature your perception, and once it is matured, the fruit is real pure perception: you see the true nature of existence, and even your location and your place in it is perceived as heaven. You see all these great things. That is the result of the actualization.

VAJRASATTVA PURIFICATION

THE INTENTION

As USUAL you are requested to formulate your intention, bringing all the sentient beings under the vast horizons of the sky to the realm of your mind.

THE TEACHING ON THE VAJRASATTVA MEDITATION

Today's teaching will be the Vajrasattva meditation. As we have discussed, we circle in samsara because we perpetuate adharmic actions and create bad karmas. Why is there no expansion of your experience, why is it obstructed? Your experience is obstructed by your defilements. The mirror's surface must be clean in order for it to reflect an object. Likewise, if the mind is clear of defilements, realization will shine.

There are many paths to free yourself of defilements. At this time, within our tradition, the Vajrasattva meditation is considered the most important method of releasing defilements. Defilements do not have an absolute, independent existence. That is why defilements can be dissolved through confession: making confession in the very kernel of your heart and reciting Vajrasattva mantras.

We have a tendency to recite the 100-syllable Vajrasattva mantra or visualize Vajrasattva without being fully aware of the meaning and significance of the mantras. We chant mantras more as a verbal recitation than as a meaningful practice fully integrated with and supported by the mind. If it is not supported by the mind, it is simply recitation that does not carry enough weight to absolve the defilements. It almost becomes like a habit. This is common among contemporary practitioners. Should the practice become mere habit, we might recite the text without full awareness and intention. Since intention is basic to the formation of all good and bad karma, leaving it in a neutral zone will not help to absolve defilements.

There are several kinds of defilements. One is a sort of spontaneous or natural defilement that is due to habitual behavior, such as taking the lives of lesser creatures, lying, or cheating. We are so habituated to the behavior that we are not fully conscious of each and every transgression. The second type is contrived or intentional defilement, where one consciously commits a defilement. Knowingly breaking the moral and ethical codes laid down by the great teacher Lord Buddha is that kind of defilement. For example, monks are not allowed to cut grass, because doing so prevents growth. If a monk who knows this rule mows the lawn, he breaks the code and commits a defilement. If a person has taken 250 vows and breaks the vows, he or she accumulates bad karma. The third type of defilement is in the Tantra tradition, where one has a moral responsibility to abide by the vows, the samayas. If one breaks a vow, one commits a very serious defilement and the consequences are very severe. (In Hinayana, breaking the vow of self-liberation is the primary defilement. In Mahayana, taking the bodhisattva vows and breaking them accumulates the same bad karma.) When laypeople who do not know what to acquire and what to abandon commit a defilement, the consequence is not as severe as it is for the people who know what the consequence will be.

There is no defilement that cannot be absolved by confession. Yes, we commit defilements every day. We accumulate bad karma every day. However, bad karma can be dissolved by doing the Vajrasattva meditation. If the result is good, all the defilements will be dissolved. If not, the defilements will at least lessen in intensity or thin out.

The first way to absolve yourself of defilements is by being in the mind of the lama, through the power of the lama's manifestation or representation. According to guru yoga, Vajrasattva is this powerful manifestation. The confession of your defilement should originate from bodhichitta. The second way to free yourself of defilements is by speech. You recognize that the defilements are created by your actions. Then you accept responsibility for your actions, repenting verbally and pledging that such actions will not occur again in future. Having committed a defilement, you should not hide or rationalize your actions or discount the consequence of your actions because of egoic concerns. Always offer the confession (*shaka*) with true repentance. If there is no genuine repentance, the confession by itself cannot absolve you of defilements. The third way to release defilements is through the power of vows or resolutions. After realizing that you have committed certain defilements, you make a resolution that you will not repeat those actions again in future.

There are numerous ways to release one's own defilements. If you have broken samaya with your teacher through body, speech, and mind, 100,000 prostrations is the main way to discharge the defilement. The offering of lamps or candles or food to deities is another way. Offering food to yidaks also releases the defilements, and so forth. If you do not have enough wealth to make offerings and see someone else making the offering, simply feeling joyous and content, thinking, "Let that be the supreme offering," will get you the same merit. Dedicating the merit is equally important. If you broke vows or resolutions and do ten thousand 100-syllable Vajrasattva mantras to absolve yourself of defilements, then at the end you must dedicate the merit for the enlightenment of all sentient beings.

Those are the means to absolve yourself of defilements. Now we

Guru Vajrasattva

shall discuss the recitation of the mantra while meditating and visualizing Vajrasattva.

THE VAJRASATTVA VISUALIZATION

The Vajrasattva Purification Recitation

Ah! In my ordinary form, on the crown of my head,
in the center of a white lotus and moon seat is a Hung that turns into
   Guru Vajrasattva, radiantly white, (in the form of) the sambhogakaya,
holding the vajra and bell and embracing his consort.
I implore your protection: purify my defilements.
I confess (my misdeeds) with strong repentance.
In the future, even at the cost of my life I shall abstain.
Upon a full moon, the heart letter Hung encircled by (the hundred-
   syllable) mantra;
by invoking with the recitation of mantra
from the point of union of the bliss-enjoying consorts,
a cloud of the nectar of bodhichitta descends like camphor powder.
Of myself and the sentient beings of the three realms,
the karma and mental afflictions, the causes of suffering,
our illness, harmful spirits, defilements, transgression of vows, and
   contamination
I implore you to purify without remainder.

The 100-Syllable Vajrasattva Mantra

Om! [i.e., vajra body] O Vajrasattva samaya, please grant me your
   protection.
O Vajrasattva, reside (in me).
Reside firmly in me.
Be pleased with me.

Grow within me.
Be passionate toward me.
Grant all of the siddhis as well as (the fulfillment of) all activities.
Make my mind virtuous.
Hung! [*i.e., vajra mind*]
Ha Ha Ha Ha Ho [*The laughter of joy in the four boundless attitudes,*
four wangs, four joys, and four bodies.]
O Conqueror, vajra of all the tathagatas,
do not abandon me.
Make me a vajra holder, O Great Samayasattva.
Ah! [*i.e., vajra speech—unite indivisibly into oneness.*]

The Invocation and Dissolution of the Visualization

O Protector, because of my lack of knowledge and ignorance,
I have transgressed and weakened the sacred samaya;
O Lama Protector, please give me refuge!
O Lord Vajradhara, Nature of Great Compassion, Lord of Beings, to you
I go for refuge;
I confess and acknowledge all the transgressions of the sacred samayas of
body, speech, mind, root, and branches.
Please cleanse and purify all the stains of defilements, obscurations, and
transgressions.
By praying thus, Vajrasattva, with joyfully smiling countenance [says],
"O child of noble family, all your wrongdoings, defilements, and
corruptions are cleansed."
So giving pardon, he melts into light and dissolves into me.
By this means I become Vajrasattva, apparent but empty like a reflection
in a mirror.
From the heart syllable Hung encircled by four syllables, Om Vajra Satto
Hung, rays are emitted.

Then all the beings and realms of the three worlds become enlightened in
the nature of buddhas and pure lands of five classes of Vajrasattvas.

(Repeat many times)

The meaning of each word shall be explained.

> *Ah! In my ordinary form, on the crown of my head,*
> *(Ah daknyi thamal chiwo ru)*

Ah daknyi means "myself." *Thamal* means "ordinary person." Now,
contrary to the practice of guru yoga, where you visualize yourself as
Dorjé Naljorma,[25] here you are an ordinary person, not an enlightened person. *Chiwo ru* means on top of the crown of one's head. In the
space above the crown is a lotus with many petals. It says a thousand,
but that doesn't mean you have to have exactly one thousand. It just
means numerous, a lotus with many many petals.

The text continues with the description of the lotus throne shown
in the thangka-image of Vajrasattva.

> *In the center of a white lotus and moon seat is a Hung that turns*
> *into Vajrasattva*
> *(Pekar dawa dan gyi ü)*

Pe means *padma*, lotus. *Kar* means white. *Dawa* means moon. *Dan*
means throne. *Ü* means the central top. On top of that lotus throne
is the moon throne. It is a full moon, a complete circle.

Every deity has a seed syllable. *Hri* is Chenrezik. *Hung* is for Guru
Rinpoché. There are different syllables for each deity. There are
also different colors for the five different Buddha families. *Hung*
is the white seed syllable of Vajrasattva. It turns or manifests into
Vajrasattva.

Radiantly white, [in the form of] the sambhogakaya,
(Karsal longchö jepai ku)

The color of Vajrasattva is radiant white. He manifested in the realm of sambhogakaya and is represented in the ornamentation of the sambhogakaya. The Sakaymuni who is nirmanakaya (*tulku*) form is different from the sambhogakaya (*long ku*) form that has ornaments in the headdress.

Holding the vajra and bell and embracing his consort
(Dorjé dril dzin nyem ma tril)

Vajrasattva has the vajra (indicating diamond-like spiritual firmness) in his right hand, holding it next to his chest at the center of his upper body. He holds the bell (*dril*) in his left hand, the open end of the bell facing toward his body. He is seated in the position of the *dorjé kyiltrung*. Some say it is the vajra lotus position or something like that, the soles of two feet facing upward. *Nyem ma* is the name of the consort. *Tril* means the position they are in together.

When you visualize images you should not see them as made of material things, like mud or iron or any kind of material. You should not visualize them as a painting, as a surface upon which an image has been painted. They should be visualized as a body you can perceive but that do not have a real, concrete essence. The image perceived should be like a reflection in the mirror or the reflection of the moon in water. You can see the reflection of the object in the mirror but you cannot catch or hold the reflected object. You must visualize the image in the same way, perceiving it in its full form but not as something you can grasp or hold. You should not visualize it as a human body of flesh and bones. The image should be visualized as the enlightened mind of your root lama and the collected consciousness of all the buddhas of the three times. Also, Vajrasattva should not be visualized as simply a painting out there, or a body shape out there that doesn't have any kind of feeling. He has a feeling of compassion toward all sentient beings and perceives all sentient beings through the radiant light of supreme compassion.

This visualization involves four ways of absolving. First, it dissolves defilements through the power of manifestation. Second is confessing (*khyöla kyabsol dikpa jong*).

> *We, all the sentient beings throughout the vast horizon of the sky,*
> *have been committing defilements since the very beginning*
> *and we would like to confess to you, the great Vajrasattva,*
> *without hiding, without rationalizing our defilements.*
> *To you, Vajrasattva, I will confess without hiding, confess with*
> *repentance.*

Third is taking responsibility for the mistake:

> *I will take responsibility for what I have done and admit I made a*
> *mistake.*

Fourth is making a resolution that from now on even if it costs my life, "I shall not perpetuate such action in the future."

The next line:

> *Upon a full moon in your heart*
> (*Khyö thuk dawa gyé pé teng*)

Khyöthuk refers to Vajrasattva. *Dawa gye pe teng* means the full moon in the heart center of Vajrasattva. This moon is as big as a mustard seed pressed flat. On top of this full moon disc, there is the letter *Hung* written with a line as thin as a hair of your body. On the periphery, going around in a clockwise direction, are all 100 syllables of the mantra. The letters stand up, barely but not really touching. The syllables *Om Vajrasattva samaya, manupalaya, Vajrasatto tvenopatistha, dridho mebhava…* go around the moon disc of the heart of Vajrasattva. Don't view the heart as the physical heart, but the heart of the body center.

The next line:

> *By invoking with the recitation of mantra*
> *(Depa ngak kyi gyü kulwé)*

Depa means to recite, and *ngak kyi* means reciting the stream of the mantra, which is of Vajrasattva and his consort.

> *From the point of union of the bliss-enjoying consorts*
> *(Yab yum derol jor tsham ne)*

From the joining point of the consort and Vajrasattva.

> *A cloud of the nectar of bodhichitta*
> *(Dütsi jangchup semkyi trin)*

From the rotating mantra originates the amrita, essence water, that will flow down in the bodies of Vajrasattva and his consort, and come out of their union point, and flow out to the crowns of all sentient beings.

(Again it is important that one does not localize or personalize as "my defilements," but rather see this as all the defilements of all sentient beings.) The falling of the amrita, or nectar, should be seen as camphor dust falling. After the nectar enters the body, all the diseases of the body will come out as blood and pus. All the effects from evil spirits and their possessions come out in the form of animals, such as fish, snakes, frogs, and so forth. All the defilements will come out like black smoke or smog, and everything will come out from the soles of the feet and all the cells of the body through the pores. All will come out.

> *The karma and mental afflictions, the causes of suffering,*
> (*Lé dang nyönmong duk ngal gyu*)

Lé is karma; *nyönmong* is defilements that are the seeds of suffering.

> *Our illness, harmful spirits, defilements, transgression of vows,*
>   *and contamination*
> (*Nédön dik drip nyétong drip*)

Ned is disease. *Don* is any kind of possession, effects from the evil spirits. *Drip* is the kind of effect that results in sickness. One of the most important defilements is breaking the vows (samaya) with your teacher. One begins to get sick or feel unwell. Also, there are different kinds of obscurations. Effects such as allergies to one's food or clothing or even the sunshine are due to breaking one's vows or resolutions.

Then under the surface of the earth there is Shinjé (Yamantaka, Lord of Death). He is a deity or spirit residing under the earth with his paws lifted up. All the defilements that come out of the soles of your feet and the pores of your body go into Yama's mouth.

You must visualize that everything is absolved and that all the remnants of the carryover karma are also absolved. Carryover karma is the karma of your previous life that manifests in the present. This means if you have killed a sentient being even once, you will be killed like that five hundred times. That is the manifestation of carryover karma. For example, you have never done anything bad to a person but that person is always doing something wrong to you. You are bewildered and think, "I have never done anything, never said anything bad, to him. Yet he keeps blaming me and accusing me falsely." That is because of remnant carryover karma. In your previous life, you did something bad to him and now you are facing the consequences. You should visualize and think that all the remnant karma is now being dissolved. Also that the spirits who are waiting to take revenge are now pacified and all the bad karma or defilements are dissolved. Thinking that way, you should recite the 100-syllable mantra. After that you recite the short mantra that is essential to Vajrasattva, *Om vajra sa to hung.*

It is essential that one practice every day, since it is the supreme means to absolve yourself of defilements on this path. The best result is that one discharges all the defilements. If one cannot clear all the defilements, this practice will definitely lessen them. This practice has to be done in the very kernel of your mind, realizing and taking responsibility for the adharmic action and making a sincere confession.

There is another issue in visualization I want to mention. Although everyone seems to persevere in their practice, there is one common complaint—not having a clear visualization or not having a higher realization. This complaint is common among the learned ones also. Now, how does this come about? As I mentioned, one practices Vajrasattva meditation, but most of the time the practice becomes habitual and is done in a karmic zone of neutrality that reflects your neutral activities that are neither virtuous nor nonvirtuous. The practice becomes a part of your habits rather than deeply realized. So you wander here and there, doing Vajrasattva mantras. Your eyes, distracted, dart here and there while you recite the 100-syllable mantra. You recite a lot in this manner, but there is no result. So you try to find other means, easier and more powerful means, to absolve yourself of defilements, to get some kind of strong realization right now. But you must understand that such searching is very superficial and external, oriented outwardly. A genuine result depends on your own mind that is oriented inwardly.

If you do the Vajrasattva mantra and the 100-syllable mantra with clear intention and devoted, consciously concentrated thoughts, then the practice will begin to earn virtuous karma and will begin to lessen the unvirtuous karma or the defilements. It is said that recitation of the 100-syllable mantra once in the state of samadhi, or concentration, is like reciting it 100,000 times. If you can recite the 100-syllable mantra one syllable at a time, with distinct and very clear pronunciation, and in a state of concentration, it is equal to reciting it a hundred times without distinct pronunciation and so on. It is equal to that. The result is realization and the lessening of one's own defilements.

Thus it all depends on one's own conscious effort rather than just verbal recitation. The Vajrasattva meditation acquires not only the ultimate result but the immediate result as well. It can do away with diseases or the effects of evil sprits. The disease that cannot be cured by medicine or the disease that cannot be analyzed by the doctors can be cured through the Vajrasattva meditation. There are many historical cases where, when people meditated on Vajrasattva, their diseases came out of their bodies as blood and pus; they also vomited their disease out, or got rid of their poison through vomiting blood. All sorts of things have happened.

People have healed themselves through this process, but that is not the ultimate goal. That is simply the byproduct of Vajrasattva meditation. Do not be confused by teachings on different aspects of the practice, like, for example, the meditation on taking refuge or generating bodhichitta or developing the bodhisattva mind or doing Vajrasattva mantras. All these are taught not as separate teachings but as a part of the main path, which is guru yoga.

Guru yoga is the path leading to the ultimate realization and experience. It is like the sun or the ultimate essence that is within you. Like the sun in the sky on a cloudy day, we cannot see it because the sky is overcast and cloudy. It's the same with your own true nature, your enlightened nature that has been covered by defilements. In order to drive away the clouds covering the sun—that is, to drag out the defilements and dissolve them in the face of your true nature—this Vajrasattva meditation is required and necessary. It is like wanting to go to a higher floor of a house. First, you open the door and walk in, then you go up the stairs for the upper floors. This is also the process of ultimate realization, the ultimate opening to the true nature, or the opening up to the real sun.

A person having all the limbs needed for the survival is different from a person who is deprived of those limbs. A person having one arm is different from a person having both arms. The capacity for action is different. Likewise, the path that has all the necessary limbs can lead to the ultimate realization.

This Vajrasattva meditation, like the meditation on taking refuge or bodhichitta, can be a path in itself. However, at this time, it is a limb of the main path or a part of the mainstream path that can lead you to the ultimate realization.

THE DEDICATION

Today the teaching on the Vajrasattva ends. As usual, please dedicate all the merits from hearing the teaching for the enlightenment of all sentient beings.

MANDALA OFFERING

THE TEACHING

The earth anointed with perfumed water and strewn with flowers,
Mount Meru and the four continents ornamented with the sun
* and moon,*
by offering them visualized as a buddhafield,
may all sentient beings enjoy the pure land.

WHY WE MUST COMPLETE THE PRELIMINARY PRACTICE

We offer the mandala to earn merits and do away with defilements. This is a very important practice for accumulating merits and eliminating defilements.

To attain full enlightenment, one has to accomplish both the virtues with thought and the virtues without thought. We accomplish these virtues in three ways: earning merit, abandoning or dissolving defilements, and coming into contact with the compassionate powers of the lama. At this level of teaching the mandala offering, we try to acquire the three aspects of earning virtuous merit, eliminating the defilements, and being in touch with the compassionate heart of the realized lama.

There are varieties of ways to offer the mandala. At this point, it is not really necessary to explain the very detailed mandala offering. I myself do not know that much about Dharma. However, at the request of my students I try to teach this doctrine. These days, everybody wants to practice and likes to have the Dzokchen teaching, which, however, cannot be given like doses of medicine.

I taught the Ngöndro Dharma practice last year. The Tibetan term *ngöndro* means going ahead. It is an essential practice that must be fully accomplished before enlightenment can be reached. Ngöndro practice is the root of enlightenment, and the practice must be rooted deep within the very kernel of our hearts. Now, since Ngöndro is the condensed teaching that we can apply without neglecting any of Buddha's teachings, perhaps many of you think the preliminary practice is over and it is time for Dzokchen. However, it is not that easy. It is important that one knows Ngöndro very well. The preliminary practice of guru yoga somehow must be grafted onto or integrated with one's nature and have affected one's mind. It must be fully accomplished. Only then can one be firmly established on the path to receive the Dzokchen practice. Without that, the meditative experience cannot be achieved in full strength. Without Ngöndro as a basis, other practices will bring obstacles, not enlightenment.

As I've mentioned, the detailed version of Ngöndro, or the preliminary practice, is vast (according to Kunsang Lamai Shalung). It takes months and months to complete the teaching and one needs a lot of free time. However, in general people these days do not have vast amounts of free time. Given our time constraints, we are trying our best to take one section of the teaching at a time every few days. Once one gets the teaching on the preliminary practice, it is inappropriate to say, "Now I know it very well." But it is appropriate to say, "Now I am aware of it."

An incomplete sequence of practice is like a person without complete sense organs. Not having one eye will hinder a person. That's what will happen if one does not get the complete sequence of the teachings. Our inability to take the full course of teachings will affect our experience. Because of our incomplete practice, we will not be able to further our realization. Then we begin to look for faults. We begin to find faults in the teaching or the teacher rather than inside of one's own mind. Thus one becomes dissatisfied. It is analogous to driving on an interstate highway and missing your exit. You have to go a long distance before you can turn around and come back to the exit you wanted, and the way back to that exit is not straightforward and easy. The effect of doing only the incomplete sequence of the teaching is similar. If the preliminary teaching or the path of the meditation is not fully complete, it will be difficult for you to have a thorough realization. It can also cause great harm to one's life.

THE MANDALA OFFERING

Now for the mandala offering. The base of the mandala is like a plate that is placed upside down. When you make the mandala offering, you rub the base as if you are cleaning it. You are not cleaning dirt, you are cleaning your thoughts. You are cleaning out all the defilements and unvirtuous thoughts. With such intention, you rub the base of the mandala with your hand. This mandala offering is called *tsawa dunma* ("constructed with seven heaps of rice").

The first line:

> *The earth anointed with perfumed water and strewn with flowers,*
> (*Sashi puchuk shing metok tram*)

Meaning, the earth anointed with incenses, water, and strewn with flowers.

Mount Meru and the four continents ornamented with the sun
   and moon,
(Rirab lingshi nyidé gyenpa)

Ri rab is Mount Meru at the center of the base, the front of which faces east. Mount Meru has four faces—the eastern, southern, western, and northern faces—each of a different precious substance. *Ling zhi* means the four main continents of the universe, facing in the three remaining directions. With Mount Meru in the center, the sun is high up in the east and the moon is high up in the west. *Nyi de gyen pa* means ornamented with the sun and the moon. Thus Mount Meru, the four continents, and the sun and moon compose the seven major aspects of the mandala. All three thousandfold universes of this mandala, empty in nature, are offered as the Dharma field. Visualize it as the pure region of all the buddhas and offer it, the east side of the mandala facing oneself.

The last line:

By offering them visualized as a buddhafield,
may all sentient beings enjoy the pure land.

All perceptions are pristine in their primordial nature. They are pure. All these absolutely pristine perceptions are not made at this moment but originated from the Dharma realm from beginningless time. That's the mandala offering.

THE TEACHING TRADITION AND RITUAL CEREMONY

Although we are doing a shorter practice, it is good to be aware of the tradition. As I mentioned earlier, in Tibet, monastery lamas have to learn for years and all ceremonies are performed with great care as a continuous stream within the tradition.

Once there was a lama who had a head monk, a *chöpön*, who pre-pared altars and made tormas.[26] The lama was ready to perform the ceremony but the chöpön had forgotten to make a torma. The lama had bad eyesight and had trouble seeing. So the chöpön dipped his finger in butter, put the plate in front of it, and raised his finger. Since the lama couldn't see well, he assumed it was a torma standing upright on the plate. The chöpön then offered the plate, saying "Here is the torma." The lama said, "OK," and dedicated the torma to the spirits. Soon thereafter the chöpön caught leprosy and lost his finger. Because such consequences can happen, you have to be careful.

Here is another example demonstrating the necessity of following tradition carefully. Some of you have gone to Nepal and Sikkim and must have seen the god's eye. In the Dharma tradition we make an elaborate god's eye with string, or weave strings to make a kind of house for a spirit to come in. Lamas will invoke the spirits in that woven structure. Once they are invoked, they are asked to leave.

The structure has to be woven and set in a particular way, with cor-rect color combinations. You cannot innovate or improvise in any way. One time a chöpön wove a structure and the lama asked, "It seems the spirits are having a tough time getting into the house. Are you sure you wove it right?" The chöpön said, "There was no mistake." But the lama responded, "There is something that is troubling them. They are unable to go inside." Later they found that the chöpön wove the structure in the wrong way. If you do not do things properly, as they should be, there are real consequences of that nature.

As for offerings on altars: this ritual also has great significance. The tradition is not just to set a few bowls in front of the altar; it has a deeper meaning. The first level of the altar is the exterior offering. There are seven offerings: water for drinking and washing, flowers for the eyes, incense for the nose, a light or lamp for the eyes to see, perfume for smell, food for the mouth, and music for the ear. In esoteric practice the interior offering will include medicine, blood, and tormas. This should be done according to the empowerment. Sometimes in an invocation and offering ceremony, for example, the medicines and blood are offered to the deities.

If you are not careful while you are offering and if you happen to drop something where you are not supposed to, it can create bad consequences. The arrangement of the offering should be complementary to the sequence of the path. My insisting on having the altar set properly is so that we can arrange all the offerings appropriately. The exterior offering comes on the lowest level, according to the path. The interior offering comes on a higher level, and so forth. You have to place the offering according to the sequence of the path. Also, in setting the altar, it is better that you do not put your picture or anybody's picture on the altar. I have insisted that my picture not be put on the altar, but here someone did it. It is important that one does not put one's picture on the altar.

At one time in India, there was a tradition to worship one's own parents. They used to put the dead bodies of their parents in a coffin and worship the remains as a form of respect. Maudgalyayana, one of the closest disciples of Buddha, visited the realm of hell and found these people burning in hell. They requested Maudgalyayana to tell their living relatives not to make offerings to their dead bodies. Whenever their relatives burned the lamp for the offering, the people in the hell realm received a shower of fire, scorching them. They told Maudgalyayana, "Whenever they make offerings we are burned. Please tell them not to do that." So Maudgalyayana came back and, hesitating a bit, told the Hindu teacher that relatives in hell sent a message to not make offerings because such offerings caused them suffering. The Hindu thought this Buddhist lama was trying to insult their teaching. So they beat him almost to death.

It is all right to put a picture of Dudjom Rinpoché on the altar. However, if you put a picture of someone else and if a bodhisattva or a great lama comes and worships at that altar, it will diminish your karma and result in a bad consequence for you. We don't put pictures on the altar because ordinary people will not recognize an extraordinary person, like a bodhisattva or a true incarnate, although an incarnate person recognizes ordinary persons. But if he happens to bow to that ordinary person, that would diminish him and bring bad consequences to the ordinary person, diminishing all his virtue. Since we, as ordinary persons, cannot recognize or judge an extraordinary person, it's better not to put your picture or anyone else's on the altar. That's why you must not put a picture of anybody else on the altar. You might think you are paying respect, but ultimately you might be doing harm to them and yourself.

PART 4

The Practice: Merging with Guru Rinpoché

THE VISUALIZATION

One's perceptions spontaneously arise as the totally pure land,
the fully arrayed Glorious Copper-Colored Mountain.
In the center visualize one's own body as the holy Vajrayogini,
with one head and two hands, transparently red, holding a curved blade;
her two legs are in the "advancing posture" and her three eyes gaze up
   into space.
On the moon and sun within the blossoming hundred-thousand-petaled
   lotus seat on the crown of her head,
inseparable from one's tsawai lama, the union of the refuges,
is the emanation body of Tsokyé Dorjé (Padmasambhava).
His complexion is white with pinkish hue, a youthful appearance.
He is attired in a gown, monastic robe, brocade cape, and inner gown.
With one face and two hands, he sits in the royal playful posture.
In the right hand he holds a vajra and in the left a skull cup containing
   a vase.
He wears the lotus hat on his head.
In the cleft of his left arm he holds his divine consort, embodying the unity
   of bliss and emptiness,
concealed in the form of a sacred trident.
He sits amidst rainbow rays and auras of radiant light.
In the outer perimeter, in the vastness of the exquisite lattice of five
   colored lights

(are seated) the twenty-five emanation disciples: the king and subjects;
the spiritual scholars and sages, knowledge-holders of India and Tibet;
*   and tutelary deities,*
dakinis, dharmapalas, vow-holders: all are gathered together like
*   a cloud.*
Visualize them in the state of the great equanimity of luminescence
*   and emptiness.*

In the center of Guru Rinpoché's region, the Copper-Colored Mountain (Zangdok Palri), the pure land that is complete with all the qualities of heaven, or the region of the Buddha, visualize one's own body as the holy Vajrayogini (Rang Nyi Shilu). This line means my body of flesh and blood is Dorjé Naljorma, the essence or the true nature of Yeshé Tsogyal.

Visualizing one's nature as Dorjé Naljorma originates from the fact that Yeshé Tsogyal is the secret consort of Guru Rinpoché. In order to be blessed, one transforms one's true nature, one's essence, into the form of Yeshé Tshogyal. She stands on the throne of lotus. Her body is red in color and in her left hand she holds the knife that cuts off the roots of poisons. Her raised right hand plays a drum that awakens the beings from the ignorance and confusion. She has three eyes looking ahead , as if looking toward the heart of the tsawai lama.[27]

In the front space, visualize the lotus. On top of the lotus is the sun throne. On top of the sun is the moon and on top of the moon is Guru Rinpoché. Guru Rinpoché has one face. On his right hand he holds a five-spoke dorjé at his heart. His left hand is placed on his lap and on his palm is a vase that has the amrita of deathlessness. On his left side is a trident. He wears a hat with a five-petal lotus shape. This visualized image is called "samaya deity" (*damtsikpa*). Surrounding Guru Rinpoché are rainbow-colored radiant lights. Around him are circular disc lights of rainbow color with eight rikzins, the supreme

Dorjé Naljorma

knowledge-holders, like Hungkara, Shantigarbha, Nagarjuna, and so forth.[28]

On the outskirt of that gathering are eighty-four siddhas, like Saraha, Naropa, Tilopa, and so forth. And then come twenty-five disciples, twenty-five siddhas of Tibet, and also the great saints, scholars, and panditas of Tibet and India.[29]

Outside of that are the dakinis Vajrasadhu, Ekajati, and Rahula, and so forth, who are the protectors of Dharma.[30] All other protectors and other dakinis who surround this visualized gathering are like the clouds in the sky. They are not made out of the aggregated organism or the elements—that is, the flesh and the body, but the bodies of radiant lights.

THE INVITATION

THE SEVEN-LINE PRAYER

HUNG! In the northwest of the country of Oddiyana,
(born) on the pistil stem of a lotus,
endowed with the marvelous supreme attainment,
renowned as the Lotus-Born,
surrounded by a retinue of many dakinis,
following you, I shall practice.
Please come and bless (me), Guru Padma Siddhi Hung.

THE SEVEN-LINE PRAYER will invoke Guru Rinpoché to the place. While you are reciting the prayer, visualize Guru Rinpoché coming down from the lotus palace on the Copper-Colored Mountain. Visualize Guru Rinpoché as the samaya deity in front of you. This visualized image descending from Copper-Colored Mountain is called the "wisdom deity" (*yeshepa*, Skt. *jnana*).

Guru Rinpoché

ACCUMULATION OF MERIT

THE SEVEN PRACTICES FOR THE ACCUMULATION OF MERIT

My body, as numerous as the atoms in the universe,
by emanating, I offer prostrations to you.
The material offerings are well set out, and the mental offerings emanated
*   by meditative power;*
all phenomenal existents as the form of the offering, I offer to you.
All my demeritorious karma committed through the three entrances I
*   confess in the state of the luminous dharmakaya.*
Within the sphere of the two truths, I rejoice in the entire accumulation of
*   merits.*
I request you to set into motion the Dharma wheel of three vehicles.
Until the emptying of samsara, I pray you not to go into nirvana.
All the merits accumulated in the three periods of time, I dedicate to the
*   purpose of the great enlightenment.*

THE PRAYER for the seven practices for the accumulation of merit is the prayer for prostrations. At this time you invoke Guru Rinpoché, who appeared and became one with the visualized guru; also all the retinue as wide and vast as an ocean. In front of this vast ocean-like visualization or manifestation, you begin to recite:

My body, as numerous as the atoms in the universe,
by emanating, I offer prostrations to you.
(Daklü shing gi dulnyé tu, nampar trulpé chak tsal lo)

Basically, the meaning is that by emanating oneself as innumerable bodies as numerous as the dust of this earth, you prostrate to Guru Rinpoché and the gathering. At the same time you visualize your present father on the right side and your present mother on the left side of Guru Rinpoché, while in front of Guru Rinpoché you visualize your present enemies and all sentient beings under the wide horizon of the sky. Together, all bow to Guru Rinpoché.

This is the first of the seven practices for the accumulation of merit. There are great, detailed explanations of the offering that we cannot go into right at this moment. However, it is important to realize that without earning merit, it is difficult to see one's own true nature or attain enlightenment.

The next practice:

The material offerings are well set out, and the mental offerings
emanated by meditative power;
all phenomenal existents as the form of the offering, I offer to you.

The first offering is the offering of real objects (*ngösham*), like the offering of water, lamps, and incense—materials you can perceive. Those objects that invoke joy and happiness, or the objects you are attracted to, those objects become the offering.

Then the next offering is the transformation of one's mind. Visualize those phenomena or objects that are beautiful and attractive to one's eye, that invoke happiness and joy. Bring those things into the realm of your mind and offer to all the buddhas of the ten directions, and let the offerings spread. Let these offerings be so vast an expanse that they cover all of existence and all the planets and the universes.

The third practice:

All my demeritorious karma committed through the three entrances
I confess in the state of the luminous dharmakaya.

This is doing away with one's own defilements or sins, in Buddhist terms, all the defilements that one committed through three
entrances or three doors, which are body, speech, and mind. All these
can be absolved through the radiant light emitted from the gathering
of all enlightened ones. The detailed practice of how to release one's
defilements was taught in the Vajrasattva meditation. At this time
one generates ways of thinking that were discussed in the Vajrasattva
meditation.

The fourth of the seven practices is:

Within the sphere of the two truths, I rejoice in the entire accumula-
tion of merits.

This is to be content or happy or to rejoice in the merits and actions
of others. For example, if other people perform dharmic actions,
instead of being jealous, be content and share joy with them (*jesu*
yirang). *Jesu* means after the completion of the action by somebody
else. *Yirang* means to be content or fulfilled in mind by being content
and satisfied with the action.

The fifth practice:

I request you to set into motion the Dharma wheel of three vehicles.

A request for all the buddhas, the countless buddhas of the planet, to
turn the wheel of Dharma. There are countless buddhas. There were
times when enlightened buddhas did not preach their doctrine. It was
true of Shakyamuni Buddha. After he was enlightened, he did not

preach for forty-nine days. Then Lhatsangpo and Gyashin offered lots of mandalas to him. Making offerings, they requested him to turn the wheel of Dharma. So this is the request for all the buddhas and countless buddhas in existence to turn the wheel of Dharma for the benefit of all sentient beings.

The sixth practice is:

Until the emptying of samsara, I pray you not to go into nirvana.

There are many enlightened buddhas who have absolute power over their destinations or absolute power over death. However, in order to create a sense of sorrow among untamed sentient beings, they disappeared from this earth. This is to request them to live as long as possible by turning the Wheel of Dharma and benefiting all sentient beings.

The seventh practice is the dedication:

All the merits accumulated in the three periods of time, I dedicate to the purpose of the great enlightenment.

The merit that I and others have earned in the past, present, and future, let all these merits be dedicated for the enlightenment of all sentient beings.

THE INVOCATION OF
GURU RINPOCHÉ

Revered Lord, Precious Teacher,
you are of all buddhas the glorious unity of compassion and blessings,
the only protector of all beings.
My body, possessions, mind, and heart,
I offer to you without hesitation.
From now until I attain enlightenment,
in all happiness and suffering, good and bad, high and low,
great revered Lord Padmasambhava, please watch over me.
I have no others to depend upon.
Beings of the present dark age are sinking in the mire of unbearable
  misery.
O Great Guru, protect us from this.
Blessed One, transmit the fourfold empowerment;
Compassionate One, elevate our realization;
Powerful One, purify the two obscurations in us.
When the end of my life comes,
may my perceptions become Ngayab Palri,
the manifested buddhafield in which my body becomes Vajrayogini,
a light body of brilliant radiance.
From the revered Lord Padmasambhava, inseparable, may I attain
  buddhahood.

By the power of bliss and emptiness, [may I] display of great wisdom.
For all the sentient beings in the three samsaric worlds,
to be the sacred guide of liberation,
Jetsun Pema, please empower me.
I pray to you from the center of my heart,
not just by mouthing words.
Grant blessings from the depth of your wisdom mind.
Please fulfill my aspirations.

ENLIGHTENMENT MEANS to understand or to see that enlightened part of your mind and your nature. Attaining enlightenment depends on two aspects. The first is the blessing of the lama. The second is the devotion and the confidence or trust of the student. The cause and effect relationship will bring about enlightenment.

In terms of his wisdom, your own lama is equal to all the buddhas. But in terms of his beneficence, he is more than the buddhas. That is because at this present time we do not have the fortune to see the buddhas. In order to reach supreme enlightenment, one must depend on the spiritual instruction of the lama. Only through the blessings and the spiritual instruction of the lama can one experience absolute realization. Therefore, in quality and in wisdom, the lama is equal to the buddhas. However, in reality, the lama is more beneficial than the buddhas for immediate enlightenment.

Here, *Revered Lord, Precious Teacher* is identified with Guru Rinpoché, who is one's own tsawai lama, the collected manifestation of all the blessings and the compassionate heart of all the buddhas. Then you make a pledge with the following thought: "Lama, who is one with and is identified with Guru Rinpoché, with one pointed mind, I vow and serve you and pray to you."

The next lines are:

Beings of the present dark age are sinking in the mire of
  unbearable misery.
O Great Guru, protect us from this.
Blessed One, transmit the fourfold empowerment;
Compassionate One, elevate our realization;
Powerful One, purify the two obscurations in us.

This means all sentient beings at the present degenerating time are trapped in a quagmire of defilements. In order to free them, absolute power is invested in Guru Rinpoché, who is one's own tsawai lama. Through the power of one's compassionate heart, ask Guru Rinpoché: "Please help me in my ups and downs while pursuing the path of this enlightenment."

The next lines are:

When the end of my life comes,
may my perceptions become Ngayab Palri,
the manifested buddhafield in which
my body becomes Vajrayogini,
a light body of brilliant radiance;
from the revered Lord Padmasambhava, inseparable, may I attain
  buddhahood.
By the power of bliss and emptiness, [may I] display of great wisdom.
For all the sentient beings in the three samsaric worlds,
to be the sacred guide of liberation,
Jetsun Pema, please empower me.
I pray to you from the center of my heart,
not just by mouthing words.
Grant blessings from the depth of your wisdom mind.
Please fulfill my aspirations.

When it's time for you to die, when the time for death comes, let yourself be transformed into the form of Dorjé Naljorma that blends into one's own heart. And in that one taste, let all desires and prayers be answered.

THE MANTRA RECITATION

Om Ah Hung Vajra Guru Padma Siddhi Hung
(repeat many times)

THE INVOCATION and praise prayer is followed by the recitation of
Guru Rinpoché's mantra. This includes the request and the response
of Guru Rinpoché to all sentient beings.

THE FOUR EMPOWERMENTS

THE VASE EMPOWERMENT

From the syllable Om [white], like a shining crystal in the center of the
*   forehead of Guru Rinpoché, rays are projected.*
They penetrate the crown of my head, cleansing the defilements of the
*   actions of the body and channels;*
I obtain the blessings of the ajra body,
I receive the vase empowerment and become the vessel of the development
*   stage.*
The seed is sown of "attainment with karmic residue."
In my mind is placed the capacity for attaining the state of nirmanakaya.

FROM THE MIDDLE of the forehead of Guru Rinpoché, between two eyebrows, originates the letter *Om*, white in color. White radiant light enters the crown of your head, where your hairs go in a circle. Through that light, the defilement that one has committed through one's body will absolve, and it also purifies one's psychic veins. All the blessings of the body manifestation will be empowered in you. Then one will be in a potential state of being incarnate or a physical manifestation.

THE SECRET EMPOWERMENT

From the syllable Ah shining like a ruby in the throat [of Guru Rinpoché],
    rays are projected.
They penetrate my throat, purifying the defilements of the karmas of speech
    and the wind;
the blessings of the vajra speech enter me.
I receive the secret empowerment and become the vessel of recitation.
The seed is sown of "attainment of control over life."
In my mind is placed the capacity for attaining the state of sambhogakaya.

Now from the throat of Guru Rinpoché, the letter *Ah*, red in color. From that letter originates a radiant red light that enters your own throat. Through this light, unvirtuous karma earned through speech will be purified. Also the winds of one's body will be purified. Then you will be blessed with vajra voice or speech, becoming the vessel to be able to recite mantras. You have the potential to become a vessel of recitation, the power to attain that state.

THE WISDOM EMPOWERMENT

From the sky-colored syllable Hung in the heart [of Guru Rinpoché],
    rays are projected.
They penetrate my heart, purifying the defilements of the karmas
    of mind and essence.
The blessings of the vajra mind enter me.
I receive the wisdom empowerment and become the vessel of bliss-emptiness
    heart yoga.
The seed is sown of "attainment of mahamudra."
In my mind is placed the capacity for attaining the state of dharmakaya.

Then from the heart of Guru Rinpoché, the letter *Hung* originates in light, and that touches one's heart. All the unvirtuous karma of one's own mind is absolved. One receives the blessings of the hearts of all the buddhas. Also one's nature receives the power to become dharmakaya.

The Empowerment of Verbal Indication

Again from the Hung in the heart [of Guru Rinpoché],
a second Hung bursts out like a meteor and mixes indistinguishably
    with my own mind,
purifying intellectual defilements and the karma of the universal ground.
The blessings of the vajra wisdom enter me.
I receive the absolute empowerment indicated by words and become the
    vessel of the primordially pure Great Perfection.
The seed is sown of "attainment of spontaneous accomplishment."
In my mind is placed the capacity for attaining the state of
    svabhavikakaya.

Again, from the same *Hung*, a second *Hung* originates and becomes one with one's own mind. Karma/deeds of the universal ground and intellectual obscurations are purified. One becomes a vessel to be able to practice Dzokchen. One receives the power to attain the ultimate supreme enlightenment.

THE DISSOLUTION OF THE VISUALIZATION

Finally, from the heart of the lama [Guru Rinpoché] a warm red light is
  suddenly emitted,
and just by its touching the heart of myself visualized as Vajrayogini,
I become a ball of red light
that dissolves into the heart of Guru Rinpoché
and unites inseparably as one taste.
(Remain in the ultimate nature)

THEN A RED LIGHT, which has the nature or quality of warmth, originates from Guru's heart. It touches the heart of oneself, who is Dorjé
Naljorma. Then this light, at the instant of touching the heart of
Dorjé Naljorma, becomes a disc of red light. It blends with the Guru's
heart, which is the essence of collected compassionate power of all the
buddhas. It is not like a shooting star. It doesn't hit but gently blends
with Guru Rinpoché. And one should remain in that empty state
without thoughts. All thoughts should be abandoned. One should be
one with the mind of Guru Rinpoché who is the collected essence of
all the buddhas.

As for *Remain in the ultimate nature*: According to the text of Palden
Tsawai Lama Rinpoché, this refers to the practice at night. After guru

yoga, before going to sleep, visualize the lotus in one's heart. That lotus is Guru Rinpoché. Its essence is one with one's own tsawai lama.

In daytime it is better to visualize Guru Rinpoché as the object of worship, the lotus Guru Rinpoché who is one with one's own tsawai lama. In the daytime, he is on top of the crown of your head. At night, the lotus Guru Rinpoché is in one's heart.

Following the prayer, recite the binding obligation between the lama and the disciple, not breaking the honest relationship of samaya between the lama and the student, and the responsibility of the student to the lama. This is followed by the dedication.

PART 5

Dedication of Merit and Prayer of Aspiration

Glorious Root Lama, Precious One,
dwell on the lotus seat on the crown of my head;
look upon me with the grace of your great compassion.
Grant me the attainment of body, speech, and mind.
Just as the bodhisattva Manjushri attained his realization,
and likewise Samantabhadra.
In order to train myself to follow after them,
I dedicate these merits (for the enlightenment of all sentient beings).
Beings, infinitely numerous as the limitless sky,
may they attain the Trikaya[31] without any effort;
and the beings of the six realms, (all of them) my fathers and mothers
   without exception,
together may they reach their primordial state.
May the life of the glorious Lama be stable;
may joy and happiness arise for all the sky-like (endless) beings.
May I and others without exception accomplish the merits and purify
   our defilements,
and may we swiftly attain buddhahood.
The doctrine of Longchen Rabjam, the unique ornament adorning the
teachings of the Buddha,
of Jikmé Lingpa, the master of teaching and practice,
and of the peerless Lama, until the end of samsara,

may it be maintained by teaching and practice, by hearing, pondering, and
*   meditation.*
In the state where appearances, sounds, and thoughts are divinities, man-
*   tras, and dharmakaya,*
by totally merging with the display of divine forms and wisdom,
may I unite with the profound and secret practice of Great Yoga
and become "one taste" with the heart essence (of the buddhas).

LONG-LIFE PRAYER OF THE FOURTH DODRUPCHEN RINPOCHÉ

By the power of the ocean-like infallible refuges,
may Jikmé Thupten Trinlé Palbar's
lotus feet remain indestructible and stable for a hundred eons,
and may he accomplish his vast wishes for the doctrine and beings.

This concludes the teaching of guru yoga. As we do every time, please
bring all sentient beings within the realm of your mind and dedicate
the merit we have earned by receiving the teaching for the enlightenment of all sentient beings.

RINPOCHÉ'S CLOSING STATEMENT

I WANT TO thank you for persevering in your efforts. The hardship was not without any result. The hardship did bear some fruit. Mostly the work was aided by the sincere and honest ethical bond between the lama and the student and between students themselves.

Within samsara we have to have lots of hardship. We have to face hardship in order to get anywhere. But all that hardship within samsara is essenceless. At this time, having done a lot together and gone through a lot together, there is some kind of essence that is complementary to the Dharma path. The hardship has established Dharma quite firmly in this land. The seat of the Dharma has become firmer. And if you look at your own lives, conditions have improved. One progresses a long way with persistent study. When you look into your own light, you see immediate effects. Everything goes by way of karma. Everything is shaped by karma, as well as by virtuous merit. Both are important to one's development and the development of others. It comes about through your efforts and by keeping good relationships.

Always understand and keep in mind karma. What result did one's actions produce; what was the karmic effect? As for Dharma, learn what to acquire and what to abandon. One's actions should be guided by this knowledge. Never react to others' actions or justify an action of yours based on what someone else has done. Always look for guidance from the Dharma. Remember that the practice of Dharma is not only to accomplish immediate goals but to attain ultimate enlightenment.

When practicing Dharma, it is important that you tone down your ego. If being a practitioner causes you to become more egotistic, then you have only succeeded in adding one more poison, the poison of ego, on top of what you already have. Dharma practice is not an object to sell. It is not an object to show. It is done to help one's own nature. Listening to the teaching is done to guide one's attitude. The meditation on the teaching is done to affect one's mind, to tone down or to eliminate the poison of one's own mind. Dharma practice is completely for oneself, not to tell others what to do.

Telling others what to do is like having lots of medicine and, without taking any yourself, showing it off to everyone, saying, "Well, I got the medicine. I got the medicine." All you have done is to show off the medicine. But the effect of the medicine is in taking it, not just piling it on your table and showing off. If you don't take the medicine, you still have the disease. By taking it seriously and using it yourself, you get rid of the disease and the defilements that are the poisons. Anyone can practice Dharma because Dharma shows what to acquire and what to abandon. By toning down one's ego, one practices anonymously and will achieve one's goal.

Questions and Answers

Q: What are the ten directions?
A: Directions are things like north and south that you can find in magnetic fields, the four cardinal directions being north, south, east, and west.

Q: Is each direction the consciousness of mind?
A: It cannot be said that eight directions are consciousnesses. Direc-

tions are directions, and consciousness is consciousness. They are separate things and cannot be blended.

Q: The lotus is on top of your head with Guru Rinpoché facing you?

A: It is above the crown of your head, not touching the head but above the crown of the head, in the space in front of you with Guru facing you.

Q: After dissolving the visualization, does Rinpoché recommend sitting long?

A: Yes, it is necessary to stay for a longer period of time if you can. With this preliminary practice it is very difficult to get the feel of the state of mind without conceptual thoughts. The teaching of staying empty of thoughts is another whole path.

Q: Are the bum nga practices included in guru yoga? Are you thinking of those five practices?

A: Before you do guru yoga, you have the four contemplations and so forth. The five aspects—such as taking refuge, the intention, the mandala offering, and the 100-syllable mantra and prostrations—are completed before guru yoga.

Q: At some point Rinpoché mentions there are prostrations. During taking refuge and guru yoga, at these points, is it appropriate to do prostrations or do we just visualize the prostrating attitude?

A: People doing the easier Ngöndro do the prostration while doing the taking refuge. Those who have lots of time (this varies from monastery to monastery) can do prostrations during the seven-line prayer and at the end of the seven-line prayer.

Q: Does one prostration to each seven-line prayer take a long time?
A: You don't have to keep count of the seven-line prayer, just count the prostrations.

Q: Rinpoché, please say something about the effect of the mandala offering, at the fifth line.
A: That is the Sanskrit mantra that condenses the four previous lines of the mantra.

Q: Rinpoché, please say something about the symbolism of Guru Rinpoché's five-pronged dorjé and skullcap.
A: The five-pronged dorjé symbolizes the possession of the five supreme wisdoms (mirror-like wisdom, wisdom of equanimity, all-discriminating wisdom, all-accomplishing wisdom, and wisdom of dharmadhatu). Guru Rinpoché is the real manifestation or embodiment of the five supreme wisdoms. Within the skull is a vase that contains the nectar of immortality. That nectar was accomplished near Nepal, in Miratika where Guru Rinpoché stayed in a cave. There, he achieved the accomplishment of the power over life and death (*chimé tsewa rikzin*), which is one of the four rigdzins. So the nectar of such accomplishment is in that vase.

Q: Is that literally the nectar of immortality, or does it symbolize something?
A: It means Guru Rinpoché is free of death or any cause of death. It symbolizes his immortality.

Q: During the process of the four wangs (the four empowerments), when the light rays penetrate the body, speech, and mind, what is the visualization?
A: As commonly happens when visualizing the second light coming, the first light phases out of your mind, meaning you can't keep it

clearly distinctive. One should not be concerned with either its being there or its elimination. One should be concerned with the visualization being as spacious as possible. One must know the space. It's not like wanting to fit something in a very small cupboard and having to be concerned about the size of the thing. The nature of the mind is not the same. The nature of the mind is spacious. One can visualize the whole universe filled with lights within the realm of one's mind, it's so spacious. During the meditation you must realize it is not a limited space or jammed. It is wide and spacious. So meditate spaciously.

Q: This is true for the prostration also. Visualizing your mother and father. It should be very spacious?
A: Yes, that's true. You must visualize spaciously when you do the prostrations. There are practices within the visualization that allow a wide expansion of the mind. You have to expand the mind as wide as possible. Also, there is a time to visualize all three empty worlds. To visualize three universes in one mustard seed. All these are infinitely expandable. That is their nature.

Q: When an obstacle arises, like painful knees, should one include that experience in the spaciousness?
A: My knees also hurt when I do the prostration, becoming very sore. Lamas encouraged me to keep on going, though. I remember the life story of Milarepa, who carried stones under the command of his teacher, demonstrating so much perseverance. We are so protective of our body. The minute our knee hurts or gets irritated, we begin to have self-pity and think, "I am fatigued and it hurts," and all that. We make rationalizations. So you must persevere and endure. Through endurance you purify defilements.

Q: In the dedication of merit and prayer of aspiration, what is the meaning of the fourth line from the last line: *Nangtra riksum lha ngak chökui ngang?* The meaning is "Appearance, sound, and perception being in the state of divinities, mantras, and dharmakaya."

A: *Nang* means perception, what you see. *Trag* means sound. *Rik* means knowledge. Whatever you see is transformed into enlightened gods. Whatever you hear, which is the sound *ngak*, is the sound of Dharma. Whatever is understood within one's self—*chöku*, knowledge—is the dharmakaya. After this transformation, after merging totally with the display of the divine form and wisdom (Kudang Yeshé Rolpar Jamlepé), there is nothing else. But *yeshé* means the supreme wisdom.

DODRUPCHEN RINPOCHÉ'S TALK
TO MAHASIDDHA MEMBERS

In 2010 Rinpoché visited the Mahasiddha Nyingmapa Center in Hawley, Massachusetts, for the summer. This short teaching he gave before his departure was translated by Tulku Thondup and lightly edited for this edition of *Liberation from Samsara*.

The Mahasiddha Nyingmapa Center was started in 1973, almost forty years ago. Lots of contributions were needed to start the center, your own contributions and those of others, of friends. We need friends to help one another. So we all did our best and we all had the aspiration to do Dharma. That was our intention, to establish the center and do Dharma. We all contributed our best and it satisfied my mind. Everyone must now keep trying to work as one person, as one mind, in terms of Dharma practice. That is very important and that is satisfying for me.

Today we did the aspirations. The aspirations are always important. As you know, doing them in the right way has inconceivable benefits. And we did wonderful aspirations today. It made my mind happy and satisfied.

So we are all Dharma practitioners. We are here to practice Dharma. In order to practice Dharma, you need to study in order to learn (*thöpa*), you need to ponder and think about (*sampa*) what you have learned, and you need to do the meditation (*gompa*) on what you have learned from the teaching. Those are the three most important things for anyone who wants to practice Dharma.

All these years you have relied on me as the teacher. So I started teaching and we learned Dharma. In general, however, it is not easy just to practice Dharma, because we need a livelihood, we need to earn our living. Even though I myself am supposed to be a lama, a teacher, I also have to make a living because I have to eat. We cannot abandon our daily lives but we can still try to practice and also have a healthy secular life. Doing only the Dharma would be like being Kunkhyen Longchen Rabjam and Milarepa, who both devoted themselves to the Dharma exclusively! You know all about their lives from their biographies, which have been translated and published. But it is not easy for us to become like Longchenpa or Milarepa. We cannot just abandon our daily lives. We have to survive. Still, we can remember that we are all here together to study the Dharma and to learn what daily Dharma practice is.

Buddha himself said, "Don't do evil deeds but dedicate and do virtuous deeds." That is the bottom line. If you condense the Buddha's teachings, that is the essence of the teaching. That means we should try to do whatever we can that is virtuous and try to avoid unvirtuous deeds. Just seeing the lama or listening to the lama alone won't work. You have to practice. You have to put whatever the lama has said into practice. You cannot simply listen to and repeat what the lama says, like a parrot.

So you and I, teacher and students, got together because of karmic reasons, me playing the role of lama and you playing the role of students. We did that for many years. But in order to fulfill that role or succeed in that role, you have to make Dharma practice a daily practice in your life.

There are two important aspects to integrating Dharma practice into your daily life: you must learn and you must establish consistency and stability. You should first learn Dharma and practice and do meditations, and so on. But then you have to be stable, which means you have to learn to do the Dharma practice consistently. Learning and being consistent are of the utmost importance.

The same can be said for worldly activities. If you are not stable, if you don't work in whatever job you have with dedication and consistency, you won't be successful. It is the same way with the Dharma. You have to be consistent. You have to be dedicated. Learning is important but learning alone won't work. It requires both learning and dedication, dedicating your time and energy consistently to whatever you have learned, to whatever meditation you are doing. If you do that, then you will be successful. And so you must look at yourself, at your own mind and your own heart to learn and to practice consistently.

We have now been together all these years. The teaching I gave was mainly Ngöndro, guru yoga. All the meditation materials are condensed into guru yoga. We also studied *The Words of My Perfect Teacher*. And now my talks have been translated and transcribed into books. This is a meaningful development and I am happy the teachings have been so well translated by Tulku Thondup Rinpoché and Sonam Paljor Dejongpa.

At this point, many people think, and some of you might think, "Now, what should I do? Is there something different to practice or study or learn?" There are all kinds of teachings, different levels of teachings, and so on. For example, if you are working, there are all different kinds of careers, different levels of progress. It is the same way with the Dharma. There are lots of different things. People are often interested in something else simply because there are many things around them. They are always hungry for something else instead of appreciating what's in front of them. The important thing is that you shouldn't be looking for something new, for something other than what is in front of you.

I taught you to just think about the difficulty of obtaining a human life, and the impermanence and preciousness of a human life. Learn, think, ponder, and meditate on these important matters. Don't get too many ideas, too many interests in this and that. Just relax and focus on what you already have. Apply those teachings to your mind. The teaching is not something you study and collect as information. These are teachings that you have to apply to your mind so that the mind can improve. So I say again, the important thing is to apply what you have learned to your mind. That means not just learning more and different things but using and enjoying what you already know.

When we first got together many years ago, everybody was young. Now, forty years later, you are not young anymore and it is important to focus your mind in meditation and dedicate your life to meditating on what you have learned. So don't look for something else, just focus on the material in *The Words of My Perfect Teacher*, which we learned and thought about. This is the most important thing.

You can also look and compare yourself with someone who never learned and never practiced Dharma. Having learned, studied, and practiced Dharma for forty years, when you compare yourself with them, you should feel a little better. Are you not more aware, more focused, and more dedicated than the ordinary person who has not learned Dharma? It is not that you are comparing yourself with others to make some sort of arrogant judgment. But you should feel better, having dedicated all this time to Dharma. It should make you proud.

The important thing now is to continue your studies and meditation. Don't give up. Keep doing it. Diligence is very important. If you don't have diligence, whatever you know won't help. So use diligence to gain experience in applying what you have learned and meditated on. I say, again and again: Maintain the continuity. Don't break the continuity. Maintain the continuity of learning and meditating on the teachings.

There is a Tibetan proverb that says, "Diligent people can turn even a mountain into dust because they are very diligent in their work." If they start something, they will finish it. They can even flatten a mountain if they set out to do it. The proverb continues, "The intellectuals go empty-handed at the time of death." They know so much, but they don't do meditation or hold an experience in their hearts. So when they die, although they know so many things, they don't have much experience or feeling. They will die empty-handed. In the same way, you know enough about how to meditate and practice. Now be diligent and meditate on what you know.

That's all you need to do now. Just try to focus on what you have already learned and continue practicing. Keep doing what you are doing. Don't look for new things, but be happy and focus on what you have learned. That's all I want to say.

NOTES

1. The mendicants' way of making merits and cutting off (*chö*) ego clinging, as well as the transference of consciousness into the pure lands (*phowa*), are in the Ngöndro texts and commentaries but are not included in this book.

2. Rinpoché condensed the practice for Western students, but it is "a full and complete practice" to buddhahood [—Tulku Thondup].

3. Bum nga is "the five hundred thousand" accumulations of the preliminary practice. They are repetitions of the lines on taking refuge, 100,000 times; repetitions of the lines of developing bodhichitta (the mind of enlightenment), 100,000 times; repetitions of the one hundred syllable mantra of Vajrasattva for purification, 100,000 times; repetitions of the mandala offering for accumulation of merits, 100,000 times; and doing prostrations for purification and making merits, 100,000 times. These five trainings constitute the main preliminary trainings for the serious meditators of Tantra and Dzokchen.

4. Ngöndro is the preliminary training of Longchen Nyingthik as well as of many other Tibetan Buddhist traditions. Thematically it contains three major parts: (1) the four levels of common preliminaries to turn the mind toward Dharma; (2) the five uncommon preliminaries; and (3) guru yoga, the meditation training of Guru Rinpoché and unity with him for high esoteric attainments, which is the main training [—Tulku Thondup].

5. Mahaparinirvana is the attainment of great peace, the cessation of suffering without residues. It is also the term for the death of the Buddha.

6. In Tibet there are four major Buddhist schools: Nyingma, Kagyu, Sakya, and Geluk. Nyingma is the oldest of all, founded by Guru Padmasambhava (Guru Rinpoché).

7. For sample works, see Tulku Thondup's translation of *Practice of Dzogchen* and Herbert V. Guenther's *Kindly Bent to Ease Us*.

8. Jikmé Lingpa was the holder of the Longchen Nyingthik lineage who transmitted it to the First Dodrupchen Rinpoché. See the lineage diagram on p. 15.

9. *Si sum miten tönké trin dang dra* ("The three worlds are as impermanent as the clouds of autumn"). Shantideva was an eighth-century Indian Buddhist scholar at Nalanda University and an adherent of the Madhyamaka philosophy of Nagarjuna. *Bodhisattvacharyavatara*, or *Bodhicaryavatara*, sometimes translated as *A Guide to the Bodhisattva's Way of Life*, is Shantideva's famous Mahayana text written in Sanskrit verse. It has ten chapters dedicated to the development of bodhichitta (the mind of enlightenment) through the practice of the Six Perfections (Skt. Paramitas).

10. Each monastery has a handprint (*chakjé*) of its own lama. That means there are certain ways to perform ceremonies: how to ring a bell, how to begin to chant, how to chant, the tone of the chant, at what point you should ring the bell, at what point you should pick up the bell from the table, how you should hold a dorjé in your hand, and how you should do your mudras (ritual gestures). All these things are done without deviation from the lama's teaching. That's why monastery lamas have to learn for a long time, to make the ceremony performance one continuous stream within the tradition rather than innovating or creating a new way of doing things. Everything is done in the traditional way with great care.

11. There are numerous deities in tantric teachings that individuals meditate on, pray to, and from whom they receive common and uncommon blessings. If a person chooses a deity as his or her main focus of meditation training, that deity is called the "personal" or "tutelary" deity.

12. There were numerous highly accomplished siddhas (adepts) in India, but eighty-four are most known; they include Saraha, Tilopa, Naropa, Luipa, and Virupa.

13. Chorten are used by Buddhists as a place of worship; they are mound-like structures containing Buddhist relics.

14. According to ancient Indian literature, this world is made up of a giant mountain called "Mt. Meru" or "Mt. Sumeru" at the center of the ocean, surrounded by four continents and eight subcontinents, all encircled by a wall.

15. Arhats, often referred to as "Destroyers of the Foes," are Buddhist sages who have realized a high state of attainment. They have overcome the dual defilements: the emotional and intellectual defilements of their minds.

16. A purification retreat where one recites mantras and makes offerings and prostrations.

17. Tilopa (988–1069), born in Bengal, was a tantric practitioner and a mahasiddha (a great spiritually accomplished adept). He developed the mahamudra method, a set of spiritual practices that greatly accelerates the process of attaining bodhi (enlightenment). He is regarded as the founder of the Kagyu lineage of Tibetan Buddhism. He was the first Kagyu teacher and master of mahamudra and tantra, and is, in effect, the primordial dharmakaya buddha Vajradhara. Naropa (956–1041) was an Indian Buddhist yogi, mystic, and monk, a great Nalanda scholar and disciple of Tilopa.

18. In the actual practice we visualize Guru Rinpoché as the object of the practice who embodies not any individual teacher but all the parts of the refuge in one, and all the buddhas, bodhisattvas, and teachers of the lineage, so that our faith is in the nature of our own mind, our buddha nature; the only infallible refuge and the true nature of the lama being this mandala of essence, nature, and compassion.

19. In the Vajrayana tradition of the Nyingma school, where the practitioner progresses beyond Ngöndro (preliminary) practices that have purified the mind of its defilements to the various yoga practices of tantra, Kuntu Sangpo (Skt. Samantabhadra) is considered a primordial buddha, or dharmakaya buddha. Dorjé Chang is Buddha Vajradhara. Samantabhadra Buddha and Buddha Vajradhara are cognate deities in Tibetan Buddhist cosmology, with different names, attributes, appearances, and iconography, but both are dharmakaya buddhas. Samantabhadra is unadorned (depicted without any attributes), while Buddha Vajradhara is often adorned and bears attributes, generally the iconographic representation of a sambhogakaya buddha. Both are generally depicted in *yab yum* unity (the primordial union, or interpenetration, of wisdom and compassion) with their respective consorts and are primordial buddhas, embodying void and ultimate emptiness.

20. Dorjé Phurba (Skt. Vajrakila), Shinjé (Skt. Yamaraja), Tamdrin (Skt. Hayagriva), and Guru Drakpo (Wrathful Guru Rinpoché) are all names of deities who are peaceful and loving but visualized here in their wrathful forms. Khandroma Sengé Dongwachen (Skt. Dakini Simhamukha) is the lion-faced deity who repels any negative forces and black magic. Kurukulé is the deity who brings others under one's power. Shakya Thupa (Skt. Shakyamuni) is an epithet of the historical Buddha.

21. Jampalyang, Chakna Dorjé, and Chenrezik are among the eight bodhi-sattvas, the principal bodhisattvas of Mahayana Buddhism.
22. This chorten is the famous stupa in Nepal, standing at Boudha Jarung Kashor even today.
23. Milarepa (c. 1052–1135 CE) was a student of Marpa and a major figure in the history of the Kagyu school of Tibetan Buddhism. He is generally considered Tibet's most famous yogi and poet.
24. The Indian philosopher Nagarjuna (c. 150–250 CE) founded the Madhya-maka school of Mahayana Buddhism. He is credited with developing the philosophy of the Prajnaparamita sutras and was closely associated with Nalanda University. The story is a karma parable: Nagarjuna passed away when he offered his head to a greedy prince who thought he could ensure his own longevity by killing Nagarjuna. No blade would cut Nagarjuna, but he told the prince that in a past life he had killed an insect with a blade of kusha grass, so his head could be cut off with a blade of that grass, which then happened.
25. Dorjé (Skt. Vajra) is usually translated as "diamond," to symbolize supreme eternal indestructability.
26. Tormas, figures made mostly of flour and butter, are used in tantric rituals or as offerings in Tibetan Buddhist practice.
27. In 1977, based on Khyentsé Wangpo's commentary, Kyabjé Rinpoché instructed us to visualize Vajrayogini holding a curved knife in her right hand and a skull filled with blood in her left. However, in his later teachings, based on the commentaries by Paltrul Rinpoché and others, Kyabjé Rinpoché instructed us to visualize Vajrayogini playing a skull-drum in her right hand and holding a curved knife in her left hand resting at her hip, as shown in the illustration. You can visualize her in either form. [—Tulku Thondup]
28. The eight rigdzins are the eight great accomplished adepts of India belonging to the Nyingma lineage of the Vajrayana tradition of Tibetan Buddhism. Hungkara, Shantigarbha, and Nagarjuna are among the eight Vidyadharas of the Nyingma lineage in the Vajrayana tradition.
29. Siddhas are great spiritual adepts, the twenty-five chief disciples of Guru Rinpoché. Saraha, Naropa, and Tilopa are among the great adepts of New Tantric (Sarma) lineage in the Vajrayana tradition of Tibetan Buddhism.
30. Dakinis are female deities (human or nonhuman) with mystical powers. *Dakini* is also an honorific term for the consorts of high lamas in Tibet. Vajrasadhu, Ekajati, and Rahula are the three principle Dharmapalas, protectors of tantras in the Nyingma tradition.

31. In the Dzokchen or Mahamudra tradition, the Trikaya describes the three bodies, or modes of being, of the Buddha: the dharmakaya (the essence body, the unmanifested mode and the supreme state of absolute knowledge, which is emptiness), the sambhogakaya (the enjoyment body, the heavenly mode, which is luminosity, the cognizance of emptiness), and the nirmanakaya (the appearance body, the manifested mode suffused with self-existing awareness).

ILLUSTRATION CREDITS

Cover photo by Lama Chödak Gyatso Nubpa.
1. Official seal of His Holiness Kyabjé Dodrupchen Rinpoché.
2. Courtesy of Eileen Latshang.
3. © Deorali Chorten Gonpa, Sikkim, India.
4. Photos courtesy of Deorali Chorten Gonpa, Sikkim, India.
5. Courtesy of Tulku Thondup and Harold Talbott.
6. © Deorali Chorten Gonpa, Sikkim, India.
7. © Deorali Chorten Gonpa, Sikkim, India.
8. Courtesy of David Dvore.
9. © Deorali Chorten Gonpa, Sikkim, India.
10. © Deorali Chorten Gonpa, Sikkim, India.
11. Courtesy of Konchog Yonten.
12. © Deorali Chorten Gonpa, Sikkim, India.

INDEX

karma and, 76–77
perfection of, 195–98
goddess of the earth (Sayi Lhamo),
    12, 101–2
god's eye, 231
gods' realm, 22, 38, 45, 51, 75
  anger and, 98–99
  liberation to, 122–23
  suffering and, 100–103, 119–20
gossip, 110, 115, 116
greed, 72, 75, 78, 111
Guna Parba, 28
Guru Drakpo, 157, 275n20
Guru Prayer, 3, 5–7
Guru Rinpoché, 44, 169, 219, 242
  invocation of, 247–50
  lineage of, 14–16
  oral teachings of, 16
  prayer to, 5–6, 14, 27
  symbolism of dorjé and skullcap of,
    264
  taking refuge in, 154–56, 159–60,
    275n18
  twenty-five disciples of, 14, 28, 240
  visualization of, 238–40, 241, 244
guru yoga, x, 3, 33, 211, 226, 228,
    269
  accumulation of merit in, 243–46
  dedication of merit in, 259–60
  dissolution of visualization in,
    257–58
  four empowerments and, 253–55
  invitation for, 241
  invocation of Guru Rinpoché,
    247–50
  mantra recitation in, 251
  as root practice, 40
  taking refuge and, 136
  visualization for, 237–40

H

happiness
  Dharma as source of, 33, 39–40, 92,
    172, 201
  karma and, 54–55
hardship, bearing, 101, 199, 261
harm from others, patience and, 199
harmful thoughts, 110, 115
harsh speech, 109, 116, 131
hearing the Dharma, 1, 32
  wisdom of, 208
hell realms, 22
  anger and, 75, 85, 111, 173, 189
  cold hells, 67–68
  hot hells, 59–67
  meditation on, 62–63
  as perceptions, 86
  relative and utmost hell, 70–72
  short-lived hell, 68–70
  timescale in, 72
Hinayana path, 10, 123–24, 125, 160,
    182, 214
hot hells, 59–67
human birth, fortunate, 19
  difficulty of obtaining, 22, 25–27,
    54, 87–88, 270
  freedoms and endowments of,
    21–25
  turning away from samsara and,
    42–43
human life
  generosity of giving, 197
  impermanence of, 38–39, 201
human realm
  rebirth in, 75, 122, 123
  suffering in, 81–84, 88
Hungkara, 240, 276n28
hungry-ghost realm (yidaks), 22,
    72–80, 88, 111

ABOUT THE AUTHOR

KYABJÉ DODRUPCHEN RINPOCHÉ is one of the most important living masters in the Nyingma and Dzokchen traditions of Tibetan Buddhism. He was born in 1927 in the Golok province of Far Eastern Tibet. He was recognized as the reincarnation of the most celebrated master, the Third Dodrupchen Rinpoché. At the age of four, he was enthroned at the famed Dodrupchen Monastery. From his conception until the age of six or seven, he displayed endless miraculous signs of high attainment. For example, at the age of five, he spontaneously recited many verses from memory that include the following:

> I am inseparable from enlightenment,
> the unchanging vajra-wisdom.
> In the vajra-womb [or source] of (all the) male and female
>   yogis,
> I have become the realization of the Great Bliss.
> In the ultimate sphere of the unchanging vajra,
> I praise the essential quality and also vajra-protectors.
> I am the Vajra-Master, and I have achieved the Great Bliss.

But then he stopped exhibiting miraculous signs and would not approve of others showing them either. He studied with Lushul Khenpo Könchok Drönmé, Chökhor Khenpo Gangnam, Kyala Khenpo Chechok, and other scholars of Dodrupchen Monastery. He received Nyingthik Yabzhi and Longchen Nyingthik transmissions from Khenpo Kunpal, a disciple of the Third Dodrupchen. He received numerous transmissions from Khyentsé Chökyi Lodrö, Shechen Kongtul, and Gyarong Namtrul. From Yukhok Chatralwa and Apang Terton he received the ultimate Dzokchen teachings and transmissions. At Dodrupchen Monastery, he built a scriptural college, and he subsidized the many woodblocks for printing texts such as the *Seven Treasures of Longchenpa*. He gave major teachings and transmissions of Nyingthik Yabzhi, Longchen Nyingthik, Nyingma Kama, Lama Gongdu, and Rinchen Terdzod and many others at numerous places, especially at Dodrupchen Monastery. Then, due to the changing political situation, Rinpoché left his beloved monastery and settled in Sikkim in 1957—as had been clearly prophesied by the Third Dodrupchen and Apang Tertön. In Sikkim, he established the Chörten Gönpa near Gangtok with about five hundred resident monks and nuns and made it his permanent seat. He also established other monasteries and nunneries in Sikkim, Bhutan, and Nepal and conferred endless teachings and transmissions. Rinpoché has also visited Dodrupchen Monastery in Golok province many times since 1984, and has helped to restore his famed monastery to its original eminence. He has made frequent visits to the West, his first being in 1973 when he established the Mahasiddha Nyingmapa Center in Massachusetts. Rinpoché has also visited a number of European and Southeast Asian countries repeatedly to impart teachings and transmissions. On one of his visits to the United States, in 1977, Rinpoché taught the Ngöndro of Longchen Nyingthik to his students at the Mahasiddha Nyingmapa Center over a number of days. For a complete explanation of the Longchen Nyingthik tradition, see Tulku Thondup Rinpoché's *The Tantric Tradition of the Nyingmapa*, published by The Buddhayana Foundation in 1984.

ABOUT THE TRANSLATORS

TULKU THONDUP RINPOCHÉ

Tulku Thondup was born in Eastern Tibet. He was recognized as a tulku at age five and studied at Dodrupchen Monastery. He came to India in 1958 and taught in its universities for many years. In the 1980s he came to the United States as a visiting scholar at Harvard University. For the past three decades he has written, translated, and taught under the auspices of the Buddhayana Foundation. His numerous books include *The Healing Power of Mind* and *Boundless Healing*. Tulku has given many teachings at Mahasiddha Nyingmapa Center, the seat of Dodrupchen Rinpoché in the United States.

SONAM PALJOR

Sonam Paljor was born in Sikkim, India. He studied Tibetan Buddhism under the tutelage of Dodrupchen Rinpoché. He earned a BA in anthropology from Brown University with a focus on Buddhism, and then served as a translator for Dodrupchen Rinpoché and his designee, Lama Jikmé Dorjé, while also actively involved with the growth of the Mahasiddha Nyingmapa Center. Upon returning to India, he was active in the affairs of Chorten Gonpa, Rinpoché's monastery in India. Sonam and his wife Maria and son Pintso were founders of Taktse International School in Sikkim, and he is still actively involved in its operations.

Dorjé Naljorma

WHAT TO READ NEXT
FROM WISDOM PUBLICATIONS

APPROACHING THE GREAT PERFECTION
Simultaneous and Gradual Methods of Dzogchen Practice
in the Longchen Nyingtig
Sam Van Schaik

"An important work for its breadth and attention to detail, this book contains translations of ten texts from the widely practiced treasure cycle called the *Longchen Nyingtig*, as well as a survey of Nyingma history and Jigme Lingpa's corpus. Van Schaik's lucid explanation of the issues and technical vocabulary in the 'seminal heart', or *nyingtig*, teachings provide the reader with an essential framework for tackling the extensive primary source material found in this work."—*Buddhadharma*

MIPHAM'S BEACON OF CERTAINTY
Illuminating the View of Dzogchen, the Great Perfection
John W. Pettit

"A riveting and wonderful work, which gives the reader a real education in some of the most compelling issues of Buddhism, especially their impact on Dzogchen."—Anne Klein, Rice University

THE EASY PATH
Illuminating the First Panchen Lama's Secret Instructions
Gyumed Khensur Lobsang Jampa
Edited by Lorne Ladner

"A marvel."
—Jan Willis, author of *Dreaming Me: Black, Baptist, and Buddhist*

MANJUSHRI'S INNERMOST SECRET
*A Profound Commentary of Oral Instructions
on the Practice of Lama Chöpa*
Kachen Yeshe Gyaltsen
Translated by David Gonsalez (aka Losang Tsering)

"I am delighted that Wisdom is publishing *Manjushri's Innermost Secret*. The authentic translation of this important commentary will enhance and add to the in-depth understanding of the essential practice of Lama Chopa. The translator, the late David Losang Tsering, was a devoted practitioner of this lineage and his efforts will bring tremendous benefit to earnest seekers."
—Sharpa Tulku Tenzin Trinley

PRACTICING WISDOM
The Perfection of Shantideva's Bodhisattva Way
His Holiness the Dalai Lama

A *Shambhala Sun* "Best Buddhist Writing" selection

A LULLABY TO AWAKEN THE HEART
The Aspiration Prayer of Samantabhadra and Its Tibetan Commentaries
Karl Brunnhölzl

"Among translators, Brunnhölzl is unsurpassed in his knowledge of Tibetan and Sanskrit Buddhist literature. His deep practice experience brings the meaning and intent of texts to life. In *A Lullaby to Awaken the Heart* he brilliantly presents the teachings in *The Aspiration Prayer of Samantabhadra*, a gateway into the profundity of the Dzogchen teachings."—Andy Karr, author of *Contemplating Reality: A Practitioner's Guide to the View in Indo-Tibetan Buddhism*

About Wisdom Publications

Wisdom Publications is the leading publisher of classic and contemporary Buddhist books and practical works on mindfulness. To learn more about us or to explore our other books, please visit our website at wisdomexperience.org or contact us at the address below.

Wisdom Publications
199 Elm Street
Somerville, MA 02144 USA

We are a 501(c)(3) organization, and donations in support of our mission are tax deductible.

Wisdom Publications is affiliated with the Foundation for the Preservation of the Mahayana Tradition (FPMT).